AUSTRALIA'S NATURAL DISASTERS

RICHARD WHITAKER AUSTRALIA'S

NATURAL DISASTERS

Richard Whitaker

First published in 2005 by Reed New Holland Publishers
This edition published in 2021 by Reed New Holland Publishers
Sydney • Auckland
Level 1, 178 Fox Valley Road, Wahroonga, NSW 2076, Australia
5/39 Woodside Avenue, Northcote, Auckland 0627, New Zealand

newhollandpublishers.com

Copyright © 2021 Reed New Holland Publishers
Copyright © 2021 in text: Richard Whitaker
Copyright © 2021 in maps and diagrams: Ian Faulkner
Copyright in photographs: As credited

All rights reserved. No part of this publication may be reproduced, stored in a retrieval system or transmitted, in any form or by any means, electronic, mechanical, photocopying, recording or otherwise, without the prior written permission of the publishers and copyright holders.

National Library of Australia Cataloguing-in-Publication Data:
Whitaker, Richard, 1947– .
Australia's natural disasters.
ISBN 9781760792626
1. Natural disasters - Australia. I. Title.
363.340994

Publisher: Louise Egerton
Project Editor: Yani Silvana, Liz Hardy
Designer: Andrew Davies
Research: Jan Whitaker
Production Director: Arlene Gippert
Printed in China

2 4 6 8 10 9 8 7 5 3 1

Keep up with Reed New Holland
and New Holland Publishers
 ReedNewHolland
 @NewHollandPublishers and @ReedNewHolland

Acknowledgements

The author and publishers would like to thank the following organisations and individuals for the use of their pictorial material.

page 1 Vicky Ackx/Shutterstock
pages 2–3 Jamen Percy/Shutterstock
pages 6–7 josh.tagi/Shutterstock
page 8 Picture courtesy of *The Mercury*, Hobart
pages 10–11 *The Advertiser*, Adelaide
pages 14–15 Watercolour by S.T. Gill, Mitchell Library, State Library of New South Wales
pages 16–17 Australian National Maritime Museum
page 18 Dixson Galleries, State Library of New South Wales
page 20 NASA
pages 22–23 Drawing by Bruce Swann from a copy held by Mitchell Library, State Library of New South Wales
page 24 Photo courtesy of State Library of South Australia
pages 26–27, 28–29 State Library of Queensland, negative nos 64182 and 74951
pages 30, 31, 33 Photo courtesy of *The Courier-Mail*, Brisbane
page 36 Bruce Elder/Fairfaxphotos
page 37 Bureau of Meteorology
pages 38–39 Mitchell Library, State Library of New South Wales
pages 42–43 National Library of Australia
pages 46–47 Maud Gibson Collection, Kuringai Municipal Library
page 48 Steven Siewert/Fairfaxphotos
pages 52–53, 55–56 John Oxley Library, State Library of Queensland
pages 58–59 Brighton Historical Society
page 60 Newspix
page 65 State Library of Victoria
page 68 Macarthur Job
page 69 Milton Kent/Charles Ulm National Aviation Collection, National Library of Australia
pages 70–71 Photo courtesy of State Library of South Australia
pages 73, 74, 76 Photos courtesy of O'Reilly family
pages 80–82 North Bondi Surf Life Saving Club/Waverley Library
pages 84, 86 Macarthur Job
page 89 Newspix
page 91 Newspix
page 95 Bob Rice/Sydney Sun
page 100 Milton Speer/Bureau of Meteorology
page 101 Newspix/Milan Scepanovic
pages 102–103 Emergency Management Australia
pages 107–108 *The Advertiser*, Adelaide
pages 111–117 Photos courtesy of *The Courier-Mail*, Brisbane
pages 119, 122 Newspix
page 125 State Library of New South Wales
page 127 Macarthur Job
page 129 Bureau of Meteorology

pages 130–131 Macarthur Job
page 135 National Archives of Australia
pages 138–139 *The Mercury*, Hobart
page 141 National Archives of Australia
page 143 National Library of Australia
page 146 Australian News and Information Bureau, via National Archives of Australia
pages 148–153 Emergency Management Australia
page 154 Newspix
pages 158–159 Neville Bowler/Fairfaxphotos
page 160 Heath Missen/Fairfaxphotos
page 163 National Library of Australia
pages 165, 167 Miscellaneous 2 collection, Northern Territory Library
pages 170–171 Katsuhiro Abe/Bureau of Meteorology
pages 173, 174, 175, 177 Newspix
pages 178–179 Emergency Management Australia
page 180 Newspix/Mike Arthur
page 181 Bureau of Meteorology
pages 183, 184 *The Courier-Mail*, Brisbane
page 186 Mrsdonnamari/Shutterstock
pages 189–193 Emergency Management Australia
pages 196–197 *The Courier-Mail*, Brisbane
pages 198–199, 202–203 Emergency Management Australia
pages 204–205 Dallas Kilponen/Fairfaxphotos
page 207 Leo Meier/NHIL
page 209 Mike Rosel/Bureau of Meteorology
page 212 Andrew Taylor/Fairfaxphotos
page 213 Newspix/Michael Klein
page 215 Newspix/David Crosling
pages 216–217 Newspix/Grant Turner
page 218 Newspix/Mark Evans
page 221 NASA
page 224 Peter Rae/Fairfaxphotos
page 225 Newspix/Jeff Herbert
pages 226–227 Newspix/Darren Edwards
page 231 NASA
page 232 Nick Moir/Fairfaxphotos
page 233 Andrew Taylor/Fairfaxphotos
page 234 Andrew Meares/Fairfaxphotos
page 236 Ben Jeayes/Shutterstock
page 242 Jonathan Berry/Shutterstock
page 244 Matt Makes Photos/Shutterstock
page 246 Alan Bilsborough/Shutterstock
page 249 NASA Goddard MODIS Rapid Response Team
page 252 Jacques Descloitres, MODIS Rapid Response Team, NASA/GSFC
page 253 Leah-Anne Thompson/Shutterstock
page 256 Zorro Stock Images/Shutterstock
page 257 NASA EOSDIS/LANCE and GIBS/Worldview

Contents

	Introduction	8
1857	**The Wreck of the *Dunbar***	13
1865	**Goyder's Line Ignored**	19
1893 & 1974	**Brisbane Floods**	25
1902	**The Federation Drought**	34
1903	**A Fatal Race up Mount Wellington**	40
1914 & 1991	**Storms Hit Sydney**	45
1918	**Cyclone Terror in Mackay**	51
1918 & 1976	**Twisters across Victoria**	57
1929	**Tasmania in Flood**	62
1931	**The *Southern Cloud* Disappears**	66
1937	**O'Reilly and the Stinson**	72
1938	**Mass Rescue at Bondi Beach**	77
1938	**The Crash of the *Kyeema***	83
1939	**Black Friday in Victoria**	88
1947 & 1999	**Sydney's Eastern Suburbs Devastated by Hail**	93
1948	**The Adelaide Tempest**	105
1954	**East-Coast Cyclone**	110
1955	**Maitland Goes Under**	118
1961	**The Flight of Tango Victor Charlie**	126
1967	**The Apple Isle Burns**	134
1967	**Prime Minister Lost**	142

1968 & 1989	Earthquake: Meckering and Newcastle	147
1972 & 2003	Flash Floods in Melbourne	156
1974	Cyclone Tracy Flattens Darwin	162
1983	Dust Storms and Bushfires Sweep Victoria	169
1985	Huge Hail Hits Brisbane	182
1990	The Big Wet in the East	187
1992	Twisters, Wind and Hail across Queensland	195
1997	The Thredbo Landslide	201
1998	Disaster Strikes the Sydney to Hobart Yacht Race	206
1999	A Deadly Sleep – The Snowboarder Tragedy	214
2002	The Millennium Drought	220
2003	Canberra Burns	229
2007	The *Pasha Bulker* Storm	235
2009	The Black Saturday Fires	238
2009	The Eastern Australian Dust Storms	241
2010 & 2011	Queensland floods	245
2011	Tropical Cyclone Yasi	248
2019–2020	Blazing Summer – The East-Coast Bushfires	251
2020	After the Fire Came the Flood	255
	Glossary	259
	Bibliography	261
	Index	262

Introduction

*If history repeats itself, and the unexpected always happens,
how incapable must Man be of learning from experience.*

George Bernard Shaw (1856–1950)

This book looks at a collection of unusual events in Australia's history, events that have been triggered in some way by natural forces. In the majority of these cases, weather has been the natural force in question, but earthquakes and landslips have also been involved. Also included are specific air and sea disasters that resulted, either directly or indirectly, from weather phenomena. Although these events have caused tragedy, they have also led to progress, both in the prevention of a repetition, and in more effective responses to similar situations in the future.

Natural disasters occur over various time scales. Earthquakes, for example, may be over in a matter of seconds. Severe thunderstorms that produce flash flooding, tornadoes, large hail and destructive wind gusts usually unfold over a two to three hour period. Bushfires can flare and ease over a day or two, whereas broad-scale flooding, which often covers hundreds of square kilometres, can take several weeks to develop and dissipate. Drought – that most insidious and damaging phenomenon – is probably the slowest evolving event, sometimes afflicting an area for several years. But drought, in turn, may be associated with an even longer term phenomenon – climate change. History will be the ultimate judge of this.

In Australia, extreme events of this nature – excluding drought and earthquake – usually occur during spring and summer, and there is a perfectly logical explanation for this. Late spring and summer correspond with the peak of the tropical cyclone season over northern Australia and, as well as cyclone damage, flooding from monsoonal rains can extend well south of the tropics and affect the southern States. In addition, most severe thunderstorms, with their associated hail, destructive winds and flash flooding, occur over mainland Australia during late spring and summer.

Bushfires also largely occur during this time, at least in the southern States with the most populated areas. The conditions most favourable for fire outbreaks, including low humidity, high temperatures and strong winds, are most likely to occur during summer, and occasional rapid wind changes caused by frontal activity also affect the southern States during this period.

On the other hand, droughts often extend over a period of several months or even years, and earthquakes, although not common in Australia can happen at any time.

Do we really learn from such tragedies? The answer is probably yes and no.

Aircraft crashes caused by a lack of technology have resulted in improvements such as in-flight communication, accurate navigation systems, the use of radar and closer communication with the Bureau of Meteorology. These developments virtually eliminated an entire raft of problems from Australian commercial aviation.

Weather forecasting has also improved tremendously over the past 50 years. The advent of satellite photography and the continuous refinement of computer simulation of the weather, together with improvements in weather radar and the growth of automatic weather station networks, have all resulted in significant advances in the accuracy and timeliness of severe weather warnings.

Weather warnings are also more easily and quickly disseminated. A century ago the main mass-communication system was the daily newspaper. Now we have radio, television, the internet and mobile telephone technology. All this, combined with improvements in disaster management – both before and after – has created advanced disaster readiness and response over the last few decades.

But this is only part of the problem. The other, more intransigent part involves human nature itself – how the public, and indeed government authorities, react to warnings of extreme situations. The main issue is that extreme events are rare. In fact, apart from thunderstorms and drought, most Australians will seldom experience such situations and thus the lessons of the past are either never learned or soon forgotten.

Tropical cyclone Tracy in 1974 was a classic example. Despite an effective meteorological watch that provided some four days' warning of the approach of the cyclone, the response of the population, as well as the various emergency authorities, was inadequate.

As Alan Stretton was to later remark in his book *The Furious Days*: 'When Cyclone Tracy hit Darwin just after midnight on Christmas morning 1974, it found the local authorities in Darwin completely unprepared'. Various factors contributed to this state of inaction, including the all-pervasive 'Christmas cheer' and the fact that Darwin had not been seriously devastated by a cyclone for some 37 years. There were few left in the city who remembered.

A more recent example was the tragic 1998 Sydney to Hobart yacht race. Despite the unprecedented issue of a storm warning only two hours into the race, the event ended in tragedy.

Complaints about lack of warning were also received following the Canberra bushfire holocaust of January 2003, with some residents lamenting that they were completely unprepared for the ferocity and speed of the fires. Debate about controlled burning was also common to the Canberra fires and the Black Friday fires of 1939, some 64 years before, indicating that controversial issues are still connected with such events, even several decades later.

A continuous program of public education is a good response. The catastrophic eastern Australian fires of 2019/20 showed the public to be better prepared than ever before for such a disaster and this undoubtedly saved many lives and assisted with the recovery process.

It therefore becomes one of the main roles of various government organisations to act as the 'memory' of society, and to ensure that as much information as possible is recorded and processed. Disaster exercises and simulations based on this information help ensure an effective state of readiness for the various State and Commonwealth emergency services. Key government organisations such as Emergency Management Australia and the Bureau of Meteorology perform some of these functions routinely, and this collected information forms a vital part of the national interest.

Over the last decade there has been a rising interest in severe weather events. Part of this is because of our ability to photograph and record these through mobile telephone technology, and also because of the rising interest of the media in such events. Social media has also been a valuable contribution, with severe weather 'clubs' attracting the attention of like-minded people who collect information, images and stories that are placed on the internet.

Although there has been significant progress in planning for, predicting and reacting to natural disasters, three main challenges stand out from the rest.

The Human Factor

While the various government agencies and emergency services organisations have developed considerable expertise, and they train regularly for natural disasters, the general public do not, and for most,

This couple's tent was wrecked by the 'Adelaide Tempest' of 1948 (see page105). The tempest was described by media sources as the 'Storm of the Century' and produced widespread damage across the Adelaide area.

the lessons of the past are inevitably forgotten. Public reaction to disaster warnings can be unpredictable or even counterproductive. Therefore there is a constant need to educate, train and practise all aspects of natural disasters, in a similar way that the armed forces ready themselves for war-time situations. However, because of the expense involved in training of this nature and the difficulties in reaching a significant number of people, this area is likely to lag behind other technological and organisational progress. Perhaps a more effective method may be to teach 'severe weather' as a subject in secondary schools, thereby imparting the necessary knowledge to the majority of the population.

Drought

This remains one of the most damaging natural hazards in Australia. The reasons for its onset are insufficiently known to enable reliable prediction. However, over the last two decades there has been an increasing understanding of the link between drought in Australia and the El Niño/Indian Ocean

Dipole phenomena. If this knowledge can be extended, it may eventually be possible to accurately forecast the onset and duration of drought.

The national implications are enormous. For example, if forecasting of this type were possible, we could accurately plan the type and amount of crops to plant in the following season, as well as the agistment of stock and the management of irrigation. Water restrictions for city areas could be accurately managed and timed for maximum saving and minimum inconvenience.

The social and financial benefits of these activities alone would be massive, so research that may provide us with this information should be given a high priority.

The Severe Thunderstorm

Thunderstorms are at the other end of the time scale to droughts. In a period of only one to two hours they can inflict enormous damage. The Sydney hailstorm of 14 April 1999 produced a damage bill of around $2.3 billion making it one of Australia's most expensive disasters.

The extension of the national weather radar network, increased frequency of satellite photography and a quantum leap in computing power have resulted in significant progress in understanding severe storms over the past 20 years or so. However, the timely issuing of forecasts and warnings remains a real challenge for several reasons.

For the meteorologist, forecasting the development and movement of a severe thunderstorm remains one of the most difficult tasks. And as the life cycle of a thunderstorm is only short, warnings must be disseminated quickly. The most effective dissemination methods are radio, internet and social media technology, and all of these have improved substantially over the last decade.

The recent way the Bureau of Meteorology displays severe thunderstorm warnings has been a major step forward. It is essentially an explanation of current radar imagery and identifies which thunderstorm cells may contain hail and which are considered the most dangerous. These are updated regularly when thunderstorm warnings have been issued.

Then there is the question of what people should do when they hear the warnings. It is impossible to prevent the roof being damaged or trees being blown down. But the risk of personal injury can be minimised by staying indoors, and the damage bill will be reduced if the car is placed under cover. This is a public education issue and significant progress has been made over the last 20 years.

Our ability to plan, forecast and react in relation to natural disasters is constantly improving and has been hard won from the lessons of the past. The future holds remarkable promise of even more exciting progress.

1857

The Wreck of the 'Dunbar'

The ankers brak, and topmast lap,
It was sic a deadly storm:
And the waves cam owre the broken ship
Till a' her sides were torn.

'Sir Patrick Spens', Anonymous

These days, the captains and crews of commercial passenger ships sailing in Australian waters always have on hand the latest forecasts and warnings issued by the Bureau of Meteorology. This enables them to plan a safe voyage. But during the nineteenth century, before this infrastructure was in place, ships put to sea with little or no knowledge of the weather en route, and this contributed to many tragic shipwrecks.

No more terrible example of this can be found than with the *Dunbar*, a 1347-tonne passenger-carrying sailing ship which arrived outside the heads of Sydney Harbour on the night of Thursday 20 August 1857.

The *Dunbar* had departed England nearly three months before carrying 122 people, including passengers and crew. All were anxious to finally arrive and come ashore in Sydney. But the night was bad, with gale-force winds, big seas and low visibility due to driving rain.

Captain James Green was in command, and he was faced with a dilemma: should they take the safe course and head back out to sea and wait till next morning, or should they try to enter Sydney Harbour in obviously marginal conditions? The former course of action would mean yet another night at sea in strong winds and a turbulent ocean. On the other hand, once in Sydney Harbour, they would be safe and comfortable. He decided to enter the harbour.

Captain Green and his crew began their approach to the harbour. But nineteenth-century square-rigged sailing ships were very limited in their manoeuvrability, particularly in strong winds, and once

The Dunbar smashes onto the rocks of South Head, Sydney Harbour. Artist unknown. Courtesy of Mitchell Library, State Library of NSW

committed to a course, could not readily come about and reverse direction. Too late they realised that they had misjudged, and desperately tried to come about. They soon heard the boom of the surf breaking at the base of South Head, and saw explosions of white water through the gloom as the vessel was driven inexorably towards the shore.

Soon after 11.15 pm, the vessel was smashed abruptly onto the rocks just to the south of the harbour entrance. The masts came down and the hull began to break up. As each great wave broke across the vessel it was dragged back and forth over the rocks, and over the next few hours reduced to a tangled mass of ropes, iron and shattered timbers. Passengers desperately fought for survival in the boiling seas, but as the night wore on, they were repeatedly smashed on the rocks and either died through impact or were drowned.

The next morning, residents of Sydney's eastern suburbs noticed wreckage floating around the entrance to the harbour. Soon people began walking around the top of the cliffs of South Head to investigate and were horrified to see a great mass of wreckage below, as well as scores of mangled bodies, stripped of their clothing, being rolled about on the rocks by the still mountainous seas.

A large force of volunteers travelled to the

scene to begin the dangerous and difficult rescue attempt, but the foul weather and driving rain made the task impossible. Indeed, the waves breaking on the rocks below were so large that spray was drenching those along the cliff tops. However, by 22 August, the weather had moderated and rescuers were finally able to reach the wreck.

They found a scene of utter destruction. Wreckage and dismembered bodies were littered all over the rock shelf. Miraculously, they also found the sole survivor, a shivering Able Seaman James Johnson, who had been thrown ashore by a large wave. Somehow he had become wedged in a rock crevice where he clung for the next 36 hours before his rescue. Eventually he was hoisted to the top of the cliff by a long rope.

His report was printed in *The Nautical Magazine* of December 1857 as follows:

> *She made Botany Bay on the 20th. August and then sail was shortened to close-reefed topsails. The mizen top-sail and spanker were taken in. About seven in the evening Sydney Light was seen, the weather being squally with thick rain; the captain and chief officer were both on the poop. It was raining hard and the light was only seen at intervals but distinctly. She stood along the coast until they had fetched the light up to the lee mizen rigging (about 11 p.m.). All hands were then piped up by the boatswain to wear ship. She was however kept away and the foresail reefed, and she ran in on a heavy sea. It was now blowing fresh and in squalls with thick rain. The second and third mates, with the two look-out men, were stationed on the forecastle, when the captain sang out – 'Do you see anything to the North Head?' the officer replying that he saw nothing of it. Shortly after this the second mate sang out, 'Breakers ahead.' The helm was then put down and the yards braced up sharp – about two minutes after she went broadside on the rocks.*

The news created a sensation in Sydney, and eventually, as the news spread to other parts of the colony, the other capital cities as well. As many bodies as possible were pulled from the surf and a mass funeral was held on 24 September 1857 at St Stephen's Cemetery, Camperdown. The funeral procession, which left the morgue at about 5 pm, was delayed and the service was held in an eerie moonlight.

A direct result of the tragedy was the construction of the Hornby Light on the inner tip of South Head in 1858 to improve safety for vessels approaching the harbour at night. And in a bizarre replay of history, the sole survivor of the *Dunbar*, James Johnson, helped to rescue the only survivor of the shipwrecked *Cawarra* in 1866, while he was employed at Newcastle Lighthouse.

Over the years, dredging operations recovered many artefacts from the site. In the early 1900s the *Dunbar*'s anchor was raised and in 1930 was mounted on a cliff

A contemporary drawing depicting the Dunbar tragedy, showing the voyage, the wreck, Johnson being rescued, and the funeral procession. In the centre is a sketch of Johnson.

face at Watsons Bay, near the wreck site, as a memorial.

A tablet affixed to the cliff face is engraved:

> The 'Dunbar' was wrecked about 500 yards south of this spot in a heavy north-east gale at night August 20th 1857. From a total of 122 there was only one survivor. This, her anchor, was recovered by local residents 50 years later and is now set up in memory of the tragic event.

It is possible there is an error here. The great majority of gales off Sydney are from the south-east not the north-east. This is also supported by a report from a nineteenth-century issue of *The Australian Encyclopaedia* which, in relating the event, stated:

> During succeeding days wreckage of all description and mutilated bodies on the beaches of Middle and North harbours ... Bodies continued to be found after the funeral; the remains of one person were buried in the vicinity of Manley [sic] Beach.

17

This report certainly indicates the likelihood of strong winds from the south-east, as the bodies and wreckage appear to have been carried northwards.

In addition, the testimony of Able Seaman James Johnson indicated that the *Dunbar* had arrived off the coast near Botany Bay before sailing northwards towards Sydney Harbour. This would have been an unlikely course to take if a gale-force north-easter had been blowing; little headway would be possible with such a strong headwind. Again, a strong south-easterly wind appears to have been more likely.

The *Dunbar* was also carrying a number of bells, which were recovered and installed in St Patrick's Church at Parramatta in the 1880s.

From the 1950s the wreck site became a popular diving area, being within easy range of modern scuba-diving equipment.

Concerned with the widespread collection of artefacts by divers returning to the site, the Commonwealth government conferred protective status on the wreck by legislation in 1989. Whilst divers can still visit the area, unauthorised removal of artefacts is now illegal.

Shipwrecks off the Australian coast involving commercial passenger vessels now happen rarely, although they still occur from time to time with private boats and during yacht races.

Improvements in ship design and construction have boosted safety, as has progress in weather forecasting and communications. The issuing of strong wind and gale warnings well in advance of the onset of dangerous weather has provided a big increase in safety margins for all maritime traffic in Australian waters.

An 1857 photograph of the sole survivor of the *Dunbar* shipwreck, Able Seaman James Johnson.

1865

Goyder's Line Ignored

In nature, there are no rewards or punishments; there are consequences.

Horrace Annesley Vachell (1861–1955), British writer

An unusual contribution to the Australian weather scene during the nineteenth century was made by a man who was not primarily occupied with meteorology, but was in fact the Surveyor General of South Australia during the mid 1860s.

George Woodroffe Goyder was a 'small man of unimpeachable character' who had come to South Australia in 1851. By dint of hard work and attention to detail he had progressed through the Colonial Engineers Office to the prestigious position of Surveyor General in 1861.

Early in the 1860s, much of the good farming land in South Australia had already been taken up, and the government was under great pressure to open up the vast tracts of land further north towards the Flinders Ranges. Accordingly, the Surveyor General was instructed to report on the feasibility of this enterprise.

Late in 1865, at the height of a severe drought, Goyder made several trips to the north of the State. He travelled over 5000 kilometres on horseback, noting the type of vegetation and condition of the soil. After his return, he defined a line on a map: south of the line rainfall was deemed to be reliable enough for various agricultural pursuits; north of the line conditions were considered suitable only for grazing. The line coincided roughly with the southern boundary of the saltbush country in the area.

'Goyder's Line', as it came to be known, runs up the eastern side of Spencer Gulf, along the southern flank of the Flinders Ranges and then south-east, passing near Peterborough, Jamestown, Burra and Swan Reach.

Goyder's observations on the vegetation

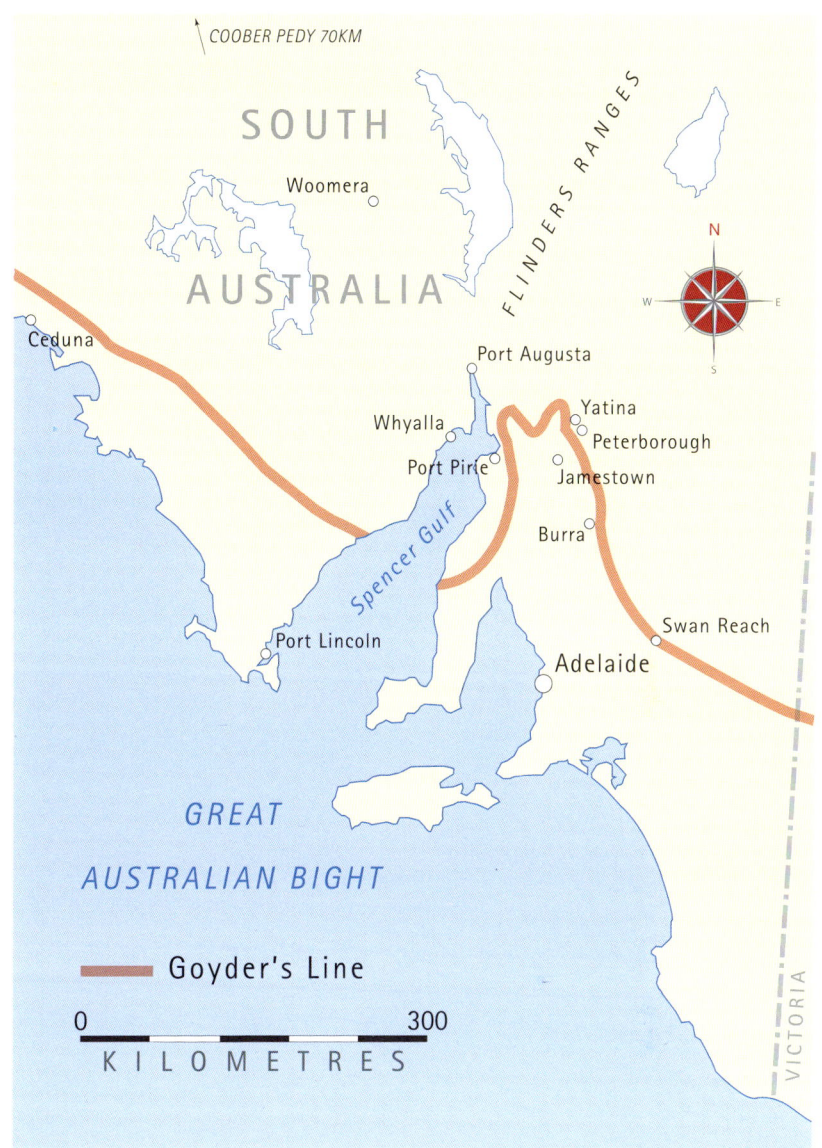

A comparison of the sketch of Goyder's Line (right) with a photograph taken from space in 2001 (left). The difference in the vegetation colour corresponds quite well with the line.

had led him to believe that outside his line, farming would be unsustainable due to insufficient rainfall. This was a bold prediction. Firstly, no detailed rainfall records were then available on which to base his belief. Secondly, it was not what the politicians of the day wanted to hear, as it put added pressure on them to make the unpopular decision to keep the backblocks of South Australia closed to agriculture.

Predictably enough, Goyder's Line created a turmoil of tirade and controversy. During parliamentary debate it was urged that the line be pushed further north, preferably out of South Australia altogether. The line was referred to by some as 'Goyder's Line of Foolery'. It was even suggested that Goyder was on the payroll of the pastoralists who wanted to protect their land from agricultural farming. This was a great injustice to Goyder, who was a man of 'stainless steel' integrity.

However, caving in to this pressure, the government went against Goyder's advice and allowed farming allotments to be bought up well north of his line. Hundreds of people began wheat farms in the northern plains of South Australia. Wheat-growing became general in the districts around Port Augusta during 1877 and 1878.

As with so many other areas of human endeavour, 'Lady Luck' seemed to smile on beginners. For the next few years, good rains came resulting in bumper wheat crops in 'the Golden North'. Wheat bags were stacked 'like mountains' beside the railway line for

eventual transport to Port Augusta and shipping overseas.

What Goyder had forgotten, said the farmers, was the truth of the old saying 'rain follows the plough', which was a relic from the European folkloric era. By breaking up the soil, so the theory went, more moisture was released into the air and became available for rainfall.

Encouraged by this apparent success, the South Australian government surveyed new towns to be built in the general area, such as Hammond, Bruce, Cradock, Gordon, Johnburgh, Yatina, Wilson, Carrieton, Chapmanton, Farina and Amyton. Yatina, in particular, was earmarked for great things, and was expected to become the biggest settlement in South Australia outside of Adelaide.

Then reality rudely arrived. Protracted drought during the early 1880s forced many wheat farmers into ruin. Most eventually walked off their land and returned to Adelaide disillusioned and embittered.

Derelict homesteads and abandoned farm machinery still dot the area, monuments to the fact that climate cannot be ignored and must be legislated for in our day-to-day activities. The proposed grand city of Yatina never realised its potential; only one or two buildings remain in the middle of what is for the most part a desert-like landscape.

Goyder had been right, of course, and he had made one of the early comments on the climatology of the continent, namely that most areas of South Australia have insufficient rain to support general agriculture.

A contemporary drawing of Yatina by Bruce Swann. This was intended to be the 'biggest settlement in South Australia, outside of Adelaide'. Lack of rainfall determined otherwise.

It turned out that where Goyder's Line fell corresponded roughly with the so-called 'Ten Inch Line' of average rainfall or, in more modern terms, the 250-millimetre rainfall isohyet.

The surveyor general, in performing his task with characteristic thoroughness, had also shown the folly of attempting to modify the climate by use of parliamentary decree.

Goyder's work was eventually officially recognised and a number of features have been named after him: Goyder's Lagoon on the Birdsville Track; Goyder Railway Station; Mount Woodroffe, the highest mountain in South Australia; Wheal Goyder, a copper mine near Wallaroo; and on Kangaroo Island there is the Goyder Range and the Goyder Range Branch Creek.

The Surveyor General of South Australia, George Woodroffe Goyder (1826–1898).

1893 & 1974

Brisbane Floods

Bedad, he'll have to stay the night; the rain is going to pour –
So make the rattling windows tight, and close the kitchen door.

'Around the Boree Log', John O'Brien

The meandering Brisbane River is believed to be several million years old and, as such, is one of the oldest waterways in the world. It flows from above Lake Wivenhoe, which is nearly 60 kilometres inland, across rural areas and finally through the Brisbane metropolis, before emptying into Moreton Bay.

The Brisbane River was once an important trade and transport link, but the old wharves and shipyards have mostly disappeared, and the main parts of the river within the CBD now form a picturesque tourist attraction and public amenity, lined with parks and walkways.

Numerous tributaries feed into the river, including the major waterways of the Stanley and Bremer rivers, as well as smaller flows such as Lockyer, Enoggera and Breakfast creeks. The various elements of this fairly complex catchment react differently to heavy rain. The creeks tend to rise quickly and fall just as rapidly when the rain eases, a process which might take less than 24 hours. However, the Brisbane River itself responds much more slowly, and may take two or three days to peak and remain in flood for a week or so. Given the right conditions, the river can turn from a tranquil flow into a raging torrent flooding the surrounding countryside.

Floods in the Brisbane River are certainly not rare but two of the worst were 1893 and 1974. Since then we've seen a further major flood in 2011 – and this was just short of the 1974 event.

The 1893 Flood

In February 1893, a tropical cyclone moving north of Brisbane generated a large cloud band across south-eastern Queensland, producing tremendous rains across the area. As the downpour increased, local reports told of the Aborigines coming in from all round the district and camping at One Tree Hill (now Mt Coot-tha). They warned the local residents of a massive flood developing because 'the fish had left the Bay and the ants were climbing high into the trees' – sure signs of big trouble to come.

Their advice turned out to be perfectly accurate. The Brisbane River burst its banks and flooded prodigiously across the city, 'covering areas of the town that had never been flooded before'. Houses were torn off their foundations and carried off downstream. An eyewitness account in *The Queensland Times* stated that 'Debris of all descriptions – houses, haystacks, factories, sheep, ships, snakes, bullocks, timber – all went floating down the river.'

Much of the debris piled up against the Victoria Bridge, which eventually buckled under the pressure and broke up. Refugees moved to high ground and huddled together, waiting to be rescued by boat. *The Queensland Times* further reported that 'Houses on

Extensive flooding to a depth of well over a metre along Brisbane's Edward Street in the city in February 1893. Many people sought refuge on rooftops and verandahs.

A flooded Albert Street near the corner of Elizabeth Street in Brisbane city in 1893. Some were lucky enough to get their hands on a boat, while others had little choice but to wade through the waist-deep water.

all the rising ground were completely packed with human beings, and an empty building, after Saturday afternoon, was not to be had for love or money.'

The flood eventually reached a height some 5.5 metres above the previous record in 1890 before eventually subsiding. The toll was high: 11 people had drowned, including seven miners when the Eclipse Colliery at Tivoli was flooded. Hundreds of houses were destroyed or damaged and there was significant loss of livestock. The overall damage bill was estimated to have been in excess of £2 million ($4 million), which was a colossal sum in 1893.

The 1974 Flood

January 1974 was an unusually wet month right across the tropical north of Australia. Normally, the so-called 'monsoon trough' that triggers the wet-season rains is not established across the area until early in each new year, but in December 1973 it was already in position and began moving southwards during January 1974. Heavy wet-season rains inundated much of Queensland, the Northern Territory and tropical Western Australia, producing widespread flooding across the inland. Many locations received record falls for January, and some even reported exceeding their average annual totals by the end of the month.

Serious trouble began in Brisbane when tropical cyclone Wanda crossed the Queensland coast near Double Island Point on the night of 24 January. As far as winds were concerned, Wanda was not intense, and caused only minor damage. But what it lacked in puff it made up for in rain; it dumped around 200 millimetres over the city during the next 18 hours. The soil of the area was completely soaked, meaning that any future falls would tend to run off into the waterways.

Left: At the height of the 1974 flood a large gravel barge jammed under the Centenary Bridge at Jindalee. It was deliberately sunk to save the bridge.

Opposite: Young residents of suburban Brisbane attempt to clean up, rescuing whatever they can from the deep mud left behind by the 1974 floodwaters.

As Cyclone Wanda moved inland, it triggered intense falls of rain across the entire catchment of the Brisbane River during the next three days. From 24 to 29 January Brisbane received approximately 75 per cent of its average annual rain, with falls of between 500 and 900 millimetres recorded in various suburbs. Saturday 26 January was the wettest single day in Brisbane since 1887.

The Brisbane River and all its tributaries flooded across large areas, with the river reaching a width of over 3 kilometres in some parts. Witnesses described a 'sea' covering the suburbs, reaching roof height.

Flooding at the junction of the Brisbane River and Breakfast Creek totally submerged nearby Albion Park racecourse. A large barge jammed hard up against the Centenary Bridge at Jindalee and had to be scuttled to reduce stress on the structure. The 67,000-tonne oil tanker *Robert Miller* broke from its moorings in the swirling waters of the river and swung broadside, threatening to dam the flow. Quick work from two nearby tugboats averted this emergency, which could have resulted in a substantial intensification of the local flooding.

The river height finally peaked at 6.6 metres as registered at the Brisbane Port Office at 2.15 am on 29 January, and then slowly receded over the next three days.

Sixteen people died and 300 were injured as a result of the floods. Some 8000 people were made homeless, 56 houses were totally destroyed and about 1600 were heavily damaged. In all, 13,000 buildings were affected, with insurance claims exceeding $200 million in the terms of the day, although the total cost was far more than this because of damage to roads and bridges.

As well as the obvious physical damage, there was a heavy social impact. Many people discovered, too late, that their insurance did not indemnify them against flooding, adding financial hardship to the general devastation.

The official report into the incident, compiled by the then Director of Meteorology, Dr W. Gibbs, noted that 'Some people have been permanently affected, both physically and mentally, by the shock of the flood and its aftermath'.

Given the massive population increase during the time between this flood and the one in 1893 (when 11 people died), it is remarkable that the 1974 flood did not result in a far greater loss of life. Almost certainly, the advance warnings available through improved weather forecasting and communications, combined with an organised emergency services response, were powerful contributing factors.

Opposite: Guests of Brisbane's Parkroyal Hotel in 1974 carry their belongings and sometimes each other through the muddy waters to dry ground.

1902

The Federation Drought

Praise the Lord and pass the ammunition.

Howell Forgy, US Army Chaplain at Pearl Harbor

Towards the end of the nineteenth century, a succession of abnormally dry seasons occurred across much of eastern Australia. Between 1895 and 1900 drought gradually extended across large areas, and instead of entering the new century with optimism, much of rural Australia had become increasingly desperate, with repeated crop failures and stock losses.

This dry trend continued during 1901 although, ironically, the opening of Australia's first parliament, in Melbourne on 9 May 1901, was a wash-out, with strong winds and rain driving across the city.

The situation grew so desperate that on 26 February 1902, the New South Wales government declared a public holiday and a day of 'Humiliation and Prayer' in an attempt to finally break the drought. *The Sydney Morning Herald* reported 'Large congregations at the Churches' around Sydney, and although this was a Wednesday, the city 'presented the usual characteristics of the Sabbath'.

'No doubt some of the small retail shops were open,' continued *The Herald,* 'and also the hotels, but in the wholesale establishments of every kind, there was a strict abstention from trade.'

Sydney's St Andrew's, St Mary's, St James' and Christ Church, St Laurence all reported bumper crowds at services during the day, which was, in keeping with the drought, one of 'bright sun and midsummer heat'.

Cardinal Moran led the congregation at St Mary's in a recitation of 'Ad petendam pluviam', or prayer for rain. He then issued instructions to all the clergy in his diocese that this prayer was to be repeated in each mass until 21 March.

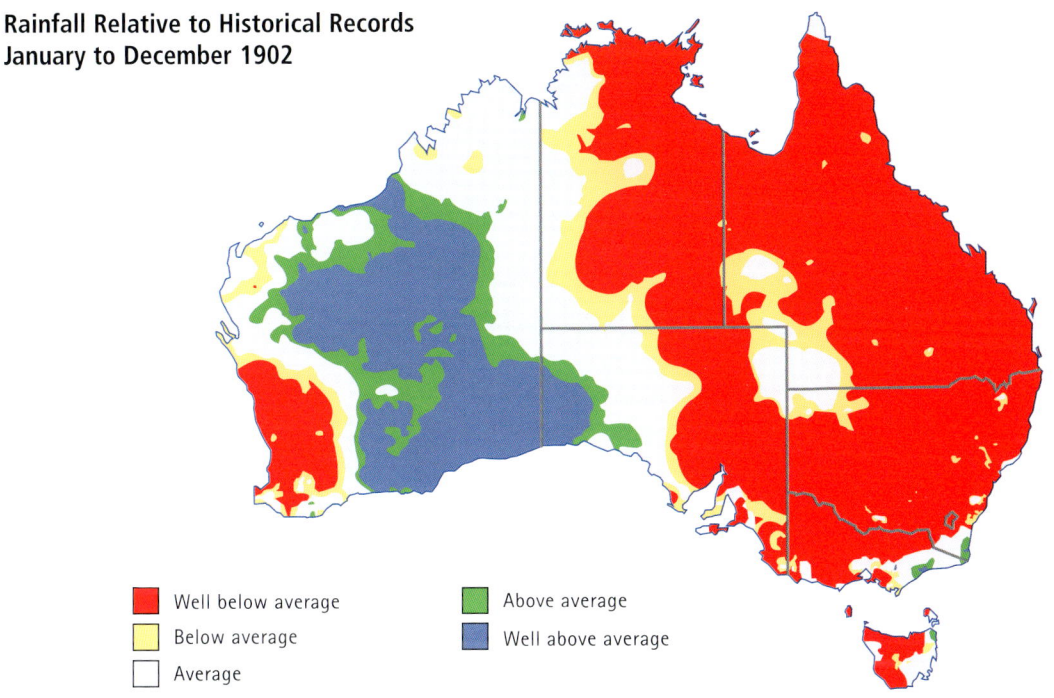

**Rainfall Relative to Historical Records
January to December 1902**

- Well below average
- Below average
- Average
- Above average
- Well above average

The rainfall pattern that was recorded in 1902 shows large areas of extremely low rainfall across eastern Australia. 1902 ended up being Australia's driest single year of the twentieth century.

The Premier of New South Wales, Mr See, was highly pleased with the way the day had gone. He noted that 'A very large proportion of the commercial and trading community had ceased from business'. So far as he could observe, 'no more solemn or holy day could have been spent'. Despite the fact that the hotels had remained open, the premier was also encouraged by the fact that he had observed 'very little drunkenness' about town, which was also a good sign.

However, the drought progressively tightened its grip and became far worse during the second half of 1902, which turned out to be the driest single year of the twentieth century. Stock losses steadily mounted and several of the great inland rivers, including the Darling and the Murray, became chains of muddy waterholes for many kilometres. Massive dust storms swept across the land, stripping the topsoil and converting vast tracts of the inland into desert.

Other attempts were made to coax rain from the copper-sulphate blue skies, with perhaps the most celebrated effort coming from the Queensland Government Meteorologist, Clement Wragge.

Wragge, a highly eccentric character, was not universally admired in scientific circles, where he was variously known by several nicknames, including 'Inclement', and 'Wet Wragge'. But among the general public he attracted considerable popular support.

He proposed to break the drought by simultaneously firing several large cannons into the air. He had a ring of six of these – called Stiger Vortex Guns – installed around the inland Queensland town of Charleville, situated ideally on the Warrego River.

Wragge announced: 'The Warrego will

The Stiger Vortex Gun

The Stiger Vortex Gun was an unlikely device invented in Europe in the early nineteenth century. It was supposed to prevent hailstorms from destroying vineyards. Theoretically, explosions from the gun should prevent raindrops within thunderstorms from forming into hail that would wreak havoc on the grapevines. Why Wragge thought that this machine could be used to generate rain is not clear, but the connection is at best tenuous.

The plans for these guns were imported from Europe. On Wragge's suggestion, local newspapers raised the money for their manufacture, which was undertaken in a Brisbane engineering factory. They were large, cone-shaped barrels about 4 metres high. When fired, they produced huge explosions, rapidly rising smoke rings and a bell-like 'singing' tone that lasted for several seconds afterwards.

So-called 'hail guns' that fire salvoes of acetylene explosive into the air are still used by some orchardists today to prevent hail, but many scientists are dubious as to their effectiveness.

Pictured is one of the guns used by Wragge, now on display at Charleville, Queensland.

behold the unique spectacle of a regular bombardment. Jupiter Tonans and his brother Pluvius will blush with astonishment.'

On 26 September 1902, the cannons were put to work and the surroundings of Charleville shook to the explosions of gunpowder charges, while much of Australia followed the story with intense interest. At noon the guns fired ten shots each, primed with 7.5 ounces (212 grams) of gunpowder, and a few drops of rain fell. A redoubling of efforts was then ordered and a fusillade of fire followed, with two of the cannons eventually bursting under the strain. But this time no rain fell at all.

Predictably, the experiment had failed. With no rain forthcoming, Wragge was subjected to a large amount of public ridicule from around the country, and he later left Australia for New Zealand.

The terrible drought continued. Australia's wheat crop for 1902 was almost totally lost, over 30 million sheep and 4 million cattle were dead and many farmers had been forced off their land.

Finally, in mid-December the drought began to break, and Victoria received substantial rain. Over the following three months, there were good falls also in New South Wales and Queensland. The magical effect of the coming of the rains was well captured by Bernard O'Reilly, whose family lived in the Blue Mountains to the west of

Sydney around the early 1900s. In his book *Green Mountains and Cullenbenbong* he recounts:

Rain was coming! Dad came back from Merriman way to say that a little spring up the hillside was showing moisture. It had been dry for many months and this new phenomenon had sent Dad home as quickly as possible with the glad news. No man who had battled against other droughts could mistake that sign; still, there was a disinclination to believe, for the scourge of 1902 was not as other droughts; there was a hopelessness which had entered the hearts of the people – a feeling that rain would never fall again.

But evening brought other signs: the ants began carrying their eggs to higher levels – long armies of them moved with military precision, for Great Nature had given the evacuation order and warned them that their nests would soon be flooded with storm water. Down on the creek banks, the ants swarmed high into the water gums and found retreats under shingles of bark.

Rain was coming, and animals knew it too. Cattle mooed with new energy and bellowed loudly; horses whinnied; foals and calves almost too weak to stand made a game pretence at frolicking; hens set about oiling their feathers.

A thick haze spread itself across the landscape from the east, subduing and mellowing the last of the sunlight.

Then clouds appeared, great golden fellows blown up like giant balloons, and poised themselves high above the dark bulk of the Blue Mountains. For a while they stood in all their dignity, like actors of the old school pausing after an effective entry. Then they bent towards us, cascading over the mountain slope to the valleys; they came heavy with moisture and trailing long purple streamers of rain across the stricken countryside. The royal afterglow which lit the wild advancing march of the rain was symbolical of the eternal glow of hope that

The Queensland Government Meteorologist in 1902, Clement Lindley Wragge (1852–1922).

arises in the valiant heart of the land-holder at the breaking of a drought.

The Federation Drought produced a massive shift in the mindset of both politicians and land-holders. It was now firmly believed that the solution to farming in Australia's climate was to 'droughtproof' the country. It was proposed that this would be done through irrigation, which became a hot political topic, particularly along the Murray and Murrumbidgee rivers. In 1905 a special position was created within the New South Wales Department of Public Works to study the engineering works required for irrigation in the area. The Burrinjuck Dam and Murrumbidgee Canals Construction Act was approved by the New South Wales Parliament in 1906. Six years later, the Irrigation Act was passed and the Water Conservation and Irrigation Commission was established.

Burrinjuck Dam was the first major dam built for irrigation purposes in New South Wales. Located on the Murrumbidgee River near Yass, it was designed to supply water for the Murrumbidgee Irrigation Scheme. Construction began in 1907, and in a partially completed stage, was able to supply irrigation water in 1912. However, it was not completed until 1927.

A massive wall of dust descends upon Narrandera in southern inland New South Wales during 1902 at the height of the Federation Drought.

1903

A Fatal Race up Mount Wellington

Young lives rashly lost.

The Mercury, Monday 21 September 1903

Mount Wellington, rising to a height of 1270 metres, forms a picturesque backdrop to the city of Hobart, its peak often covered with snow during the winter months. However, because of its southerly latitude, snow-producing cold fronts racing up from the far Southern Ocean can reach the area at any time, even during summer, triggering extreme changes in temperature. When a strong cold front moves through Tasmania, snow can extend down to quite low altitudes, and there are several recorded cases of snow actually reaching sea level around Hobart.

It was Mount Wellington, with its notoriously capricious weather, that formed the stage for a gruelling athletics race in 1903, a race that was to end in a double tragedy. In the early 1900s there was an Australia-wide athletics craze. Numerous running and walking competitions, involving both sprinting and distance events, were staged around the country. Unlike today's fun-running phenomenon, these events mostly involved only trained and sometimes professional athletes, with prizes given and a good deal of public betting on the side.

However, the first major race up Mount Wellington was an all-amateur affair organised by the Tasmanian Amateur Athletics Association. The first prize was not money, but a brand new double-barrelled shotgun presented by the sponsor, Watson Whisky.

The race was organised for Saturday 19 September 1903. Its course was from Lower Elizabeth Street to the top of Mount Wellington and back – a distance of some 27 kilometres. It was a 'Go As You Please' race, meaning that the runner could decide his own route – provided he reached the

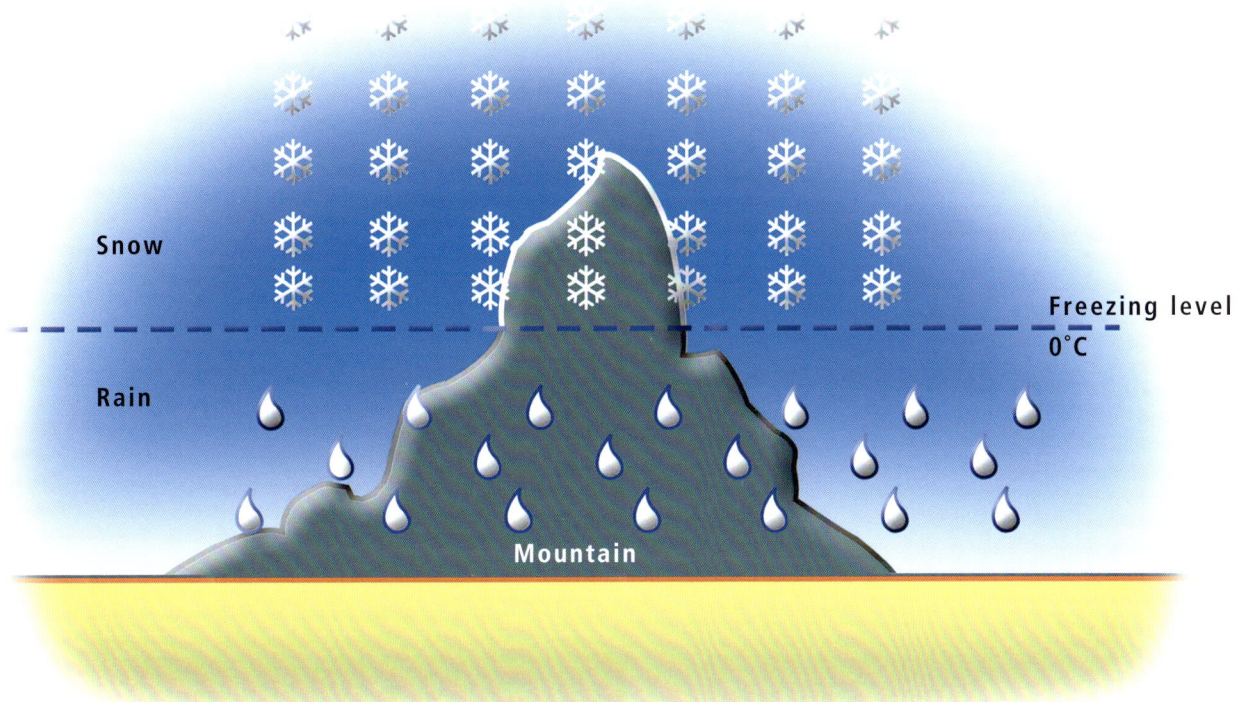

Precipitation over a mountain often occurs in two forms. Above freezing level (0°C), snow can fall; below freezing level rain will fall. The height of freezing level varies from day to day, but during a 'cold outbreak' it can fall to below 500 metres. During the race, the rain initially encountered by runners soon turned to snow above the freezing level.

checkpoint at the top of the mountain, he could go any way he wanted.

On the morning before the race, the weather was described as 'very unsettled', with snow drifting low on the mountain. There was talk of postponing the start, but eventually 39 out of the 70 original entrants began the race in the early afternoon. The pace was a cracker out of the city but naturally slowed as the runners began the arduous climb up the mountain.

Part of the way through the climb, snow began to fall, and the athletes, clad only lightly in athletic singlets and shorts, found themselves in freezing conditions. A strong south-westerly wind produced a chill factor that effectively further reduced the temperature.

The going became too tough for several, and only 23 out of the 39 starters reached the pinnacle and began the downhill run home.

One member of the group of officials at the summit reported that 'He had never met with worse weather on the mountain. With the heavy snow beating on them [the athletes], their clothes got frozen hard'. Leading at the halfway mark was a runner

A view of Hobart in the early 1900s clearly showing a cover of snow around the peak of Mount Wellington. The lower level of the snowline gives a rough idea of the freezing level in the area at that time.

42

called Charles Beard, followed closely by a group that consisted of Betts, McDonald and Cockshutt. Another athlete, Mark Richards, also reached the summit but complained of feeling faint and dizzy. He was about to drop out but, 'encouraged by another competitor', was persuaded to run on.

As a result of the steep downhill grades on the return journey, the pace picked up considerably, but many of the athletes became exhausted in the freezing conditions and dropped out. More than half of the 23 men who reached the summit failed to reach the finish, and only a small band eventually raced into the city, applauded by a large crowd. The eventual winner was Cockshutt in the very respectable time of 2 hours 44 minutes.

However, the euphoria of the finish of the first organised race up Mount Wellington was soon eclipsed by news filtering back from the mountain: Mark Richards had collapsed and died part way down, and another athlete, George Radford, was missing. Local police, together with race promoters, immediately organised search parties, which continued in failing light and falling snow until well after midnight, but no trace of Radford was found. Next morning the search resumed at sunrise, and a little later, Radford's body was found in the snow on the 'Old Fingerpost Track', where he had fallen backwards and frozen to death.

The deaths cast a pall of gloom over the race and its organisers, and a full coronial inquiry was ordered. The inquiry found that both Richards and Radford had died from a combination of heart failure and prolonged exposure to below-freezing conditions.

Such a tragedy is unlikely to happen today. Recognised distance running events involving either elite athletes or 'fun-runners' are carefully planned, with medical assistance available to all competitors. In addition, the weather forecasts from the Bureau of Meteorology are routinely monitored so that race organisers can plan for extreme conditions such as very hot or very cold temperatures.

As far as Tasmania is concerned, not only Mount Wellington, but the State as a whole, can experience great temperature variations. Cold changes can produce snow across many parts of the Tasmanian highlands even during summer, and the Bureau of Meteorology issues 'Bushwalker's Alerts' when such changes are expected.

Today the Radford Track on Mount Wellington is both a memorial and a reminder of the tragic events of September 1903.

1914 & 1991

Storms Hit Sydney

And there fell upon men a great hail out of heaven, every stone about the weight of a talent.

Revelations 16:21

Over the last century or so, Sydney's north shore has suffered several abnormally severe thunderstorms that produced widespread damage and dislocation of services. There is no obvious reason why the north shore should be more thunderstorm-prone than anywhere else in Sydney, unless it is the presence of the so-called north shore ridge – a long spine of elevated ground that the Pacific Highway follows. There is some evidence to support the proposition that 'high' ground does experience increased thunderstorm activity, but this has not been conclusively demonstrated in Sydney.

Two of the big north shore thunderstorms of the twentieth century occurred in 1914 and 1991, and in the former case it's possible that a tornado may have been generated. However, because of the patchy documentation, this is not certain.

A Possible Tornado across Sydney, 1914

On 25 November 1914, a very severe thunderstorm raged across Sydney's north. A contemporary photograph reveals heavy damage to the Lindfield shopping centre, with awnings down and wreckage on both sides of Gordon Road – now the Pacific Highway.

The Sydney Morning Herald reported that 'The roofs of the premises occupied by E. Duval, bootmaker, and H. J. Dale, grocer, which form part of a terrace facing Lindfield Railway Station, were blown completely away and debris was carried across the roadway and onto land adjoining'.

After blasting the north shore, the thunderstorm moved south-east. In the Watsons Bay area, a military tent encampment suffered heavy damage. *The Herald* continued:

> *At Watson's Bay the storm was accompanied by a particularly strong whirlwind which did much damage, flattening trees and tents on South Head, and striking Middle Head, where similar damage occurred. A big tree at Watson's Bay was struck by lightning, and was torn up by the roots. Two of the military tents were caught by the whirlwind and were carried high into the air and deposited about 200 yards away. A lot of other tents were blown down.*
>
> *Mr. T. Farrell of Watson's Bay was working on his 16ft skiff, which he had dragged up from the beach. The wind struck this and carried it up to a height of about 50 feet, hurling it over a fence and dashing it on to the ground where it was badly smashed.*

This description suggests that the storm may have produced a tornado, but the reporter, in describing it as a 'whirlwind', was possibly unfamiliar with the phenomenon.

Heavy damage inflicted to the Lindfield shopping centre by the severe thunderstorm of 25 November 1914: 'The roofs ... were blown completely away and debris was carried across the roadway and onto land adjoining'.

A Terrible Storm, 1991

As bad as the 1914 storm was, a far more intense system struck Sydney's North Shore on Monday 21 January 1991.

The first echoes of the storm were picked up on the Sydney Bureau of Meteorology's radar at about midday on the ranges to the west of Sydney. Later in the afternoon, a large thunderstorm, which had developed near Goulburn to the south-west, was moving towards the metropolitan area.

Meteorologists tracking the storm on the Sydney radar estimated that it was travelling towards the city at about 50 kilometres per hour – an unusually high speed. Fast-moving thunderstorms nearly always produce strong winds, but in this case the intense radar echoes suggested that heavy rain, and even hail, were also likely. This combination can be particularly devastating, as wind-driven hail is usually far more likely to break windows and damage buildings than hail that falls vertically.

Bureau forecasters were increasingly concerned about the nature of the storm evolving before their eyes on the radar screens. At 3.20 pm, the bureau issued a Severe Thunderstorm Warning for the Sydney metropolitan area, alerting the population to the potential for 'strong wind gusts, damaging hail, very heavy rain and flash flooding'.

About 30 minutes later, heavy rain and strong wind gusts were reported from around Camden in the far south-west of the metropolitan area. But another storm system was developing further north, near Badgerys Creek, and it began to move rapidly and irregularly towards the north-east. By 4.10 pm, marble-sized hail was pummelling the Bankstown area.

Intensifying as it progressed, this storm reached the Hornsby area soon after 4.30 pm. Over the next 10 minutes, its full destructive force was unleashed, beginning over Terrey Hills, St Ives and Pymble, with golf ball-sized hail and phenomenal winds.

A resident of St Ives recalled the scene as the storm approached:

> *The skies grew dark green, and were soon almost black and all the streetlights came on. Suddenly the wind rose to a roar and all I could see outside was trees bent almost double, and bits and pieces hurtling through*

The steeple tumbled from the Uniting Church at Turramurra as a result of the thunderstorm downburst of 21 January 1991.

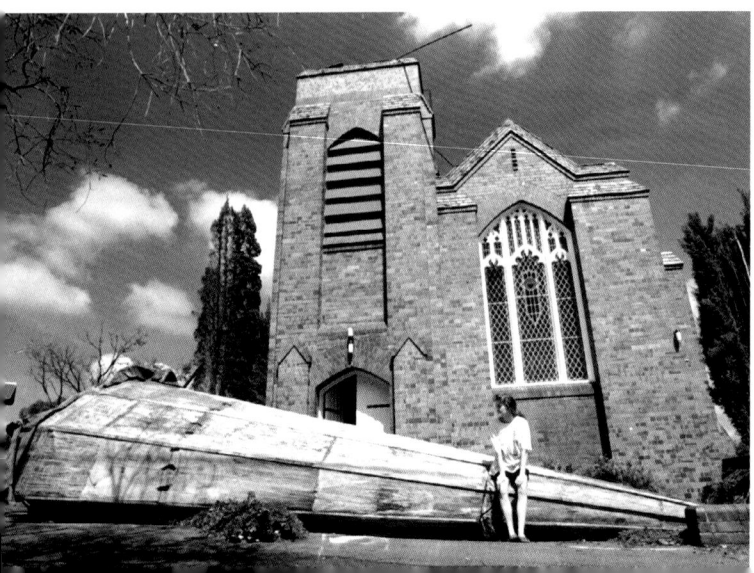

Downbursts

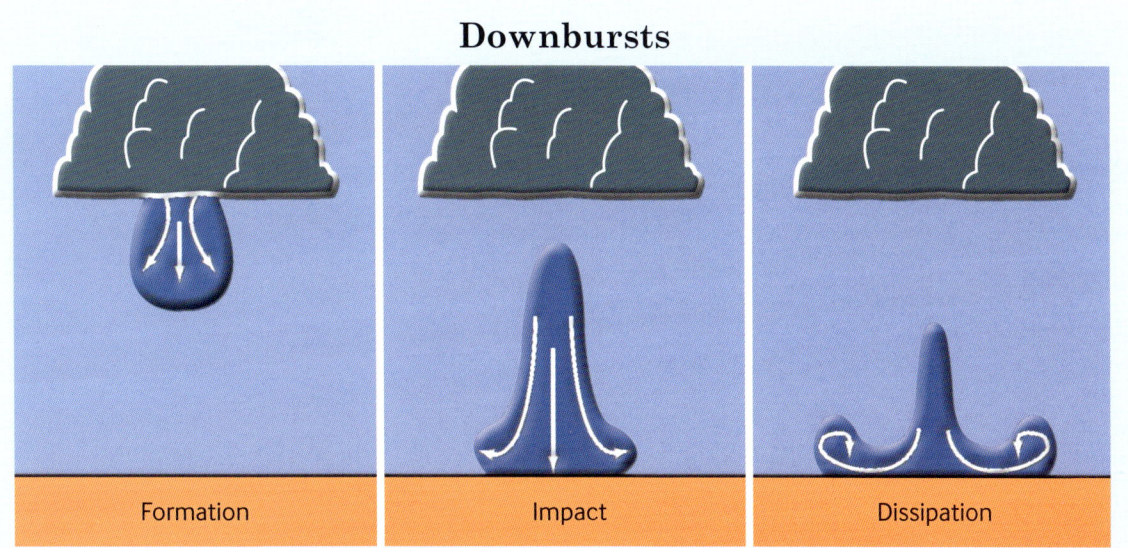

The downburst life cycle.

Sometimes, rain falling from the base of the storm cloud drags down colder, heavier air from above. This column of cold air may contain rain (a 'wet downburst'), or the rain may evaporate before reaching the ground (a 'dry downburst'). The column accelerates downwards, hitting the surface of the ground with such force that the cold air spreads out as a surge of wind, sometimes strong enough to destroy buildings and vegetation.

the air. After about five minutes I went outside and half the trees in the street were down. I had no lights and no power.

State Emergency Services, responding to requests for assistance, were astonished to see far more widespread and severe damage than they had ever envisaged. Hundreds of trees were down, many across roads, blocking access to vehicles. Along with the trees, kilometres of powerlines had been brought down. Houses had had their roofs blown off or been crushed by trees and severe hail-impact wreckage was strewn about everywhere. Hundreds of cars had been severely blasted by hail driven by high-velocity winds.

The storm raged towards the coast, producing further lashings of large hail and destructive winds before crossing the shoreline near Palm Beach and finally blowing itself out at sea.

As night fell, large parts of the north shore were in a shambles, with no power or transport. It was an abrupt transition back into the more primitive world of early local settlers – no lights, no refrigeration, no electric stoves, no hot water. Many residents turned to gas-powered barbecues for cooking, producing an immediate gas shortage in service stations across the area.

It would be up to two weeks before power was restored to some areas. Thousands of kilograms of perishable food had to be disposed of, swimming pools turned green and residents were isolated in their homes as emergency services crews struggled to clear the roadways of mountains of vegetation from fallen trees. For several weeks the entire district echoed to the sound of chainsaws as residents and local council workers alike laboured to clear the debris. This produced its own problems, with many injuries reported from chainsaws and falls from roofs, particularly involving those with lack of proper experience and training.

Gradually services were restored, but it took many months to process all the insurance claims and complete structural repairs. Many residents claimed that local council tree preservation regulations had contributed to the scale of the disaster. The overall damage bill was finally estimated to have been close to $175 million.

In the days following the storm, the damage trail was inspected by meteorologists from the Bureau of Meteorology, who also viewed photographs and film from external agencies. From these various sources a picture was constructed of what had happened.

The severity of the storm was probably due to severe downburst activity but following further investigation the possibility of an embedded tornado could not be dismissed. This conclusion was based on the nature of the wreckage trail, and the complete destruction of large trees that had existed in the area for more than 100 years.

However, the winds were still towards the extreme end of the spectrum, and destruction of several transmission towers around the Akuna Bay area indicated possible wind gusts of 200–230 kilometres per hour. In some areas mean winds of around 150–160 kilometres per hour may have been possible for short periods, and this corresponds to the sort of winds expected in a category 3 tropical cyclone.

The heavy rain and hail was also remarkable. The hail varied from pea-sized over the south-western suburbs, increasing to golf ball-sized over parts of the north shore, and up to the highly destructive orange-sized hail over Terrey Hills and the northern beaches. The recorded rainfall rates were also phenomenal, with several suburbs reporting totals in excess of 45 millimetres in 20 minutes, which represents a one-in-100-year event. This would certainly indicate that the storm was one of the most severe to hit the area since European settlement.

Thunderstorms are part and parcel of the climatology of the Sydney basin, and the events of 21 January 1991 were an extreme example. The performance of the Bureau of Meteorology leading up to this event was certainly state of the art, and continuous improvement in forecasting severe weather over the intervening years means that warnings for any future events should allow even longer lead-times for emergency preparations to take place.

1918

Cyclone Terror in Mackay

The force of the rain was terrible, Mr Shanks remarking that he was bruised all over with the driving rain and had every stitch of clothing ripped off his body.

The Mackay *Daily Mercury*, 26 January 1918

Tropical cyclones are regular visitors to Australia's northern coastlines during summer. While the tropical Queensland coast is not as affected by cyclones as is the north coast of Western Australia, which is one of the most cyclone-prone areas in the world, it is far more densely populated. In relatively unpopulated northern Western Australia, many severe tropical cyclones that could have caused immense property damage and loss of life have passed inland with a minimum of fuss.

But in Queensland, sizeable cities are in the cyclone 'strike' zone, including Cairns, Townsville, Mackay, Rockhampton and, more rarely, Brisbane itself. All of these have felt the wrath of tropical cyclones.

In 1918 there was no technology available to warn people of approaching cyclones. Weather forecasters received daily 9 am observations by telegram sent to a central office from a sparse network of ground stations. These were used to produce the '9 am Weather Chart', which was sent to the main metropolitan newspapers and finally became available to the public the next morning. Radio weather updates were only just beginning and, of course, television was still about 38 years away. Consequently, the weather information generally available to the public was about 24 hours old.

Forecasting of tropical cyclones without satellite and radar imagery, and using 'old' observations, would have been rather like playing Pin the Tail on the Donkey. Forecasters would look for falling barometric pressure, reports of increasing wind, rain and cloud, and rising ocean swell – the latter a time-honoured method used for millennia by Indigenous communities along the

Looking south along Sydney Street, Mackay, after the cyclone, with a tangle of debris piled in the centre of the roadway.

Queensland coast. In some fortunate cases a report from a ship at sea in the area was very useful. But all of this meant that community preparedness was far less than today and sometimes townships were caught unawares by the sudden arrival of a cyclone.

Such an event happened in Mackay during 20 and 21 January 1918. An extremely powerful cyclone, subsequently estimated to have been category 4 or 5, tore across the area, and made what is believed to have been a 'direct hit' on the city.

A massive storm surge, generated by the combination of hurricane-force winds and low atmospheric pressure, transported the sea inland, and huge waves crashed into the centre of the town. In fact, the barometric pressure fell to 933 hectopascals, one of the lowest figures ever recorded in Australia and considerably below that of Cyclone Tracy.

Cyclone-warning Systems

Over the past 50 years or so, Australian governments have invested considerable money and effort in the development of warning systems for the public in cyclone-prone areas. They include the installation of eight weather radar units along Queensland's east coast, and another on Willis Island, approximately 430 kilometres east of Cairns. This radar network, together with regularly received photographs from meteorological satellites, forms the front line of Queensland's tropical cyclone warning system, which is monitored and maintained by the Bureau of Meteorology.

30 people died and devastating floods surged across the surrounding countryside.

On Australia Day 1918, the Mackay *Daily Mercury* published some impressions of the disaster, which give an idea of the magnitude of the storm. (The storm surge is incorrectly referred to as a 'tidal wave' in this report.)

The destructive period of the cyclone was about ten hours and it was almost incredible the amount of damage that was done in that short period. Some of the residents are able to report that not a pane of glass was damaged in their homes, but they are very few. Of the 1200 or 1400 houses within the Municipality of Mackay, not more than one quarter escaped damage of some kind, and in a great many cases the buildings were levelled to the ground.

The town on Monday afternoon presented an appalling spectacle. The damage in most cases consisted of the houses being unroofed, and this particularly applied to the larger buildings such as hotels, churches, public

This storm surge was a major factor in the death toll, with 13 people drowned.

Although there was no official tracking performed on the cyclone, contemporary reports indicated that the system was slow moving, generating about 10 hours of raging winds across Mackay.

The resulting destruction was immense. Some 75 per cent of the housing was either severely damaged or totally destroyed, *halls and two-storeyed buildings. As with other classes of buildings some of them collapsed entirely and some sustained partial damage only. The residential area suffered severely. A great many of the residences were thrown down and completely destroyed, while others were unroofed or otherwise damaged. No particular part of the town suffered more than any other part. The damage was general in town and country and confirms the opinion that the centre of the cyclone traversed the district ...*

While the cyclone was at its height, another terror, in the shape of a tidal wave, swept the town and caused consternation amongst the fear-wracked householders. It struck the coast about five o'clock when the cyclone was raging and it is alleged a wall of water 25 ft high swept over the beaches; and taking a southwesterly direction submerged the town to varying depths as far out as Nebo Road. It was 5 or 6 ft deep on Beach Road and about 2 ft deep at the Ambulance corner. The water flowed inland in waves, carrying debris of a substantial character with it. In the river the waves played havoc with the shipping, wharves, stores and houses, while a large section of the Sydney Street bridge, which is the main avenue between Mackay and North Side, was washed away ...

The cyclone also generated tremendous rainfall, flooding Mackay's Pioneer River. Over 1400 millimetres fell across Mackay in

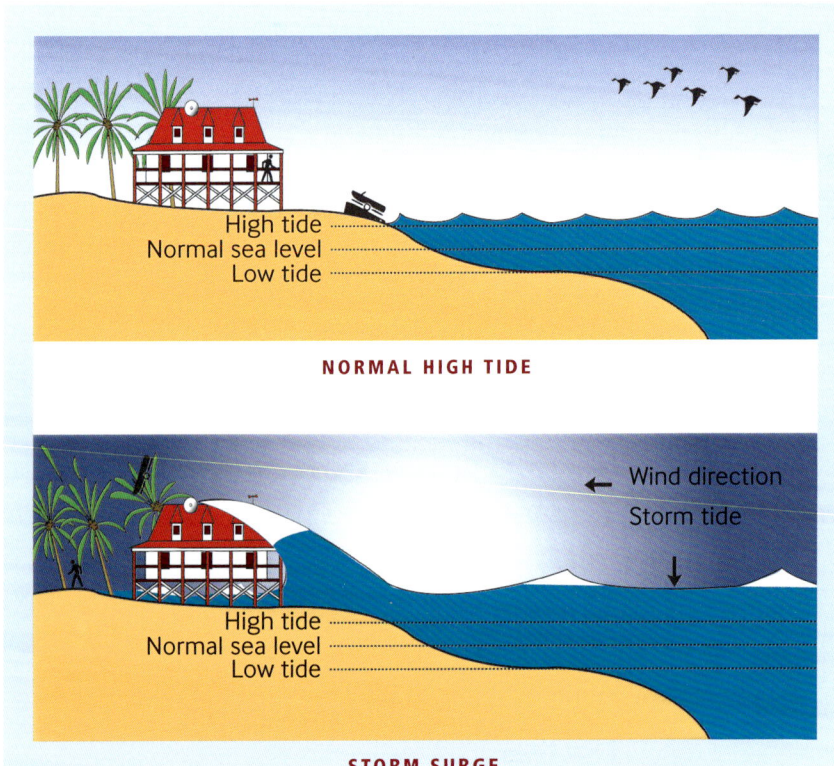

Storm Surges

Powerful winds generated by a tropical cyclone can actually drive the sea ahead of them towards the shoreline. This produces an abnormally high tidal effect, called a 'storm surge', and if superimposed on an existing high tide can result in phenomenal inundation of coastal land by sea water. This is a totally different phenomenon to a tsunami, which is produced by an earthquake, undersea landslide, volcanic eruption or meteor impact.

Washing has been hung out to dry in Sydney Street following the cyclone. Note that the tree in the foreground has been stripped of its leaves.

just three days – well in excess of Brisbane's average annual total of 1151 millimetres. *The Daily Mercury* continued:

> *The heavy rain, combined with the big tide, caused a record flood in the river on Tuesday. There is no authentic record as to the height the river rose, as the gauges were all washed away, but the Harbour Master (Captain Greenfield) states that the water rose at least 20 ft. The river broke across below Devil's Elbow into Barnes Creek and relieved the pressure in the main outlet, and on Thursday morning the back water in the land near the cemetery overflowed and, crossing Nebo Road, rushed down Shakespeare Street and a parallel street to a depth of 3 ft. It is the opinion of experienced men that had this second diversion not occurred the loss of life would have been enormous …*

The Sydney Street Bridge collapsed and sank an Adelaide Steamship Company vessel, the SS *Brinawarr*, that had been moored below. The enormous discharge from the Pioneer River caused fresh water to extend 13 kilometres out to sea from the river's mouth. (This freshwater 'plume' was later blamed for a widespread loss of coral across the adjacent reef during the period soon after the cyclone.)

The building housing Hamilton's bakery lost much of its roof in the cyclone.

Further south, Rockhampton had fared only a little better than Mackay. Six people drowned and hundreds of homes were either damaged or destroyed by the raging waters of the flooded Fitzroy River.

The devastation was so complete that all communication between Mackay and the rest of Australia was severed; telegraph lines were down and all roads into the town were cut by floodwaters. As no contact was received for several days, people in the southern capitals thought that Mackay had been obliterated, but communication was eventually re-established about five days later. (Surprisingly, this complete loss of communication also occurred 56 years later, when Cyclone Tracy devastated Darwin [see page 162] and official contact with the northern capital was lost for several hours.)

The 1918 Mackay cyclone remains one of the most devastating ever to strike an Australian city. Even today, with vastly improved warning and emergency services in place, a storm of similar intensity would certainly produce severe damage.

1918 & 1976

Twisters across Victoria

For they have sown the wind, and they shall reap the whirlwind

Hosea 8:7

Contrary to popular opinion, tornadoes associated with severe thunderstorms are not a rare occurrence in Australia, with about 20 cases reported every year. There are undoubtedly many more, but these occur over remote areas where they are not seen.

The fearsome damage wrought by 'twisters' in the USA is certainly a result of high frequency of severe thunderstorms but also the fact that this activity is occurring over comparatively densely populated areas. Australian tornadoes are also capable of inflicting serious damage if they cross inhabited localities, but thankfully this does not happen often.

However, two severe 'twisters' have occurred over the last century in Victoria, certainly not known as a tornado 'hotspot' in Australia. Both resulted in loss of human life.

The Brighton Tornado, 1918

On 2 February 1918, powerful twin tornadoes struck the Melbourne suburb of Brighton. This remains probably the most intense tornado event ever to strike an Australian capital city.

Spawned by severe thunderstorm activity associated with a cold front, the tornadoes raced across Port Phillip Bay and descended on Brighton, producing an 'orgy of destruction'. (This became rather misleadingly known as 'The Brighton Cyclone'.)

A graphic account of the event can be found in George Johnson's largely autobiographical work *My Brother Jack*. He recalls, as a young boy, the awesome

The Methodist Church in Hawthorn Road was ripped apart by the tornado.

spectacle of the tornadoes' approach:

> *... from the little jetty we saw the great storm which was to become known as the Brighton Cyclone charging towards us across the bay in a whip of white horses below a tumult of bruised purplish crepuscular cloud. Coming across the sea, the cloud would tear off in downward strips that would begin to gyrate madly, and scoop the harbour waters high in the air.*

Upon reaching the shoreline, the tornadoes unleashed their full fury across Brighton where, according to *The Age*, 'hundreds of houses were unroofed, thousands of trees snapped or twisted in two, and fences levelled to the ground … The damage done to property is computed at upwards of 100,000 pounds, and the "risk" was one of those not covered by insurance.'

Tragically, two people died. At Point Ormond, Gordon McLeod, 'a window dresser from Sydney', drowned when the boat he was fishing from capsized. Fifteen-year-old Frank Mallard was decapitated by flying sheet iron at a church picnic at Brighton.

One of the tornadoes continued raging inland, passing across Ormond, Garden Vale and Oakleigh before finally weakening. There is little doubt that the death toll and damage would have been much higher in similar circumstances today, but back in 1918, these areas were much more sparsely settled.

The Commonwealth Meteorologist, Mr H. A. Hunt, issued a press statement the next day, which noted that:

> *... the atmospheric disturbance on Saturday was something in the nature of a tornado …*

'Billilla', a Brighton mansion owned perhaps appropriately by the Weatherly family, was heavily damaged by the twister.

The disturbance, it was thought, was the marked intensification of an ordinary Antarctic storm, with the thunder accompaniments and squalls ... The velocity must have been terrific – stronger than ever I have experienced in Victoria or NSW ...

It was later estimated that the twisters had produced wind gusts of around 320 kilometres per hour, and on the Enhanced Fujita scale this would be a rating of high-end EF 4.

The Enhanced Fujita Scale

RATING	WIND SPEED (km/h)	DAMAGE TYPE
EF0	105–137	Minor
EF1	138–177	Moderate
EF2	178–217	Considerable
EF3	218–266	Severe
EF4	267–322	Devastating
EF5	More than 322	Incredible

The Sandon Tornado, 1976

Saturday 13 November 1976 was a day of increasingly unsettled weather across much of Victoria, and by around 3 pm numerous storms had developed. Although this was not an unusual weather situation for Victoria during November, what was to follow over the next two to three hours would go down in the meteorological record books as one of the more remarkable weather events in Victoria's history.

The thunderstorms continued to build and several eventually reached 'severe' status – capable of producing strong wind gusts, heavy rain, intense electrical activity and large hail. At the top end of 'severe', a thunderstorm can power up a tornado, although this is comparatively rare.

But at around 5.30 pm, a severe thunderstorm cell located between Castlemaine and Ballarat spawned a violent 'twister' that descended on the tiny settlement of Sandon, with tragic consequences. This incident

A remarkable photograph of the Sandon Tornado, taken from about 5 kilometres away. The well-developed, debris-filled funnel is plainly visible.

would be recorded as the 'Sandon Tornado'.

Several eyewitness accounts provided graphic evidence of the violence of the tornado. A group of motorists in three cars, seeing the approaching funnel, pulled to the side of the road, hoping the winds would pass them by. Instead, they watched in awe as the tornado moved slowly and erratically towards them, roaring loudly and snapping off trees in its path. As the edge of the funnel reached the leading car, it began rocking violently and all the windows burst outwards.

The second car was a small Torana, apparently with an elderly couple inside. In horror and with a sense of complete disbelief, a passenger from the first car watched the Torana being sucked up off the road and disappear in a shrieking cloud of debris.

The couple inside were ripped out of their seatbelts and killed as the car was somersaulted about 100 metres down the road by the powerful winds. Their bodies were later found stripped of their clothes some distance away. The wrecked Torana looked as though it had been involved in a high-speed collision.

The two other cars parked in front and behind the Torana rocked violently and were heavily damaged by flying debris. Every window in the front car was smashed, and the rear car was heavily dented. Some of the eight people in these two cars suffered minor cuts and abrasions, but they were otherwise unhurt.

Continuing on its deadly but erratic path, and accompanied by a maelstrom of galvanised iron, roof tiles, tree branches, dust and hay that all swirled about to a height of nearly 100 metres the twister descended on a farm in the nearby hamlet of Sandon.

For about 15 minutes the farmer, his wife and daughter had watched the monster growing larger and larger as it spun towards them, producing a terrible whine 'like a squealing pig' and ripping trees out of the ground and scattering them about as though they were so much straw. The family did not know whether to stay in the house or attempt to flee. They decided to stay, which turned out to be a good decision.

In the bedroom, the farmer tried to keep the windows intact by pushing the blinds up against the glass, but the force of the wind threw him violently backwards. The family crawled under the beds and waited in terror as the windows shattered and the entire house shook violently.

Then with a terrific roar, the tornado smashed across the remainder of the farm, flattening a chicken shed, pulling a full fuel tank off its stand and damaging other outbuildings and machinery. Eventually the funnel moved another 4 kilometres from the farm and dissipated in a heavily forested area.

The next day, police and locals discovered that in 25 minutes the twister had cut a swathe 6 kilometres long and 400 metres wide across the countryside. In addition to the two deaths, the tornado caused thousands of dollars of damage through destruction of sheds and windmills and animals being swept away. Dozens of 30-metre red gums had been 'thrown about like matchsticks', and many of these were still blocking the road the next day. Police on the scene remarked that 'there could have been another Darwin' had the tornado crossed a more populated area (see page 162).

A team from the Bureau of Meteorology later toured the Sandon area and reviewed the damage trail. Their investigation concluded that the thunderstorm driving the tornado was a full strength 'supercell' with cloud tops reaching as high as 18 kilometres into the atmosphere, more than twice the height of Mount Everest.

Tornadoes are classified according to the Enhanced Fujita Scale. The weakest tornado attracts a rating of EF 0 and the strongest EF 5. Following analysis of the wreckage trail, and in particular the distance the Torana was carried down the road, it was concluded that the tornado was generating winds of up to 300 kilometres per hour. That defines it as EF 4.

Interestingly, in 2003 a television crew travelled to Sandon to prepare a 'special' on the tornado. Locals showed them around the area and pointed to sheets of rusty galvanised iron still wrapped in the treetops after nearly 27 years!

The Sandon Tornado remains one of the most powerful twisters yet seen in Australia, and had it passed across a large township, there is little doubt that there would have been a much higher death toll, as well as a far more devastating damage bill.

1929

Tasmania in Flood

And it came to pass after seven days, that the waters of the flood were upon the earth.

Genesis 7:10

Most of Tasmania's rainfall occurs during winter and spring over the western half of the island; it is unusual for heavy rain to fall over eastern Tasmania. However, during early April of 1929 strong, moisture-laden easterly winds associated with a monsoonal depression moving south from the mainland dumped intense, torrential rains over much of eastern and northern Tasmania, causing disastrous flash flooding.

Interestingly, forecasters of the day, relying largely on barometers (a reliance that today has been substantially reduced by computer modelling, satellite photography and radar imagery), accurately predicted the flooding, noting that:

> *Barometers are now falling, due apparently to the southward movement of the depression, and further rain is to be expected, with probable flood falls in the north-east.*

Overnight on Wednesday 3 April the reasons for the falling barometric pressure became clear. Not only was the depression moving south, but it was becoming more intense, with strengthening winds and heavier rain. The weather chart at 9 am on 4 April showed a deep low-pressure cell over Victoria and a pronounced north-easterly wind flow across Tasmania. This was the perfect recipe for a flood.

From 3 April, heavy falls increased across northern Tasmania, intensifying through Thursday. The highest rainfall totals occurred across the north-eastern corner, but also extended across much of the north coast, including the Burnie–Heybridge and Ulverstone areas.

Prodigious flooding across most of the catchments in the area inundated hundreds of houses and cut transport and communications. In the worst single incident, on Thursday 4 April the huge dam on the

Cascade River above the town of Derby, constructed a few years before by the Briseis Tin Mining Company, burst 'without a second's warning' under the weight of the flood. The dam was about 1.6 kilometres long and 20 metres deep, with a capacity of 3500 kilolitres.

The Mercury reported that:

… thousands of tons of water rushed at terrific speed down the narrow gorge to the township, uprooting trees and moving boulders of many tons weight as it passed. The first warning was given, apparently by the Assistant Manager of the mine (Mr. W.A. Beamish) as the waters came in sight, travelling at terrible speed, and so far as is known, Mr. Beamish, who is numbered among the seven men who were reported last night to be missing, was able to warn only those people who were in the mines office before it was overwhelmed, and he himself was carried away.

It was later established that 14 people had drowned in this single incident.

Soon afterwards, many houses and other structures were carried away down the raging Ringarooma River and the low-lying areas of Derby were also inundated.

As the downpour continued, several major bridges were swept away, including the railway bridge over the Blithe River near Burnie and also the Scamander Bridge, isolating St Helens and St Marys. Between Ulverstone and Penguin a major landslide cut the railway line and severed all telegraphic communication. The Avoca River also reached record levels, completely washing away the local railway station. Serious flooding occurred at Fingal, where the South Esk River rose to record heights. The Swan River near Cranbrook grew to nearly a kilometre wide, isolating several houses, and many roads were blocked by fallen trees and landslips. Gale-force winds also accompanied the deluge and prevented

Tasmania's Weather

Because of Tasmania's comparatively high latitude, much of the weather affecting it during the winter and spring is associated with cold frontal activity racing across the Southern Ocean to the far south of mainland Australia. During the summer months, belts of high pressure move southwards across the State, tending to produce settled conditions. This distribution of the pressure systems means that most rain falls during the winter and spring, and mostly over the western half of the island.

Only occasionally does it rain heavily over eastern Tasmania, and this is normally associated with a burst of wind from the east, which transports moisture in from the Tasman Sea.

Such bursts of easterly winds are usually associated with the development of a low-pressure cell to the north of Tasmania, as the clockwise circulation around the 'low' will then generate an easterly flow across the State. Under these circumstances, but depending on the strength and position of the low, heavy rain can follow over much of eastern Tasmania, sometimes extending northwards across eastern Victoria and south-eastern New South Wales.

the steamship *Nairana* from entering the Tamar River above Launceston. And, in a tragedy almost on a par with the Briseis dam disaster, eight people drowned when a truck crashed off a bridge near Ulverstone.

On the South Esk River lay the major hydro-electric station at Duck Reach. This was one of the first such power stations in Australia, and began producing power for the Launceston City Council in 1895. During the planning stages there had been considerable opposition to the scheme, as some believed that it was being built in a flood-prone area. But the project went ahead despite this opinion, and over the following few years its capacity was increased. By 1919 it was producing 2 megawatts of power for Launceston.

On the night of Friday 5 April the pundits were finally proven correct when a roaring torrent of water swept down the South Esk River and demolished the Duck Reach power station, as well as a nearby suspension bridge. Longford, about 25 kilometres south of Launceston, was also flooded.

Launceston itself was in a perilous state. Located on the Tamar River, where the North and South Esk rivers converge, it lay

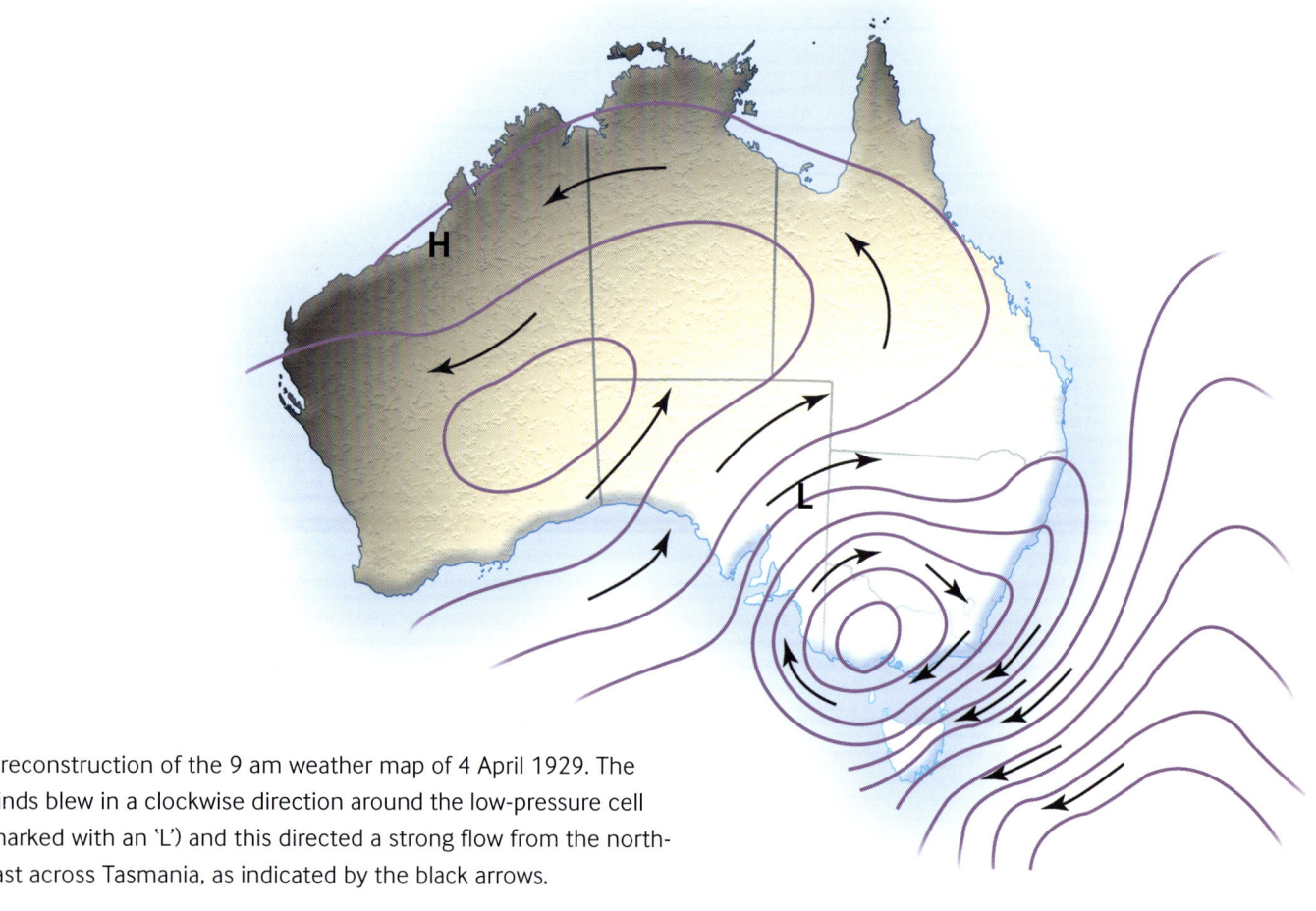

A reconstruction of the 9 am weather map of 4 April 1929. The winds blew in a clockwise direction around the low-pressure cell (marked with an 'L') and this directed a strong flow from the north-east across Tasmania, as indicated by the black arrows.

between the two areas of high rainfall to the west and east. Floodwaters converged from both directions, and on Friday 5 April the Esk and Tamar rivers rose to record levels. When the water reached Launceston, more than 1000 homes in the low-lying areas were inundated and over 3000 people were evacuated.

Finally the low-pressure cell weakened and moved away, and after three days of intense rainfall, the weather began to ease. Much of eastern and northern Tasmania had been devastated, with tremendous flood damage to housing and huge stock losses. The damage to the State's infrastructure was also immense. Railway lines were cut, roads were blocked by landslides and washaways, power and telegraph lines were down and many important bridges were destroyed. Twenty-two lives had been lost and many people had been traumatised by the ferocity of the event. It was to be several months before normal services were restored across the affected areas.

At the time there was no organised flood-warning service in operation. Should the same situation occur today, we could expect advanced warning of the development of the low-pressure cell, together with an organised response among the various emergency services. Whilst a similar situation would certainly produce massive property and infrastructure damage, this would be minimised and a reduction in stock losses would be likely. There would also be a reduced likelihood of such a large number of human fatalities, and a faster recovery time due to vastly improved 'readiness' among our emergency services.

1931

The Southern Cloud Disappears

Though far and wide they sought him, they found not where he fell
For the ranges held him precious, and guarded their treasure well.

'Lost', 'Banjo' Paterson

In the early morning of Saturday 21 March 1931, Captain Travis Shortridge, his co-pilot and six passengers boarded their Avro 10 aircraft VH-UMF, the *Southern Cloud*, for a routine commercial flight from Sydney to Melbourne. The weather was overcast, with a light northerly wind and the temperature was close to 22°C. Soon after 8 am, the plane lifted off from Sydney airport, climbed away to the south-west and set course for Essendon airport in Melbourne. It would not be seen again for 27 years, and became Australia's first major civil aviation accident.

During the late 1920s and early 1930s, passenger flights between Sydney, Brisbane and Melbourne had gradually become more common as the public was slowly convinced that flying was the safe, fast and modern way to travel.

Australian National Airways (ANA) operated daily services between the eastern capitals using their fleet of five Avro 10s, all named in honour of Sir Charles Kingsford Smith's legendary *Southern Cross*. There was the *Southern Sky, Southern Star, Southern Moon, Southern Sun* and *Southern Cloud*, all state-of-the-art aircraft designed by the English company Avro.

By modern-day standards, the Avro 10 was a primitive machine, although regarded as safe and reliable. It was powered by three ponderous Armstrong Siddeley Lynx seven-cylinder air-cooled radial engines, each generating a modest 240 horsepower. It was not a small aircraft, being 14.25 metres long, with a massive wingspan of over 21 metres, but it could only carry two crew and a maximum of eight passengers. The cruising speed was 160 kilometres per hour, with a top speed of about 185 kilometres per hour and it could reach an altitude of around 3400 metres – not a great deal higher than Mount Kosciuszko's 2228 metres.

The Avro 10 was not equipped with two-way radios, which meant that once the flight had commenced, the aircraft was completely out of contact with anyone on the ground. While this situation seems incredible from today's point of view, it was the accepted modus operandi in 1931. However, this shortcoming was to prove of critical importance in the flight of the *Southern Cloud*.

Because civil aviation was only in its infancy, meteorological services to the aviation industry were in the early stages of development, and the fast communications required to provide an efficient amendment and update service were yet to be developed. Meteorological observations were transmitted between the various weather offices by hand-delivered telegram, and the synoptic charts (or 'weather maps') were only updated once

Sir Charles Kingsford Smith

Charles Kingsford Smith (1897–1935) was one of the great Australian heroes of the first half of the twentieth century. A decorated airman of World War I, he became one of the pre-eminent aviation pioneers of the era, setting many early endurance records. In 1928, accompanied by co-pilot Charles Ulm and navigator Harold Lyon, he became the first pilot to fly across the Pacific Ocean, tracking between San Francisco and Brisbane in his famous aircraft, the *Southern Cross*. He was immediately acclaimed as a national hero. Tragically, 'Smithy' disappeared in 1935 while flying across Burma and his body has never been found.

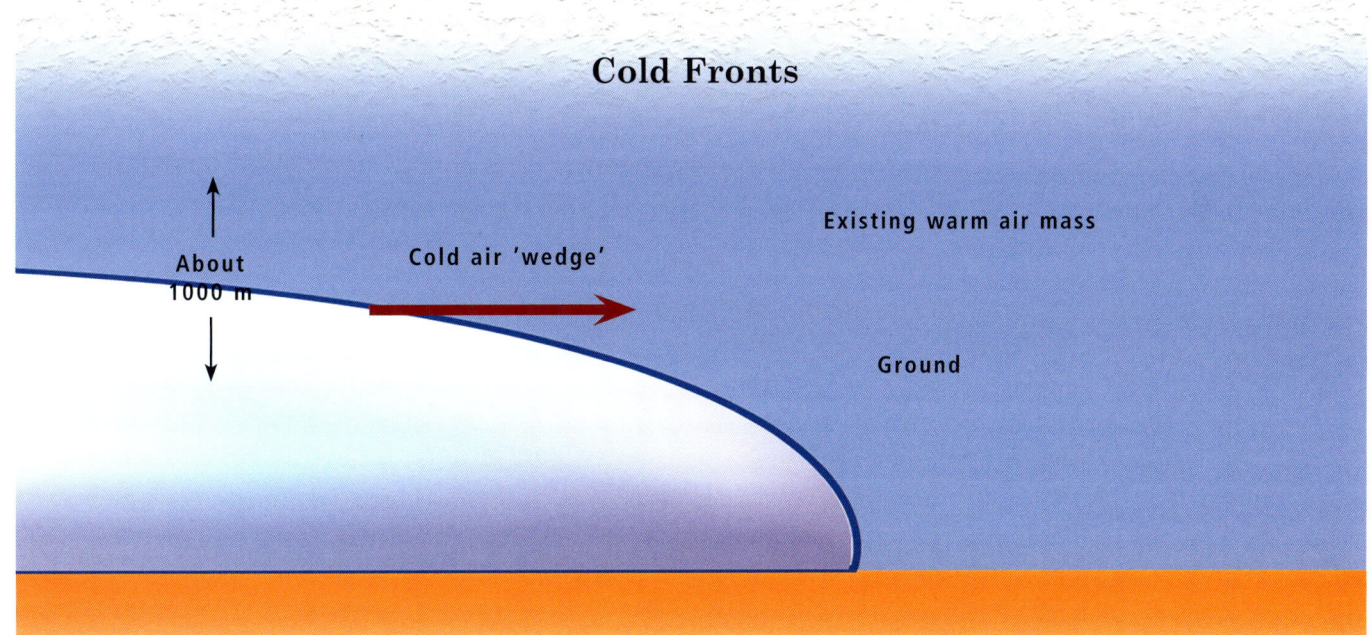

Cold fronts were named after the battle fronts of World War I. These comparatively narrow bands of atmospheric upheaval are produced when a large mass of cold air drives 'wedge-like' under an existing area of warmer air, sometimes generating massive drops in temperature, together with strong winds and thunderstorms. Cold fronts also extend well above the Earth's surface and can pose dangers to aviation in the form of airframe icing, turbulence and loss of visibility due to rain.

The Southern Cloud in flight. Note the large non-retractable undercarriage that was a feature of aircraft of the era.

per day, using the observations taken at 9 am.

When the *Southern Cloud* departed Mascot, it was carrying a forecast of weather conditions en route that had been prepared the previous day, so was based on observations some 12–24 hours old. This forecast apparently indicated no extreme conditions, although a wind change, together with some shower and thunderstorm activity, was predicted.

However, with the flight barely two hours old, the Assistant State Meteorologist in Sydney, Harold Camm, became concerned when a particularly strong cold front swept across Sydney.

The following cryptic extract from the official Sydney observations recorded in the Bureau of Meteorology's journal notes the arrival of this front:

March 21st 1931 – Light n'ly wind till 9am but strong, squally westerly change at 10am with driving rain ...

Camm anxiously awaited the arrival of the 9 am weather observations from Victoria, and when they finally reached the Sydney Bureau of Meteorology's office up on Observatory Hill by telegram delivery at about 10.30 am, his worst fears were confirmed. A major cold front had indeed whipped across south-eastern Australia overnight and raging winds from the west and south-west were surging up into New South Wales from Victoria.

Cold fronts of this nature are more common in winter, but can occur at any time of the year, and are sometimes referred to as 'cold outbreaks'. These weather systems drag cold polar air from the far Southern Ocean over south-eastern Australia and can produce highland snow, even during summer. For aviation, cold outbreaks can generate a whole

The bus-like interior of an Avro 10. To reach the cockpit, the pilot would walk down the centre aisle and step up through the doorway at the end.

raft of hazards, including very strong winds, severe turbulence, icing and reduced visibility in low cloud and rain.

In the modern era of lightning-fast communication and radar and satellite photography, it is inconceivable that a major front would ever be 'missed', but in 1931, such rapidly evolving weather events could easily slip through the network of slow-reacting observation and communication systems.

Upon seeing the Victorian telegram, Camm immediately telephoned Australian National Airways management and spoke in person to Charles Ulm, who had gained previous fame as Sir Charles Kingsford Smith's co-pilot during the late 1920s.

Camm informed Ulm that the weather situation was far worse than originally forecast and that the *Southern Cloud* was probably encountering cyclonic weather with tremendous headwinds, severe turbulence, rain and even snow. However, both men knew that, with no way of contacting the aircraft, there was absolutely nothing they could do with this vital information.

At this time, far away to the south-west, across the wild peaks and ravines of the Great Dividing Range, the *Southern Cloud* would have been bucking into turbulent headwinds, rain squalls and low cloud in a desperate battle for survival.

A grim wait began to hear if the aircraft had landed anywhere, either at its scheduled refuelling point near Wangaratta, or at any other airfield where the crew could have attempted to take shelter from the raging conditions. The nature of the front indicated that extremely strong winds from the south-west were blowing right across the flight path; the *Southern Cloud* would be struggling directly into these, slowing its ground speed dramatically. So at best, a late arrival was expected. But when the time of fuel exhaustion had passed, it was realised that something terrible must have happened. A massive land and air search was launched and continued for several weeks afterwards, but no trace of the *Southern Cloud* was found.

The Air Accident Investigation Committee soon convened a formal inquiry. Significantly, its final report recommended more frequent updates of meteorological observations and synoptic weather charts, as well as the establishment of a forecast amendment service. Just as significantly, the report recommended that all passenger aircraft should be equipped with two-way radios; in addition, ground radio stations should be established to communicate with all passenger aircraft and to monitor progress towards their destinations.

The loss of the *Southern Cloud* had a devastating effect on aviation services in general. ANA went out of business later in 1931 and public confidence in air travel fell sharply. It only gradually recovered over a period of several years thereafter.

But remarkably, the story of the *Southern Cloud* was not over. Twenty-seven years

A remarkable photograph showing the Southern Cloud and a group of passengers about to depart Essendon airport for Sydney in 1930, about a year before the crash. The pilot, Shortridge, can be seen near the centre of the group wearing flying headgear, and to the left of him is Don Bradman. The course of Australian cricket would have been changed forever had 'The Don' been flying in the same aircraft a year later.

later, in 1958, a worker in the Snowy Mountains, Tom Sonter, stumbled across some strange, rusty metallic wreckage in a wild, inaccessible part of Kosciuszko National Park. Closer examination revealed the presence of skeletal human remains. The *Southern Cloud* had at last been found, and from its position, a more accurate reconstruction of the flight was attempted. An amazing picture emerged.

The aircraft had only managed to cover 353 kilometres from Sydney, and if the flying time were calculated on a full tank of fuel, that represented an average speed of only 71 kilometres per hour. As the cruising speed

of the Avro was around 160 kilometres per hour, this pointed to average headwinds of about 90 kilometres per hour – a vindication of Harold Camm's telephone warning to Ulm all those years before. In fact, because the early part of the flight had been conducted in far lighter conditions, the strength of the headwinds was probably much greater than this, suggesting that the *Southern Cloud* could have been blown backwards during its final minutes of flight.

A certain amount of speculation still surrounds the direct cause of the crash. Did the aircraft ice up (when a coating of ice forms on the aircraft and affects its performance)? Was it forced down by severe turbulence? Or did the crew attempt to descend below the cloud base in the belief that they were nearing Melbourne? This latter scenario is perhaps the most credible, as it is unlikely that Captain Shortridge would have realised the extent of the headwinds opposing the aircraft. Perhaps it was some combination of all these, but the precise answer will never be known.

Today, a memorial for the *Southern Cloud* containing pieces from the three radial engines stands near Cooma in New South Wales. It is a reminder of the price that was paid in the quest for aviation safety.

1937

O'Reilly and the Stinson

I've found that missing aeroplane, and there are two men still alive.

Green Mountains and Cullenbenbong, Bernard O'Reilly

On Friday 19 February 1937 an intense, slow-moving tropical cyclone was located approximately 250 kilometres to the east of Brisbane and the weather across much of south-eastern Queensland was appalling. A shrieking south-easterly gale was blowing across the high mountains of the Great Dividing Range. Low cloud and pelting rain reduced visibility occasionally to near zero. Locals described the weather across the mountainous area near the Queensland – New South Wales border as the worst they'd ever seen. Wind speed was estimated to be '80 miles per hour' (130 kilometres per hour) on the ground.

But at Archerfield aerodrome near Brisbane the weather was much better. The overcast skies and gusty winds were nothing seriously out of the ordinary. A Stinson tri-motor airliner, VH-UHH, captained by Rex Boyden and carrying five passengers, began running up its engines in preparation for a scheduled flight down to Sydney via Lismore. After a normal take-off, the airliner vanished into low cloud.

But this flight was to be far from routine. It was to become one of the epic stories of Australian aviation, producing a popular hero who would be acclaimed as the embodiment of the Australian bushman.

Concern began to grow when the Stinson did not arrive in either Lismore or Sydney, and increased as the time passed when fuel would have been exhausted. Unfortunately, in spite of the recommendation arising from the crash of the *Southern Cloud* in 1931 that two-way radios be fitted on all passenger-carrying aircraft (see page 66), for a variety of reasons, including slow-moving officialdom, the aircraft had no radio. Contact with Boyden was impossible.

As soon as it became obvious that something terrible must have happened to the Stinson, a huge aerial search was

The VH-UHH in flight. Stinsons were far more modern in appearance than their predecessors, the Avro 10s. However, their safety record in Australia was far from impressive, with three of the four introduced aircraft eventually crashing.

launched – up until that time the biggest in Australia's history – involving the Royal Australian Air Force and a large number of civil aircraft. The search area was largely based on eyewitness reports of the Stinson at various locations up and down the New South Wales coast. The aircraft had not touched down at Lismore as planned, but it was assumed that because the weather had been so bad, that Boyden would have decided to bypass this stop and fly direct to Sydney. When the plane was not located, it was generally assumed that it had crashed in the ocean and would probably never be found.

Amid all the intense public and media speculation about the Stinson's fate, an unlikely figure emerged. It was Bernard O'Reilly, one of the sons of the pioneering O'Reilly family, who had established a guesthouse in the rugged mountains to the south-west of Brisbane. O'Reilly was no aviation expert; he was a bushman who had helped his family carve a living from running a tourist accommodation deep in the tropical rainforest decades before the concept of ecotourism was ever heard of. However, this unique training had given him a commonsense logic, combined with a whole host of bushcraft skills. It also provided him with a sense of self-sufficiency that meant he did not necessarily believe all that the experts said.

He had been following the story of the missing Stinson with great interest, as he had often seen similar flights passing by on their way south. O'Reilly reasoned that because the aircraft had not landed at Lismore, the most likely place to search

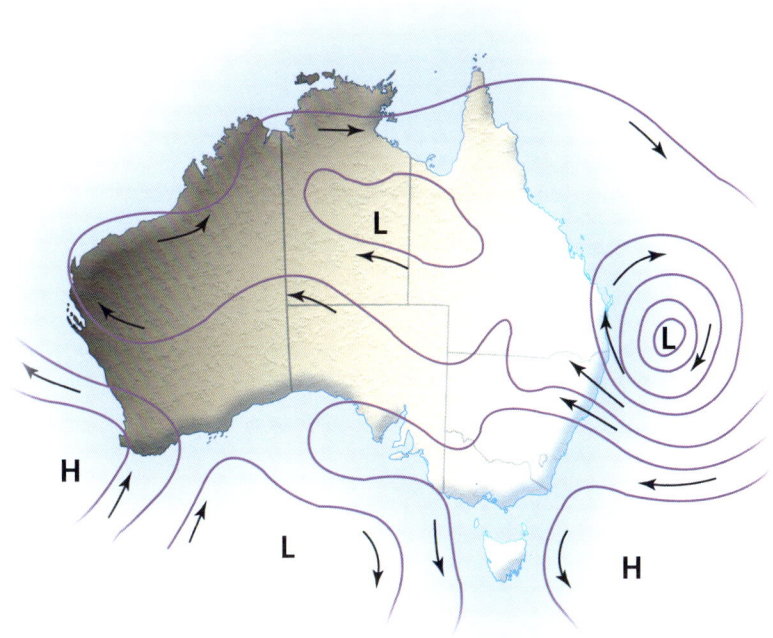

A reconstruction of the 9 am weather map of 19 February 1937. A tropical cyclone off the Queensland coastline (represented by the 'L') was directing particularly strong south-easterly winds across the New South Wales/Queensland eastern border areas.

would be on a line between Archerfield and Lismore. Part of this line was not far from the O'Reilly guesthouse in Lamington National Park, adjacent to the rugged McPherson Range that extends roughly south-west to north-east across the area with several peaks and ridges rising to over 900 metres.

Seven days after the Stinson had vanished, and after the official search had been abandoned, O'Reilly began his own investigation. He trekked through the jungle alone, moving down his pencil line drawn between Archerfield and Lismore on the map he carried with him. This was incredibly tough going, up and down steep mountainsides and through thick, tangled rainforest.

O'Reilly slept rough on the jungle floor the first night. On the second day he reached a high clearing with panoramic views of the rainforest stretching away into the distance. Then he saw something. Away across the ranges there was a small splash of brown floating in the endless green sea of the jungle. And it was just about bang on his pencil line! Could this indicate a small area of burnt tree canopy?

After another gruelling three hours, O'Reilly finally approached the area. Some years later, in his book *Green Mountains and Cullenbenbong*, he recounted what happened next:

> … a big gap in the tree tops just ahead. I tore a piece of vine aside to get a better view, the great tree beside the gap was blackened by fire, right to its branches. God in Heaven! What was this? … Before I looked down, I knew what I would see – a mass of smashed and charred metal. It was more than that; it was a horrible, unclean thing which held the remains of what once were men – a repulsive thing which I could not go near.

Incredibly, there were two survivors – John Proud and Joe Binstead – who had been able to scramble clear of the burning wreckage and had by this time been out in the jungle without food for ten days. Proud was grievously injured, with a shattered and gangrenous leg, and Binstead was suffering from hunger and exposure. A third survivor, passenger Jim Westray, had set off soon after the crash to try to reach civilisation and organise a rescue. The crew and two other passengers had been killed on impact.

After making Proud and Binstead as comfortable as he could, O'Reilly set off down

The tangled mass of burnt-out wreckage of the Stinson on the jungle floor some 10 days after the crash.

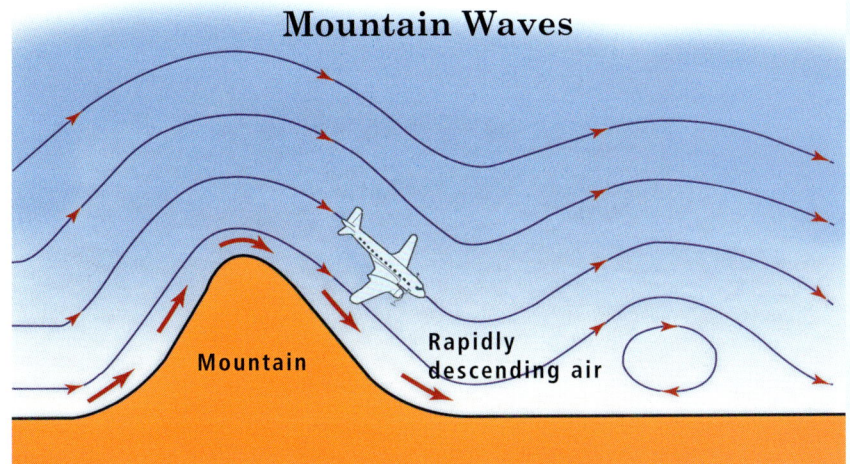

Mountain Waves

Mountain waves are generated when strong winds blow across a mountain range, causing huge 'ripples' in the atmosphere, with powerful downdraughts and updraughts. These series of wave-like disturbances in the airflow can continue for several kilometres, and extend from near the ground up to very high altitudes. When the winds involved are particularly strong, mountain waves can produce hazardous flying conditions with extreme turbulence for aircraft.

the mountain in the direction he thought the nearest settlement lay. He soon discovered the body of Westray who, having survived the crash, had died as a result of a fall down one of the treacherous cliffs in the area.

O'Reilly virtually ran 13 kilometres down the mountain, and finally established contact with some locals around nightfall. He told them: 'I've found that missing aeroplane, and there are two men still alive'.

A massive rescue operation was quickly organised, and by dawn a leading group, accompanied by a doctor, was advancing up the side of the mountain. A larger party followed behind, using axes and brush hooks to cut a trail through the scrub along which the injured men would be transported. Early next day, the two survivors were carried back to civilisation on stretchers by relays of rescuers, and finally taken to hospital by ambulance. Both survived the ordeal to tell their story.

The Stinson had flown into deteriorating weather soon after take-off, and the pilot was battling to keep control in severe turbulence, driving rain and cloud right on the ground. Finally, the aircraft was thrown about uncontrollably and smashed into a big tree, falling to the ground and bursting into flames.

The direct cause of the crash was obviously the weather, but more specifically it was possibly associated with a phenomenon called 'mountain waves'.

The diagram above shows how strong downdraughts can be generated on the leeside of mountains, and aircraft entering this region are in danger of being forced perilously low.

In this case, tremendously strong south to south-east winds driven by the cyclone were striking the wall of the McPherson Range, and it is likely that mountain waves were being generated immediately to the north-west. The Stinson could well have been forced down by the associated downdraughts.

O'Reilly went on to describe this phenomenon in his book:

On the southern side from which the cyclone blew at its greatest velocity, the range rises from low coastal country in great sheer ramparts, for from three to four thousand feet. The cyclone, striking full against these mighty walls was forced up in a great arc at more than a hundred miles an hour. It is an established scientific fact that the descending section of the arc has even greater velocity. Back a few yards from the edge of the cliff, where the wind screamed like a thousand demons, was a dead calm in which it would be possible to light a cigarette with ease.

O'Reilly was justifiably acclaimed as a national hero, and his feat of bushcraft was held up as a perfect example of the rugged nature of the Australian bushman. But he was a modest and self-effacing man who tended to shun the huge publicity surrounding his feat. However, he was to again demonstrate the commonsense and intuition that enabled him to locate the crash site in the first place when he wrote prophetically in his book:

There has been something on my mind since the crash, and this seems to be the place to say it. We all know that the safety of aviation has been built on the lessons of a thousand disasters. What then is the lesson of the Lamington crash – to me it seems this. There should be at each great aerodrome a disinterested official (preferably a

An exhausted Bernard O'Reilly relaxes with a cup of tea after the rescue.

Government official) with full knowledge of wind and air conditions along immediate air routes. This official should have the power to ground a plane, if, in his opinion, the occasion warrants it.

This system, as suggested by O'Reilly, is very close to the procedures we use today, with Bureau of Meteorology aviation meteorologists providing forecast weather conditions to all regular public transport flights on a routine basis. The flight of VH-UHH, whilst producing a tragic outcome for the victims and their relatives, was also a major stepping stone towards increased safety in Australian aviation.

1938

Mass Rescue at Bondi Beach

And the sea arose by reason of a great wind that blew.

John 6:18

Saturday 5 February 1938 was a red-letter day in Sydney. Amidst nearly an hour of colourful pomp and ceremony, the British Empire Games had been formally opened at the Sydney Cricket Ground. Scores of pigeons and gas-filled balloons were released as a prelude to the march-past of the athletes. One press report noted that during the ceremony, 'Smaller boys struggled along under the lightness of tethered gas-filled balloons, nearly swung off their feet as they met a gusty wind'. However, this little-remarked-upon occurrence was closely linked to the dramatic event that was to take place the next day in the surf off Sydney.

Sydney's surf-lifesaving clubs have become very much part of the local culture over the last 75 years, with the beach clubhouse a central feature of any seaside suburb. Perhaps the most famous one of all is the Bondi Surf Life Saving Club, and its proud history includes the greatest ever mass surf rescue in Australia on 'Black Sunday', 6 February 1938.

The lead-up to this event can be found in the records of the Bureau of Meteorology, starting two days earlier, on Friday 4 February. Official observations, as recorded by the bureau at Observatory Hill, noted 'squally to gale force' north-easterly winds on the Friday, followed by a strong south-westerly change at 2.40 am on Saturday morning. These south-westerly winds would produce the problems for the boys carrying the gas balloons at the opening ceremony later in the day. But they were also a classic sign that a low-pressure cell was developing to the south of Sydney.

The weather chart at 9 am on 5 February confirms the presence of an intense low-pressure cell off the south coast of New South Wales.

At 3 pm that day Bondi Beach was crowded. Many people were waiting to watch the start of a surf race conducted by the Bondi Surf Life Saving Club. Hundreds of people were either paddling about in the shore break or up to their waists a bit further out.

Waves are strange things. On any given day they travel along more or less routinely, but larger 'sets' can move through, often the result of newly generated swells coinciding with older swells produced by earlier weather systems.

On this day at Bondi Beach a classic example of this occurred. Big swells churned up by the newly formed low-pressure cell off Sydney lined up with older swells to produce three giant waves that bore down upon the unsuspecting crowds swimming near the shore.

The waves moved smoothly across the bay, reared in the shallow water and then crashed across the shoreline, engulfing scores of people in thousands of tonnes of churning water.

Suddenly, swimmers who had been wading, or walking about in waist-deep water, found themselves in 2 metres of violently swirling surf. After the third wave had broken, they were rapidly hauled out to sea in the receding undertow.

Complete panic followed. About 300 swimmers were swept away from the shore, and the Bondi lifesavers found themselves in a 'full-on' mass rescue situation. About 80 of them were present – many of whom had been

A reconstruction of the 9 am weather map of 5 February 1938. The strong low-pressure cell off the south coast of New South Wales (indicated by the 'L') generated large ocean swells across the area, including Sydney's beaches.

waiting to start a surf race – and all plunged into action, several using the 'belt and reel' system for rescue.

In this deadly situation of mass terror the ocean was not the main danger. Frenzied people in imminent danger of drowning seized the lifeguards and grabbed their lines, pulling them under the turbulent water.

The rescuers all commented on 'the extraordinary panic amongst the men and the comparative calmness of the women'. The men were 'crying like girls, shrieking with terror and shouting wildly for help' one of the rescuers said. 'On the other hand, the girls were calm, and seemed to wait quietly, keeping above water as best they could until they were rescued.'

Other lifesavers grabbed rubber floats from the surrounding sunbakers and plunged into the surf, paddling out to the terrified swimmers and then heading back to the beach with several in tow. Many lifesavers made several trips out and back in this way.

A surf-lifesaving emergency of this scale was unprecedented in Australia's history. Lifesavers had never imagined seeing so many people simultaneously struggling for their lives in the water. Years of rigorous surf training, combined with the superb level of physical fitness of the lifesavers, provided a very effective response to the situation.

Gradually, increasing numbers of people were rescued from the sea and pulled onto the sand. Many had nearly drowned and were unconscious. The lifesavers then began using the resuscitation techniques of the day, saving the lives of many who may well have otherwise died on the beach. Six doctors responded from the beach crowd to a call for help, providing valuable onshore assistance to the lifesaving effort.

In the words of the Bondi Surf Life Saving Club's official account:

High- and Low-pressure Circulations

The atmosphere is in a constant state of restless motion because of the heating of the sun and the fact that the Earth is also rotating. These heating and rotating forces produce chains of large, circulating disturbances in the air that move around the Earth in a complex, almost random fashion, constantly and simultaneously forming and dissipating.

There are two basic types of atmospheric circulation: low-pressure circulations ('lows') and high-pressure circulations ('highs'). Lows rotate clockwise in the Southern Hemisphere. They are normally associated with increasing cloud, strong winds, rain and thunderstorms and can generate large ocean swells along the coast. In severe cases, they can produce widespread damage of a similar scale to a moderate strength tropical cyclone. Cold fronts, which are lines delineating sharp wind and temperature changes, are also associated with lows.

Highs rotate anti-clockwise in the Southern Hemisphere, and often result in fine weather with light winds. Lows can be 1000 kilometres or more across, while highs can often be considerably larger, around 3000 kilometres across. Tracking these systems as they move around the Earth is relatively simple. However, forecasting their actual time and place of birth is notoriously difficult and has only been made routinely possible in recent times through computer modelling.

Bondi resembled a battlefield as lifesavers, doctors and first aid men fought to revive the unconscious. There were heart-rending scenes amongst relatives and friends who milled about the area where the desperate battle for life was being waged.

Tragically, five people were drowned in the incident, but nearly 300 people were saved, in what was an incredible display of bravery, strength and skill by the Bondi lifesavers.

The incident rapidly became big news, both nationally and overseas, earning the Bondi Surf Life Saving Club and the Australian lifesaving movement international renown for the mass rescue.

One of the most erudite tributes came from a visiting American physician, Doctor Marshall Dyer, who himself had performed great work in assisting with the mass resuscitation effort. He later remarked:

I have never seen, and I never expect to see again, such magnificent work as was done by those life savers ... It was a scene I shall never forget. When I get back to the United States I will tell them about your magnificent surf men. There are no men like them in the world.

The resuscitation effort goes on whilst large crowds are held back. Several doctors were on the beach at the time and assisted with the medical work.

Lifesavers desperately try to revive one of the victims – eventually five people would lose their lives in this incident.

During the coronial inquiry into the disaster, Bondi Surf Life Saving Club Captain Carl Jepperson remarked: 'The lifesavers merely did their duty, just as the police and ambulance men did.' However, the coroner noted that whereas the police and ambulance officers were fully paid and professional, the lifesavers were unpaid volunteers, and that this therefore added tremendously to the value of their contribution.

A recurrence of a disaster of this scale on a Sydney beach today is unlikely, as there have been many changes since the 1930s. Fast-powered surf-rescue vehicles can punch through the waves and reach swimmers in difficulty much more quickly than the old 'belt and reel' system. In addition, helicopter rescue services can transport victims to hospital within just a few minutes.

Also, Australia's national weather service, the Bureau of Meteorology, now issues public alerts when large ocean swells are occurring or are expected to occur along the coastline. Technologies such as mobile phones and portable and car radios enable these warnings to be broadly disseminated to the community. Such prior knowledge contributes tremendously to the safety of the Australian surfing public.

In more recent times there has been an alternative theory advanced: that an undersea 'slump', where a large slice of the ocean bed slides away from the coast, could have generated a small tsunami. There is considerable speculation here, but eyewitness reports at the time provide some credibility to this theory.

1938

The Crash of the *Kyeema*

Aviation is not inherently dangerous, but to an even greater degree than the sea, it is terribly unforgiving of any carelessness, incapacity or neglect ...

Unknown author

Compared to many other parts of the world, flying conditions in Australia are generally very favourable, with such phenomena as gales, blizzards and ice storms far less frequent than, for example, in Canada, North America and Europe. Victoria is a good case in point – conditions are usually ideal for flying and severe weather events are relatively uncommon.

But severe weather is not the only way to produce hazardous flying conditions. In light southerly winds, when the moisture content of the atmosphere is high, low cloud – called stratus – often drifts in from the ocean across southern Victoria. It can cover extensive areas of the State, often as far north as the Great Dividing Range. As long as the pilot is accurately aware of the aircraft's position, encountering cloud-covered terrain should never be an issue. But in the event of a navigational error it becomes a very different story. And although this cloud would not normally be hazardous to flight over the comparatively flat terrain around Melbourne, further east, over the Dandenong Ranges, it has contributed to a tragedy.

Following the loss of the *Southern Cloud* in 1931 (see page 66), in which lack of communications played a crucial role, two-way radio was progressively installed in passenger-carrying aircraft, and quickly proved to be a valuable contribution to safety. However, for the remainder of the 1930s, passenger aircraft were still navigated manually by estimating ground and air speed, noting reporting points on the ground below and maintaining a navigation log, a process that became

This photograph of the *Kyeema*, an ANA DC2, was taken about a year before the crash.

difficult at night or in thick cloud cover. Unlike today, when pilots are almost precisely aware of their height, location and speed, manual navigation usually produced a certain amount of error, depending on the skill and experience of the captain and first officer.

But for Captain A. C. Webb and his crew, navigational issues were probably far from their minds as they boarded their aircraft on Tuesday 25 October 1938, for a routine passenger flight from Melbourne to Adelaide and back. They were flying the *Kyeema*, an Australian National Airways (ANA) DC2, with the callsign VH-UYC.

This thoroughly modern aircraft, built by the Douglas Corporation and released in 1933, had been an instant hit with airline companies because of its superior performance and carrying capacity. Powered by two Wright Cyclone engines, each pumping out 875 horsepower, it could carry a crew of three, along with 14 passengers, at 320 kilometres per hour to a height of 6500 metres and over a range of 1600 kilometres. This was a quantum leap forward from the old Stinsons and Avro 10s of only a few years before.

The DC2 was the first Douglas aircraft to be purchased by an overseas airline, and in

1934 the Dutch company KLM entered one of its DC2s in the London to Melbourne Air Race. In an astonishing performance, as it raced, it also completed its normal tasks of picking up mail and passengers and ended up flying more than 1600 kilometres further than the race route. It finished second, behind a 'one-off' specially produced racing aeroplane, in what turned out to be a tremendous promotion for the Douglas Corporation. The Melbourne–Adelaide return flight undertaken by Webb and his crew was only a short hop in comparison, and easily within the capabilities of the DC2.

After an early morning take-off from Melbourne's Essendon airport, the aircraft landed on schedule about two and a half hours later in Adelaide. Flying conditions were generally ideal, although a light southerly wind had produced extensive cloud cover across the Melbourne basin, from the central business district across the eastern suburbs to the Dandenong Ranges. The base of this cloud was around 450 metres but with lower patches around 250 metres – well above most elevations around Melbourne, but below some parts of the Dandenong Ranges, which reach above 500 metres. These areas were in cloud for most of the day, under the influence of the cool southerly winds.

After taking on board 14 new passengers in Adelaide, the *Kyeema* turned around, took off on schedule and headed back towards Melbourne, in weather conditions that

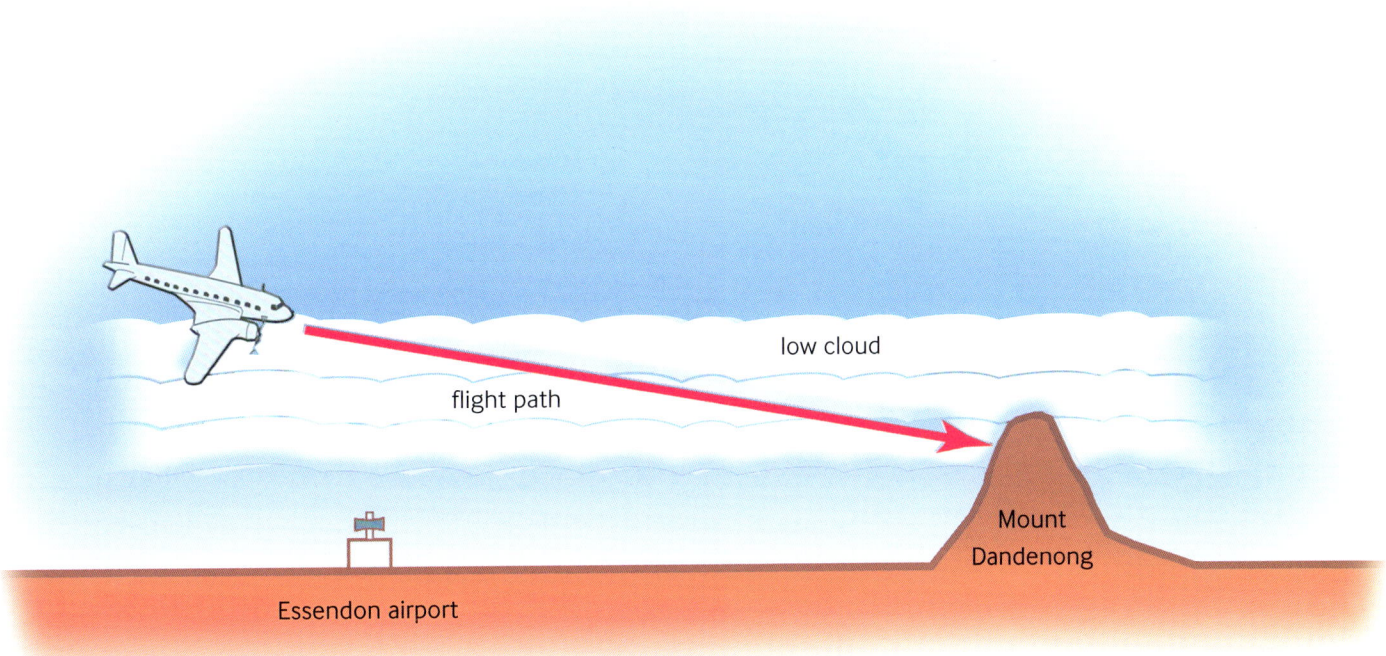

As a result of navigational error, the *Kyeema* overshot Essendon airport and descended into cloud-covered Mount Dandenong.

A reconstruction of the tragedy: the photograph was taken at the accident site looking back towards Essendon airport, showing the flight path of the Kyeema just before impact.

remained favourable for flying. Soon after 1.30 pm Melbourne time, a transmission from the *Kyeema* was received at Essendon, indicating that the aircraft was passing over Daylesford and about to enter cloud as it began its descent into Melbourne. The estimated time of arrival at Essendon was 1.45 pm. However, after another brief transmission from the *Kyeema*, nothing further was heard, and when the aircraft had not arrived by 2 pm, the authorities became concerned.

In the meantime, near the top of cloud-covered Mount Dandenong, about 32 kilometres to the east of Essendon airport, two workers were clearing undergrowth from around a roadway. Macarthur Job, in his publication *Air Crash 1,* recorded the events:

In the eerie quietness of the fog enshrouded bush, both men gradually became aware of the distant whine of an aeroplane; the sound was coming from the west, roughly in the direction of Melbourne. And it seemed to be getting louder ... It was a big one all right and it was getting nearer and nearer all the time! The noise continued to grow in intensity; it wasn't just a whine now. They could hear the powerful throb of the engines as well.

Suddenly, the noise of the engines and propellers was overlaid by a loud screeching; an instant later there was a sickening smashing of metal, then came a tremendous explosion which shook the ground beneath their feet ... and a deathly silence.

The *Kyeema* had flown straight into Mount Dandenong. It was quickly established that all 18 people on board had been killed, and an official inquiry was convened at Melbourne's Exhibition Buildings only three days after the disaster.

After a detailed deliberation, the inquiry concluded that the direct cause of the crash was a navigational error; when the *Kyeema* reported that it was flying over Daylesford, it was probably about 32 kilometres further on, possibly over Sunbury, which appeared similar to Daylesford from the air.

As the *Kyeema* descended through the cloud, Captain Webb believed he should emerge at around 1.45 pm near Essendon airport. In fact he had actually flown past Essendon, invisible below the cloud, and had descended straight into Mount Dandenong, about 32 kilometres to the east.

Although this represented a gross navigational error, it was also recognised that existing technology could have helped avoid this situation. Radio beacons were already available that provided pilots with a positive course along which to fly, and also enabled an accurate location 'fix' to be obtained. As a result of this crash, radio beacons were installed along the main inter-capital city routes.

The other major change that followed was the appointment of so-called 'Flight Checking Officers' whose job it was to maintain a watch on the progress of flights on the main air routes. This 'double check' was to guard against a pilot making a gross navigational error, as had happened with the *Kyeema*.

On 25 October 1978, the fiftieth anniversary of the disaster, a memorial plaque was placed on a cairn beside the roadway some 50 metres above the crash site. It serves as a reminder of the price paid for aviation safety in Australia.

1939

Black Friday in Victoria

It leapt across the flowing streams
And raced the pastures through;
It climbed the trees and lit the boughs,
And fierce and fiercer grew.
The bees fell stifled in the smoke
Or perished in their hives,
And with the stock the kangaroos
Went flying for their lives.

'The Fire at Ross's Farm', Henry Lawson

Winter and spring of 1938 were bad for much of Victoria. In some areas rainfall practically ceased; parts of southern Victoria registered their driest July to December rainfall on record. The situation did not improve with the arrival of summer, and in an ominous sign of what was to come, several serious fires occurred in widely scattered areas across the State.

In early January 1939, conditions were tinder dry in many areas, and with two months of a typically long, hot summer to go, a serious fire was almost inevitable. A massive heatwave gradually gained momentum across south-eastern Australia, with Adelaide initially bearing the brunt of the searing temperatures. Between 5 and 14 January Adelaide's maximum temperatures exceeded 34°C every day, peaking at 46.1°C on 12 January. This was to remain the Adelaide record until 24 January 2019 when 46.6°C was recorded. During this nine-day period, temperatures exceeded 40°C on five occasions.

Melbourne fared only a little better, with somewhat milder temperatures, although on 8 and 10 January the mercury pushed above 40°C. The maximum recorded on 10 January,

A house well ablaze in the Gippsland area of Victoria on Friday 13 January 1939. Large areas of eastern Victoria were devastated by bushfires on this day.

44.7°C, was a record for Melbourne, albeit short-lived.

These high temperatures, coupled with the dry conditions, triggered a number of severe bushfires across Victoria, and these were still burning on the dawning of Friday 13 January, traditionally an unlucky date for those who are even mildly superstitious.

The 9 am weather chart for 13 January showed a deep low-pressure cell near the border of South Australia and Western Australia, with a cold front lying to the west of Victoria near the South Australian border. There was a high-pressure cell to the east of Brisbane, and the pressure difference between this high and the low in the south-west was large.

Big pressure differences immediately imply strong winds, and the northerlies generated by this mechanism began building across south-eastern Australia early on 13 January. Soon after 8 am, northerly winds blasted across Victoria. Temperatures skyrocketed, humidity plummeted and the fires still burning from the previous few days erupted and roared through the bush as unstoppable firestorms.

At around 12.30 pm, the temperature in

Melbourne shot up to yet another new record – 45.6°C – and many of the individual fires over northern and central parts of the State amalgamated into a raging torrent of flame.

Some of the so-called 'timber towns', such as Matlock and Noojee, which were directly in the path of the fire, were burnt to the ground. Large stands of mountain ash forest were completely destroyed. Many people were trapped in the timber mills and burned alive. The fire even reached the outer Melbourne suburb of Warrandyte, necessitating mass evacuations and eventually causing heavy property damage. In the meantime, huge blazes also tore across parts of south-eastern South Australia, and extended across the border into south-western Victoria.

On 14 January *The Age* reported:

Victoria's most disastrous bushfires in history were whipped into greater fury yesterday by the scorching northerlies, accompanying the highest temperatures ever recorded in this State. Fierce fires broke out on new fronts, and at one stage, the reports indicated that practically two thirds of the State was ablaze.

One of the worst single incidents occurred in the Matlock Forest. Flames devoured five timber mills in the area, and 16 people died under appalling circumstances, mostly at James Fitzpatrick's mill. Most were overcome by the flames and smoke as they attempted to flee the inferno. In desperation, one man jumped into a water tank that stood some 4 metres above the ground but was subsequently boiled alive. Incredibly, another man survived merely by covering himself in a wet blanket and standing in the open.

The destruction of Noojee, a tiny town of about 200 people, was graphically reported by *The Age*:

The town of Noojee was wiped out today by a fire more terrifying and extensive than that which swept the settlement in 1926. The only buildings left standing are the brick hotel, a butcher's shop and another building. About 150 of the inhabitants fled to Warragul. Other women and children who remained took refuge under a water wheel while the fire passed. Firefighters, striving to save the town, were ultimately forced to take refuge in the river, 70 people thus saving themselves.

In the space of half an hour, the town was razed to the ground. At 1 pm, the fires converged on Noojee from the head of the Ada River and the Yarra Valley, and linking up in a front of many miles, they swept down with dramatic suddenness. Cars were quickly requisitioned to carry women and children who were vomiting with the intense heat to run them to Neerim Junction.

At 1 pm, the fire was half a mile from town – at 1.30 pm it was consuming buildings in the town. Women and children who remained were rushed to the Latrobe River and there covered themselves with blankets hurriedly taken from their homes.

The situation remained completely out of control until a milder southerly change extended across the area during early to mid afternoon, causing the winds to ease and the humidity to rise. The fires gradually subsided and it was time to count the terrible toll.

In total, 71 people had been killed from the beginning of the outbreak and around 1300 homes were burnt to the ground on 13 January alone. Sixty-nine timber mills were engulfed, and 'steel girders and machinery were twisted by heat as if they had been of fine wire'. The fires consumed over 20,000 square kilometres of forest, and ash is said to have fallen as far away as New Zealand.

In the public clamour that followed the disaster there was a great deal of speculation about what had triggered the fires in the first place. It was known that some land-holders routinely burnt off during the summer months in the hope of promoting a better cover of winter grass for their livestock, but there was considerable debate as to how widespread

The aftermath – this temporary hospital was established at Woods Point some time after the fire. The area had been almost totally gutted by a huge blaze that had swept through on Black Friday.

The deadly trail of destruction left by the bushfires. Over 1.4 million hectares of forest were consumed in the disaster.

this practice was. However, the Member for Heidelberg, Mr Swan, contended that 'leaseholders had been responsible for many of the fires'.

Displaying the usual political nervousness about official inquiries, the Minister of Lands, Mr Lind, said he did not favour a Royal Commission, but stated that public education was the answer. He remarked that 'many people were not aware that bush fires could be caused by actions done almost unconsciously, such as throwing away a match or lighting a fire without taking all the essential precautions. Education was the only method of reducing risks to a minimum'.

However, because of the enormity of the disaster, a Royal Commission was eventually convened to inquire into all aspects of the fires, and this was conducted under the direction of Judge Leonard Stretton. He found that most of the fires were caused by the uninformed actions of landowners and others, who routinely, and sometimes inappropriately, used fire in their land-management activities. Many of his recommendations concerning the organisation and powers of rural firefighting authorities in Victoria were eventually introduced and became policy as a result of this Royal Commission.

Footnote: Justice Leonard Stretton was the half brother of Major General Alan Stretton, who was the key figure in the relief of Darwin following tropical Cyclone Tracy in 1974.

1947 & 1999

Sydney's Eastern Suburbs Devastated by Hail

Fear no more the lightning flash
Nor the all dreaded thunder-stone.

'Cymbeline', William Shakespeare

At certain times of the year conditions in Sydney and Brisbane are meteorologically perfect for the development of severe hailstorms – warm, humid air near the surface with cold upper air temperatures developing, triggering what is known as 'atmospheric instability'.

Tropical areas such as Darwin certainly see frequent heavy thunderstorms, but any associated large hail normally melts before reaching the ground because of the high air temperatures in the tropical atmosphere.

However, Sydney and Brisbane have all the right ingredients, and large hail is a constant risk, particularly during spring and summer. Two famous examples where large hail scored a direct hit on Sydney were in 1947 and 1999, but there have been many more 'near misses' that could easily have inflicted serious damage.

Not Such a Happy New Year, 1947

New Year's Day 1947 started as a typical hot and humid Sydney summer day. Locals on the coast welcomed the eagerly anticipated afternoon north-east sea breeze, which brought some relief.

Afternoon thunderstorms are not unusual for Sydney around this time of year. They usually begin with an increase in cloud – a type of formation called 'cumulus' – over the Blue Mountains to the west of the city. Sometimes these develop into full-blown storms, which move across the Sydney basin in the mid to late afternoon.

So when cloud began to increase from the

west during the late morning, it seemed that afternoon thunderstorms were again 'on the cards'. However, there was something different in the way this storm was developing.

At that time the Bureau of Meteorology was located at Observatory Hill, near the south-west pylon of the Sydney Harbour Bridge. The official bureau report noted:

The first definite indication of cloud development at Sydney occurred towards 1300 [1 pm] when cumulus commenced to build in the west and south-west. By about 1400 [2 pm] this covered the south-west quadrant of the sky and appeared to be moving east, but keeping south of the city. The underpart of the cloud was mottled and serrated or curtained, rather than mammilated, and looked angrily black, while false cirrus tufts were discernible at the top.

This rather technical description of the cloud formation would have alerted meteorologists to the possibility that something big was about to happen. The cloud continued to increase across the city, becoming more and more menacing. The bureau report continued:

Shortly before the rain commenced at the Bureau of Meteorology, shallow cumulus was observed moving from the north-east below the main cloud structure, which was

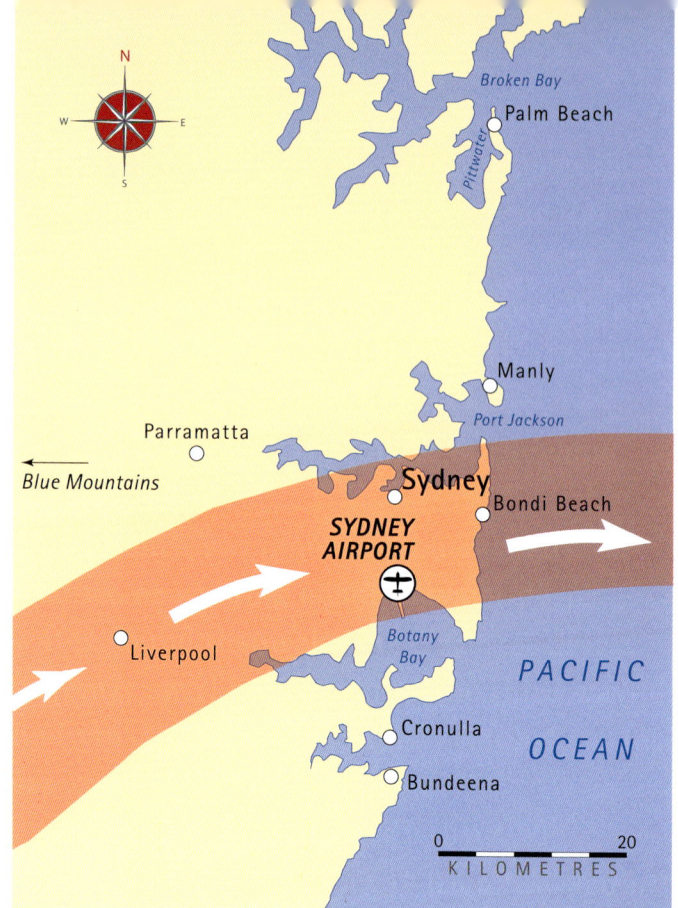

The path of the hailstorm — it smashed a trail of destruction from Liverpool to Rose Bay, with many injured whilst swimming in the surf around the Bondi/Bronte and Clovelly areas.

coming from the westward, and between this and the overlying cloud, considerable turbulence was apparent. At this time there was a terrific noise which appeared to come from the Harbour Bridge as though several trains were passing over. It was definitely not the sound of hail or rain to the south, and it is reasonable to assume its origin was in the cloud. [Although the report does not comment further about the noise, it was probably caused by several successive bursts of thunder.]

Unbeknownst to the bureau at this stage, the storm had already blasted a trail of wreckage across south-western Sydney from Liverpool to the southern parts of the CBD. Billiard ball-sized hail sliced through rooftops, battered cars and injured pedestrians.

However, the full fury of the storm finally broke as it crossed the eastern suburbs, dropping huge hailstones over Surry Hills and the Rose Bay – Bondi area. Large holiday crowds swimming and sunbaking on Bondi Beach were caught in the open and pelted with hail as large as oranges.

The Sydney Morning Herald quoted Mr H. Lacey, a returned soldier who was sunbaking at Bondi Beach at the time: 'I thought I was back in the firing line overseas. When the hail began to fall it rattled like machine gun fire. People were lying on the ground and others were bleeding from arms and shoulders'.

Fifteen-year-old Edna Menzies, the niece of the then leader of the Opposition and future prime minister, Mr R. G. Menzies, was knocked unconscious by a hailstone 'as large as a cricket ball' whilst swimming at Clovelly. She was rescued and taken to hospital, remaining unconscious as she

Amazing scenes at the Rose Bay Flying Boat Base as the sea is churned into froth by the giant hailstones.

was loaded into the ambulance.

People waiting for trains on Central Station ran for cover as hail punctured the platform roofs and they were showered with debris. The skylight running along the entire length of the old indoor area of the station was smashed and 'jagged pieces of glass up to four inches square fell among a crowd of about 100 people'.

The clock face above the station was smashed and the roof of nearby Crown Street Women's Hospital was badly damaged, terrifying both staff and patients, some of whom were in labour. The canvas roofs (or 'soft tops') common to many cars in those days were holed by the hail, injuring the drivers and passengers within.

Thunderstorms and Supercells

Most thunderstorms last about one to two hours, producing lightning, thunder, gusty winds and even hail. They begin with the 'cumulus phase', when powerful updraughts generate cumulus clouds. This is followed by the 'mature phase', when the cloud reaches its maximum height, downdraughts develop and rain and/or hail fall. Finally, during the 'dissipating phase', updraughts are overtaken and 'eroded' by downdraughts and the cloud begins to collapse. The mature phase is normally the most intense period of the storm, when ground damage is most likely to result from hail, heavy showers or strong wind gusts. However, a much more powerful type of thunderstorm, capable of lasting for several hours may be generated by what's known as a 'supercell' formation. These unusually intense storms, normally classified as 'severe' thunderstorms, are the result of a special set of conditions involving the 'upper' winds, those at high levels in the atmosphere. When a supercell enters the

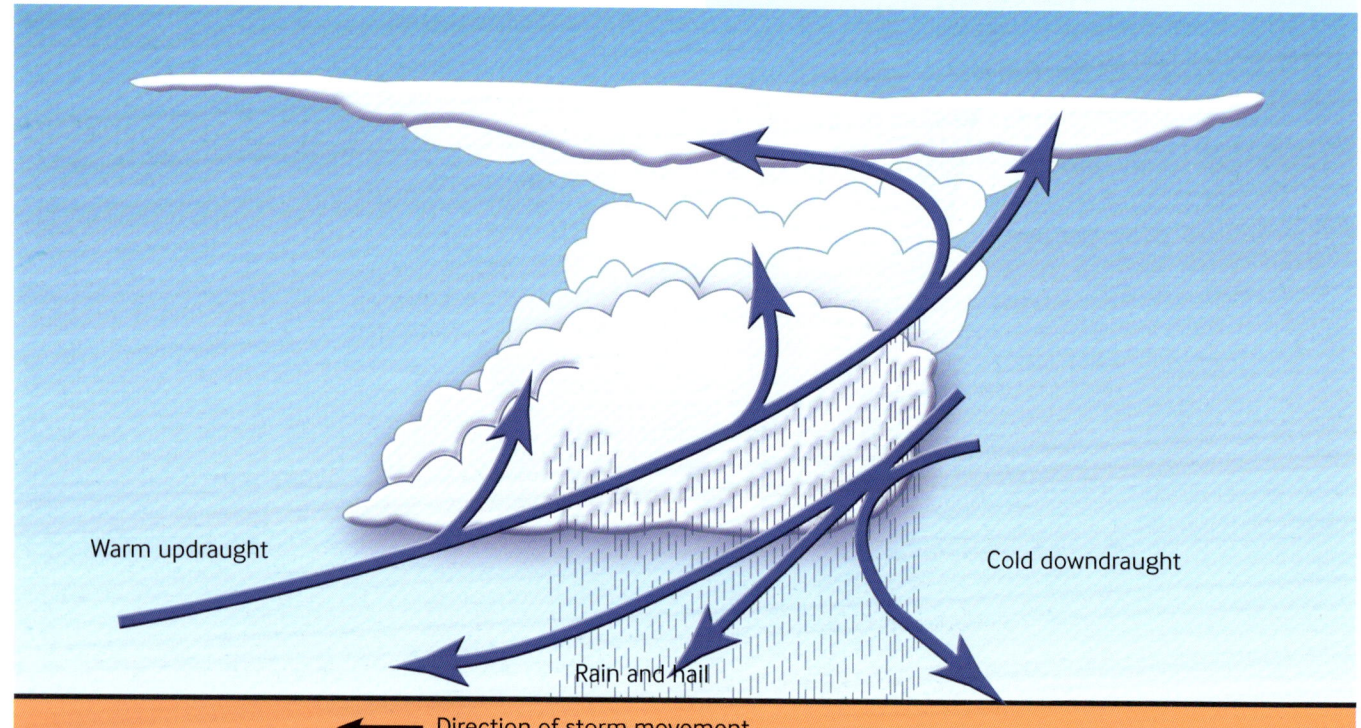

The mature phase of a supercell, showing the balance between the updraughts and the downdraughts, which can enable the storm to continue for several hours.

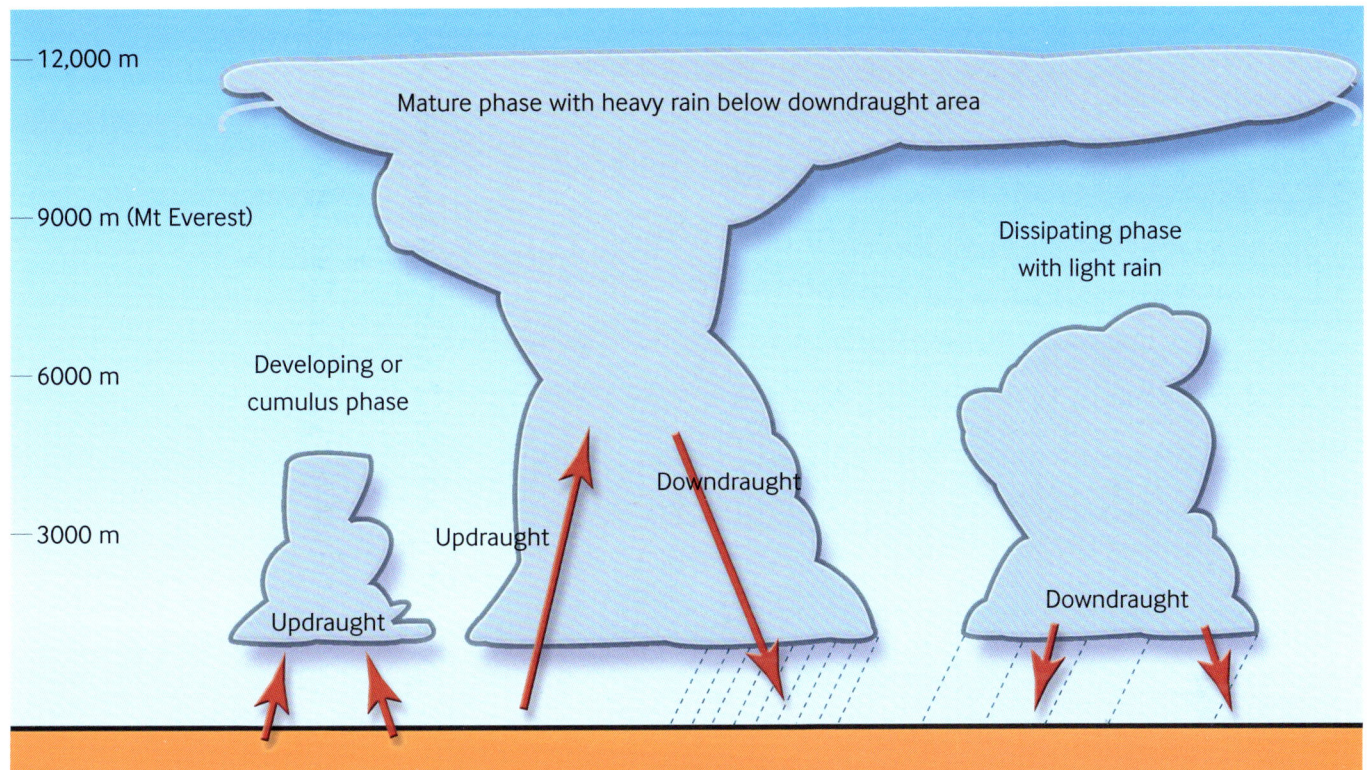

The phases of a thunderstorm.

mature phase, the updraught and downdraught areas are separated (as shown in the diagram at left), preventing the erosion of the updraughts that occurs within a normal thunderstorm during the dissipating phase. A balance between the updraughts and downdraughts within the cell can enable the storm to continue for several hours. Supercells can tower over 16 kilometres into the atmosphere.

The official definition of a severe thunderstorm is one that can produce any of the following phenomena:
- hailstones with a diameter of 2 centimetres (the size of a $2 coin) or more
- wind gusts of 90 kilometres per hour or more
- flash flooding
- tornadoes.

Meteorologists are particularly worried about supercells. During the summer months across eastern Australia, when conditions sometimes approach borderline suitability for supercell formation, radar-based thunderstorm watches carefully monitor any large cloud development.

Eastern suburbs tram windows were shattered by the ice, showering passengers with broken glass.

The Sydney Morning Herald front page banner headline the next day read 'Ice Storm Lashes City and Suburbs' and the story recounted a long list of the injuries and damage. Some 350 people were treated by ambulance officers and hospitals as a result of hailstone impact and flying debris, particularly glass from broken windows. 'For nearly three hours, ambulance wagons travelled backwards and forwards from Eastern Suburbs beaches with the injured', the *Herald* reported. Other victims were 'picked up in doorways bleeding from head wounds caused by the lumps of ice and by flying glass from hundreds of broken windows'.

Fantastic scenes occurred at the Rose Bay Flying Boat Base as hail smashed the hangar roof to pieces and churned up the surrounding water. By coincidence, Bob Rice, a *Sydney Sun* photographer, was on location. His amazing photograph shows the dense field of splashes that covered the harbour as far as the eye could see.

When it finally crossed the coastline and moved out to sea, the storm left behind widespread structural damage, many personal injuries and mounds of ice that remained intact for hours. Numerous trees, including large swathes of Centennial Park were stripped of their leaves, producing a stink of rotting vegetation across the city.

When interviewed the next day, the acting State Meteorologist, Mr Newman, said: 'The approach of such a storm could not be forecast accurately, but it is possible that because similar conditions are expected to prevail today, that a repetition, not quite so severe, can be expected'. Happily, this second storm did not eventuate.

Sydney was staggered by the enormity of the incident, as there had not been even a remotely similar storm in living memory. Hundreds of houses had severely damaged roofs and because it was only some 18 months after the end of World War II, there was a severe shortage of building materials. Consequently some roofs were still covered by tarpaulins several years later, causing a steadily rising damage bill as they leaked during strong winds and rain.

Weather forecasting in those days was severely hampered by the lack of radar imagery and satellite photography now available to the modern-day weather-forecasting team, and rapidly developing systems, such as thunderstorms, were difficult to predict.

Also, the means of distributing weather warnings were very limited, and for 'short-term' events such as thunderstorms radio was the only way. However, portable and car radios were still not generally available, so weather warnings were not easily accessible for those away from their homes. This is a far cry from today, where information can be distributed via portable radios and mobile phones. It is now possible to view current radar images surrounding all the capital cities on a mobile phone screen, so the general public can be better informed.

As far as the Bureau of Meteorology is concerned, weather forecasters now have access to state-of-the-art, regularly updated radar and satellite images, enabling accurate identification and tracking of thunderstorms. Warnings can be issued before a population centre is threatened.

It was widely believed that the New Year's Day storm of 1947 was a freak event, unlikely to ever happen again, but just over 52 years later, history repeated itself. Against all the odds another similar storm devastated eastern Sydney in 1999.

A Freak Storm, 1999

Although thunderstorms can occur over the Sydney basin at any time of year, the peak period – the so-called 'thunderstorm season' – is from November to March. Severe thunderstorms – capable of producing large hail, damaging wind gusts, flash flooding and even occasionally tornadoes – are most likely to occur during this period.

But one of the most severe thunderstorms ever recorded over Sydney occurred outside this period, on 14 April 1999. And that was not the only unusual feature of the storm. Most thunderstorms occur in the mid to late afternoon, but this one struck at about 7.40 pm. The highly 'offbeat' nature of nearly all aspects of this storm presented new territory for meteorologists, emergency services and insurance companies alike, and created unprecedented interest from the media and general public.

Conditions across the Sydney basin on the afternoon of 14 April were marginally unstable. Although there was some potential for thunderstorm activity, all the conventional meteorological indicators showed that background atmospheric conditions were not conducive to the formation of a severe thunderstorm. However, forecasters were still wary. A weak frontal system moving along the south coast of New South Wales was due to pass across Sydney during the evening; such systems always have the potential to trigger thunderstorms.

Later in the afternoon, some scattered showers developed on the ranges to the south-west of Sydney and were picked up on the local weather-watch radar. But this activity was not strong and forecasters were reassured that a severe thunderstorm was unlikely.

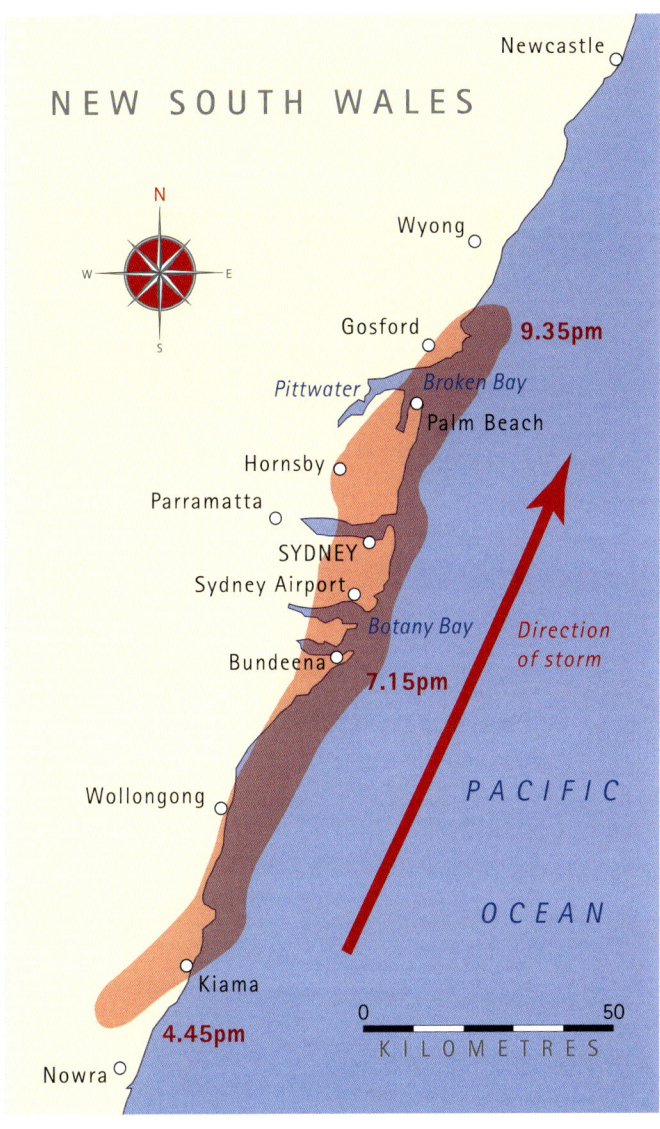

The path of the hailstorm reveals how it was confined to the coastal fringe. This was a quite different path to the storm of 1947.

However, at around 4.30 pm a large thunderstorm cell did develop just inland of Nowra and it began moving along the coastline towards Sydney. But because the upper winds which 'steer' such systems usually contain an offshore component, meteorologists believed the storm should gradually move out to sea.

And this appeared to be the case. After producing a substantial fall of pea- and marble-sized hail across Wollongong, the storm crossed the coast, but maintained a course roughly parallel to it.

At about 7 pm the virtually unpredictable happened. The storm veered left and crossed the coastline again advancing straight towards Sydney.

At Sydney airport, some 25 aircraft were damaged by large hail before they could be secured under cover, and between about

Opposite: Some of the hailstones collected from Surry Hills. They range from golf-ball size up to nearly the dimensions of a cricket ball.

Above: The roof of this car dealership was reduced to a colander by the giant hail. The eventual damage bill would top $2.3 billion making it one of Australia's most expensive disasters.

7.40 and 8.00 pm the storm unleashed its full fury across Sydney's eastern suburbs, with tennis ball-sized hail slicing a trail of destruction across the area.

Eyewitness accounts provided some insight into the unbelievable events of the evening. One Surry Hills resident reported hearing an approaching roar similar to 'a jumbo jet coming in to land in the street out the front'. Soon after, he was amazed to see giant hail crashing down across the rooftops and totally stripping the shrubbery in his front yard.

Motorists driving along nearby Anzac Parade pulled off the road in panic and attempted to shelter under the giant fig trees bordering the road, but were unmercifully pummelled by the ice fusillade. In Oxford Street, hail smashed the windshields of many cars and even sheared off side mirrors. Some drivers chose to mount the footpath in their vehicles, desperately seeking shelter. Others crashed after their windscreens were shattered. A number of injuries occurred, with people from Engadine, Rosebery and Caringbah admitted to hospital.

And in what must be an almost unique occurrence, the Sydney Swans footballers were forced to abandon their night training session at the Sydney Cricket Ground soon after the giant hail came crashing down. The galvanised-iron roofs covering the members' and ladies' stands were covered in large dents, and many of the exposed plastic seats were smashed.

Pedestrians around Central Station huddled for cover under the perspex-roofed concourse near the eastern entrance, only to be showered with broken shards from the roof as the hail punched through. The large clock-face on the Central Station tower was broken, and slate and tile roofs right across the eastern suburbs were smashed as the onslaught continued.

Heavy rain accompanying the storm poured in through the thousands of damaged roofs, exacerbating the damage. Frantic residents tried to cover the gaps with plastic sheeting and tarpaulins, with little success.

By around 8.15 pm the storm had cleared the city to the north. About an hour later it moved out to sea east of Gosford. Radar imagery showed that by 10 pm it had dissipated out at sea.

The eastern suburbs of Sydney remained in uproar. State Emergency Services were inundated with calls for assistance and supplies of tarpaulins soon ran short. Traffic throughout the area was chaotic for hours and residents attempted to clean up the mess surrounding their properties as best they could. Sydneysiders in the northern and western suburbs, unaware that anything out of the ordinary had happened, were astonished to see the scenes of destruction on the television news late in the evening.

A reconstruction of the event suggested that this thunderstorm was a 'supercell'. Supercells virtually create their own environment, and this at least partly explains

A patchwork quilt-like effect is created by all the blue tarpaulins covering shattered roofs after the storm. Many were still in place several months later, the roofs awaiting repair.

the strange and unexpected path taken by the storm in view of the surrounding wind conditions. Supercells are unusual at any time around Sydney, but unheard of at 7.30 pm in April. The 1999 storm was only the second time in recorded history – since 1795 – that hail larger than 2 cm in diameter had fallen over Sydney in April, and only the fifth time that hail of any significant size had been recorded in April.

It was estimated that about 500,000 tonnes of hail fell on Sydney during the storm. For many months afterwards, the eastern suburbs were dotted with tarpaulin-

A reconstruction of the radar imagery as the storm approached Sydney from the south. The intense red zone is the area of hail within the storm.

(see page 150) as Australia's costliest natural disaster.

There were many similarities between this storm and the New Year's Day storm of 1947. Both events produced a damage 'bullseye' across Sydney's eastern suburbs. On both occasions the clock face on Central Station was shattered. The hail was of similar size and created massive damage to housing and motor vehicles.

However, an important difference was the timing. The 1947 event occurred during a midsummer afternoon on a public holiday, when thousands of people were outdoors, particularly at the beach. But in 1999, the storm took place at night on a weekday, when most people were indoors. This important difference probably accounts for the comparatively small number of personal injuries suffered during the 1999 event. There is little doubt that there would have been a massive injury toll had this taken place on a weekend afternoon in summer.

draped houses and with each new fall of rain, further leaks occurred. Some 35,000 properties were substantially damaged, along with about 40,000 motor vehicles. Badly battered eastern suburbs cars were identifiable for a long time after. Insurance losses from the storm eventually exceeded $2.3 billion, replacing, in terms of insured losses, the Newcastle earthquake of 1989

1948

The Adelaide Tempest

They are as stubble before the wind, and as chaff that the storm carrieth away.

Job 21:18

The oceans to the south of Australia are somewhat unique in that at around latitude 60°S, there is no landmass. The prevailing westerly winds produce large ocean swells that continuously circumnavigate the globe.

Sir James Bissett, an ex-captain in the Cunard Line, describes this phenomenon in his book *Tramps and Ladies*:

The result is that the seas are heaped up by the almost continual whipping of the prevailing wind, to dimensions, in height and length, greater than those of seas anywhere else in the world. It is there that the grandest, most awe inspiring combers roll on in unending succession, attaining heights regularly of from fifty to sixty feet when the wind rises to gale force, and sometimes towering to eighty feet from trough to crest under hurricane conditions. These 'greybeards' often extend 1000 feet from crest to crest.

Occasionally, in suitable weather conditions, large waves from the Southern Ocean can migrate far enough north to impact on the southern Australian coastline.

In addition, deep low-pressure systems and vigorous cold fronts can affect the weather across southern Australia. These often produce prolonged south-westerly gales which generate large ocean swells across the southern coastal mainland and Tasmania, posing considerable danger to shipping and local coastal structures.

As well as large waves, weather situations such as this can also produce a phenomenon called a 'storm surge': ocean water is pushed ahead of onshore winds and 'piles up' against

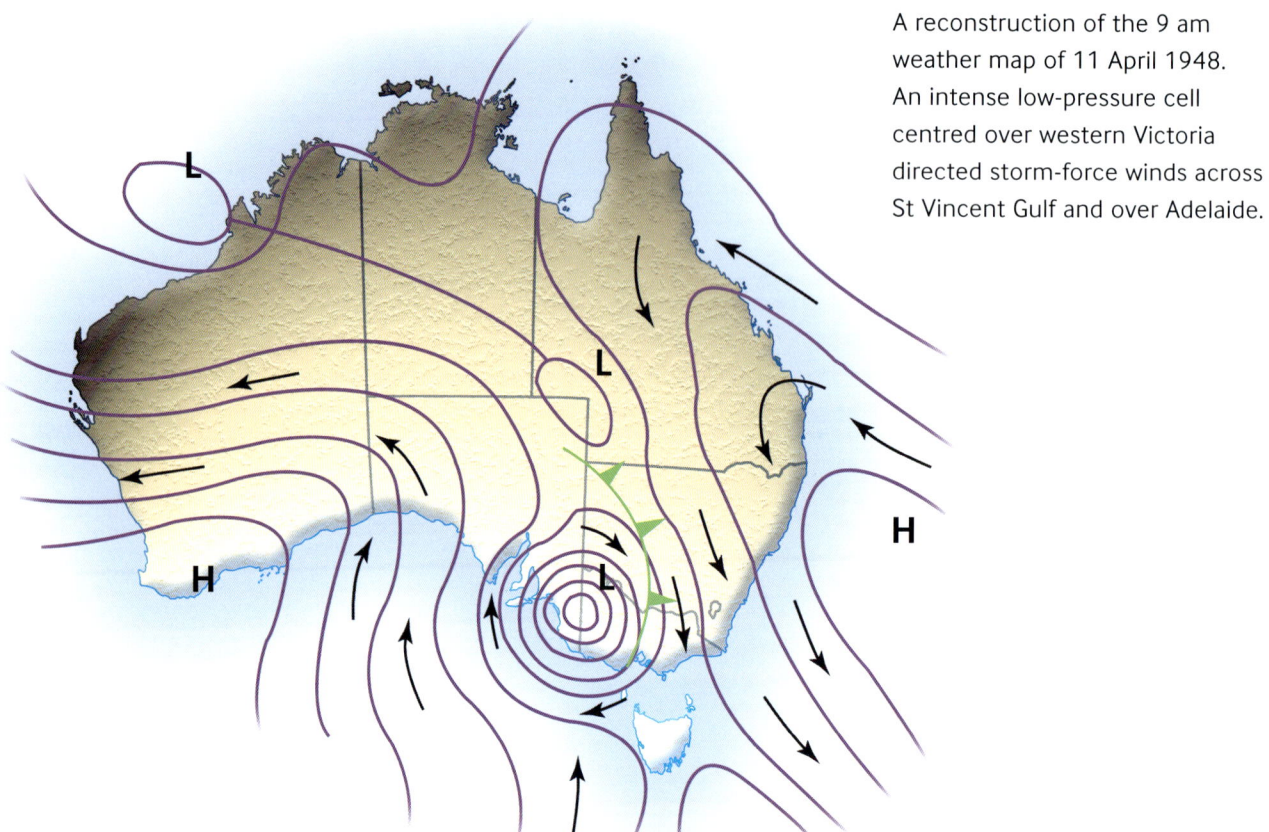

A reconstruction of the 9 am weather map of 11 April 1948. An intense low-pressure cell centred over western Victoria directed storm-force winds across St Vincent Gulf and over Adelaide.

the coastline, greatly increasing water levels, particularly if coinciding with a high tide (see the diagram on page 54).

One of the most celebrated 'big wave' events to affect southern Australia during the twentieth century occurred off Adelaide during April 1948. It was dubbed 'The Storm of the Century'.

Not far from Adelaide's central business district lies the famous seaside suburb of Glenelg, popular as a holiday resort since the mid-nineteenth century. From the very early days, the central local attraction was the Glenelg Jetty. Originally constructed in 1859, it was a favourite spot for swimming, diving, fishing and promenading. Until 1948, the jetty was over 300 metres long, with two arms jutting out laterally that housed a tea room and a large sea aquarium. No visit to Glenelg was considered complete without an excursion to the historic jetty.

But on Sunday 11 April 1948, disaster struck. Gale- to storm-force winds from the south-west tore across St Vincent Gulf for over eight hours, from roughly 4 am to midday on Sunday 11 April. Record wind gusts of 131 kilometres per hour were recorded by the Bureau of Meteorology at Adelaide. This prolonged period of high winds not only produced huge waves but also a massive storm surge on which the waves were riding. Tremendous seas rolled in, smashing

A photograph of the Glenelg Jetty, taken in 1936, shows large crowds on the pier, attracted by the tea rooms on the far end and the aquarium about halfway along.

The Glenelg Jetty on 11 April 1948. A massive storm surge, together with large rolling breakers, progressively wrecked the jetty.

onto the eastern shoreline of St Vincent Gulf, with the water rising metres above its normal height.

The huge crowds that flocked to Glenelg beach to view the awesome spectacle were amazed to see their beloved jetty under siege. The tea rooms on the far end of the pier were being continually shaken by

breaking waves, and the aquarium, about halfway along, was receiving a similar battering. The long jetty itself was completely under water, with huge curling breakers running straight over the top before crashing onto the shoreline, sending water cascading over the adjacent roadway.

It was obvious that the structure could not withstand the onslaught and eventually it began to give way. Before the gale had ceased, this charming old nineteenth-century relic was chopped into several pieces and irretrievably damaged. Amazingly, during the height of the storm, it was discovered that a man was marooned on the far end of the jetty, about 300 metres from the shore. Somehow Mr Archibald Pudney was caught in the tea rooms, and had to endure many frightening hours as the huge waves repeatedly smashed against the structure. He was eventually rescued by boat after conditions had eased sometime later.

The tragic loss of this historic and unique Victorian jetty was only part of a massive trail of damage around Adelaide. The scouring action of the high water and waves had eroded much of the sand from the famous Glenelg beach, leaving behind a barren stretch of rock and seaweed. The naval survey frigate *Barcoo* was driven ashore not far from the jetty and many smaller craft were either sunk or smashed.

The Advertiser reported that:

Dawn ... revealed scenes of great devastation. Large sections of the Glenelg and Brighton jetties have been swept away by huge seas, scores of homes have been unroofed, thousands of fences blown down and big trees uprooted. Damage estimated at hundreds of thousands of pounds has been caused by wind and rain in the city and suburbs. Never has Adelaide seen such a litter and mass of minor destruction.

It was to be another 21 years before the jetty was rebuilt, and the new structure was finally opened in 1969, although it was not as long or grand as the original.

During the 1970s, the site of the old jetty became an archaeological diving location. Many interesting artefacts were recovered, spanning the period from about 1860 to 1945. These included jewellery, bottles, medals and even bullets.

1954

East-Coast Cyclone

Expect the unexpected.

Derryn Hinch, Australian broadcaster

Many of Australia's most famous tropical cyclones are instantly recognised by the names they were given, such as Tracy, Althea and Trixie. But some of our most intense cyclones were never named at all.

The reason for this is tied up in the history of the naming of cyclones in Australia, which is an interesting story in itself. Clement Wragge, the rather eccentric Queensland Government Meteorologist from 1887 to 1902, is thought to have been the first person in the world to name tropical cyclones. He used letters from the Greek alphabet, figures from Greek and Roman mythology, female names and also the names of some of the politicians of the day, including Drake, Barton and Deakin, as names for cyclones.

In 1902, the Honourable Mr A. H. Conroy, the Member for the Sydney electorate of Werriwa, must have somehow incurred Wragge's displeasure, because his name featured in several references to one cyclone. These included: 'Conroy, looking nasty, is coming along the coast' and 'Conroy, black and treacherous, is likely to cross the Southern District …' Justifiably miffed, Conroy dismissed Wragge as 'an advertising scientist'.

After Wragge had left the meteorological scene in 1908, the naming of tropical cyclones lapsed and was not resumed by the Bureau of Meteorology in Australia until 1963. Cyclones were again given female names, but after complaints that this practice was discriminatory, alternate male and female names were used from 1975 onwards.

The upshot of all this was that from 1908 to 1963, tropical cyclones in the Australian region were not named. And it was one of these 'nameless' storms that caused tremendous damage and loss of life across

Extensive flooding throughout Rockhampton in the week preceding the cyclone raised fears about any further downpours across the area. Here, members of a Rockhampton family evacuate their house by boat on 13 February.

south-eastern Queensland and north-eastern New South Wales during February 1954.

Whereas most east-coast cyclones only affect the tropical coastal areas of Queensland, this one travelled much further south than usual, devastating the Northern Rivers district of New South Wales as well as the Gold Coast area of Queensland and, indeed, Brisbane itself.

In the week before the cyclone actually formed, heavy tropical downpours had already saturated much of eastern Queensland. Rockhampton, in particular, received a tremendous drenching that caused widespread flooding across the city that dissipated only slowly over the next few days.

The cyclone then developed over the Coral Sea on Wednesday 17 February and, to everyone's alarm, was more or less heading for Rockhampton, where further heavy rain would have been catastrophic. But providentially, on 19 February, the storm appeared to change course and began running parallel to the coast. Whilst this certainly saved Rockhampton, it produced a battering of 'gale force winds and drenching rain' from Bundaberg to the New South Wales border.

Convinced that the worst of the danger

A week of heavy rain produced floods through Rockhampton before the cyclone had developed. On 15 February this woman in Arthur Street had to wade through water a metre deep to hang out her washing.

was past, the Bureau of Meteorology's Deputy Director, Mr B. H. (Barney) Newman confidently advised the public that the situation was improving. He was quoted in *The Courier Mail*:

> *It was a lucky break. If the full force of the depression area had hit Rockhampton, it would have had serious consequences. The impact of the dry winds with the moist cyclonic winds changed the course of the cyclone. There is now no danger of it striking the Queensland coastline.*

In those days, before meteorologists had access to satellite photography and weather radar, predicting the movement of tropical cyclones was somewhat of a nightmare, relying on careful monitoring of barometric pressure, as well as infrequent reports from shipping and aircraft. Forecasters then, as now, were heavily influenced by what 'normally happens'. In this case, once the cyclone began moving southwards parallel to the coast, it would be expected to be directed out to sea by westerly winds. This expectation almost certainly influenced Newman's thinking and in the great majority of cases would have been perfectly correct. But this was not a 'normal' cyclone.

Sometime during the afternoon of Saturday 20 February the cyclone changed course again, swinging to the south–south-west, and heading towards the coast around the New South Wales – Queensland border. At around 9 pm on Saturday it passed within 50 kilometres of Brisbane, causing extremely heavy rain and gale-force winds across the city. On the way it also set two new weather records for Brisbane – one for the amount or 'run' of wind across the city over a 24-hour period, which was 898.5 kilometres, and the other the lowest barometric pressure recorded at 982.7 hectopascals.

But by far the worst was to come. As the cyclone crossed the coastline near Coolangatta, cyclonic winds and torrential rain combined with phenomenal storm surge (see page 54) generated some of the worst flooding and storm damage ever seen in settled areas of Australia, and particularly across the Gold Coast and northern coastal New South Wales.

The cyclone stripped sand from the beachfront along the Gold Coast. Boats were hurled inland by the strong winds and massive seas. Phenomenal rainfall, sometimes in excess of 500 millimetres in 24 hours, produced raging floods across the area, particularly around inland parts of the Nerang River.

However, some of the worst hit areas were far northern New South Wales towns, including Murwillumbah, Lismore, Grafton, Kyogle and Casino. The ferocious winds produced a trail of destruction, but the greatest damage was caused by the vast flooding that covered much of the area.

These towns were totally cut off from the

As a lead-up to the cyclone, flood rains had already drenched Rockhampton. On 16 February, this butcher in East Street was still trading despite ankle-deep water throughout the shop.

outside world for a period, with all roads, rail lines and electronic communications severed by the wind, rain and raging floodwaters. Radio 2LM Lismore finally managed a transmission on Sunday that provided a hint as to the severity of the disaster. This was printed in *The Courier Mail* on Monday:

It has been a night of horror. We need help. It's the worst flood in memory ... At the moment more than a thousand are sheltering on high ground without a stitch of dry clothing and food is running out. Would anyone who hears this broadcast

please contact authorities and pass a message from the Officer in Charge, Lismore Police, asking for aerial drop of 1000 blankets ... We have no fuel, no electricity and no gas. A night of misery lies in front of thousands of people, with more rain likely.

Soon after this, the RAAF responded with drops of supplies from Dakota aircraft, and the army mounted numerous rescue missions in 'Army Duck' amphibious vehicles, churning through the floodwaters and plucking people from rooftops and islands of high ground.

Kyogle was devastated, with houses torn off their foundations and debris scattered 'for hundreds of yards', the extent of the damage revealed by aerial photographs taken from aircraft hired by *The Courier Mail*.

The scene at Murwillumbah on the Tweed River was described by radio announcer Col Humphreys:

At its peak, the flood height reached 20 feet – 3 feet above the 1945 record level. The water trapped people in their homes and shops, and boats were still taking them to refuge at 2.30 am yesterday. All telephone services are broken, and people are stranded all over the district. Homes have been washed into the river, and thousands of acres of farm land are still covered by feet of water.

An aerial view of the widespread flooding in Lismore on 21 February 1954.

The swollen Richmond River cut the link between Lismore and Tenterfield when this wooden plank bridge was wrecked by the swirling floodwaters on 21 February.

Gradually the cyclone weakened as it moved south towards Sydney, and the crisis eased. The final damage bill ran into millions of pounds and tragically 26 people died, mainly through drowning in the raging floods. This cyclone remains one of the most extreme weather events in the history of the area.

While it is almost inevitable that a severe cyclone will again strike a settled area of Australia, the warning and response infrastructure has improved considerably since 1954. The Bureau of Meteorology's tropical cyclone warning system, using state-of-the-art weather radar and satellite photograph imagery, can now give up to a week's notice of the approach of a cyclone (see also page 53). This allows emergency services to be fully alerted, livestock moved to high ground and, in some cases, the local population to be evacuated before the cyclone arrives. Whilst a powerful cyclone will always cause damage, the warning system would hopefully minimise loss of human and stock life. In addition, the recovery time would be much faster because of the increased effectiveness of modern emergency services.

1955

Maitland Goes Under

I had to risk it. I heard a roar
As the wind swept down and the driving rain;
And the water rose till it reached the floor
Of our highest room; and 'twas very plain –
The way the torrent was sweeping down –
We must make for the highlands at once, or drown.

'Story of Mongrel Grey', Banjo Paterson

The 1950s was a particularly wet decade for Australia. The year 1950 itself was one of the wettest in recorded history; large tracts of New South Wales and Queensland received record rainfall and there was widespread flooding in many areas. The total annual rainfall for Sydney in 1950 was 2194 millimetres, which still stands as the record. In addition, Sydney's wettest month ever was June 1950 (643 millimetres) and Canberra's record monthly total fell in March of the same year (312 millimetres).

Three very wet years followed: 1954 was a high rainfall year for eastern Queensland, 1955 for the entire southern half of mainland Australia, and 1956 across a large area of eastern Australia.

But it was the February 1955 floods across Maitland in New South Wales' Hunter Valley that were the most devastating of the period, centred as they were over a highly populated area. Scenes from these floods were graphically captured by the media of the day, including the news segments shown at cinemas all around the country, and a very high public awareness resulted. The Maitland flood was the big weather story of the time.

As with most floods, the lead-up to the Maitland event was of considerable importance. Heavy falls across the Hunter Valley in January and early February 1955 had resulted in saturation of the soil across the area, meaning that any further rain

Hundreds of houses had to be evacuated at the height of the floods. Some residential areas were never rebuilt because they had been originally sited in flood-prone areas.

would just run off rather than soak in.

Then on 23 February a 'monsoonal depression' – an area of low pressure laden with high-moisture-content tropical air – began to form over north-eastern New South Wales, funnelling maritime easterly winds from the Tasman Sea into the Hunter Valley. This combination of tropical and maritime air masses usually produces one thing in large quantities – rain, which began falling on 23 February, increasing in intensity during the next day.

On 24 February most of the Hunter Valley received falls of over 200 millimetres in 24 hours and because of the previous saturation of the soil, this all became run-off and fed into the swollen Hunter, Paterson and Williams rivers. As the situation deteriorated, the office of the Mayor of Maitland, Alderman A. S. McDonald, made a series of radio broadcasts that were intended to keep the general public, as well as the various emergency services, constantly updated.

The first such broadcast went to air at 10 am on 24 February as reported later in *The Newcastle Herald*. Mayor McDonald said:

> *River readings are as follows: Maitland 29 feet 6 inches, Singleton 33 feet 9 inches, Sandy Hollow 23 feet 6 inches, Bulga 16 feet 4 inches. The river at Hexham has commenced to overflow and traffic should proceed with caution. No north-bound traffic*

Rainfall Relative to Historical Records
January to December 1954

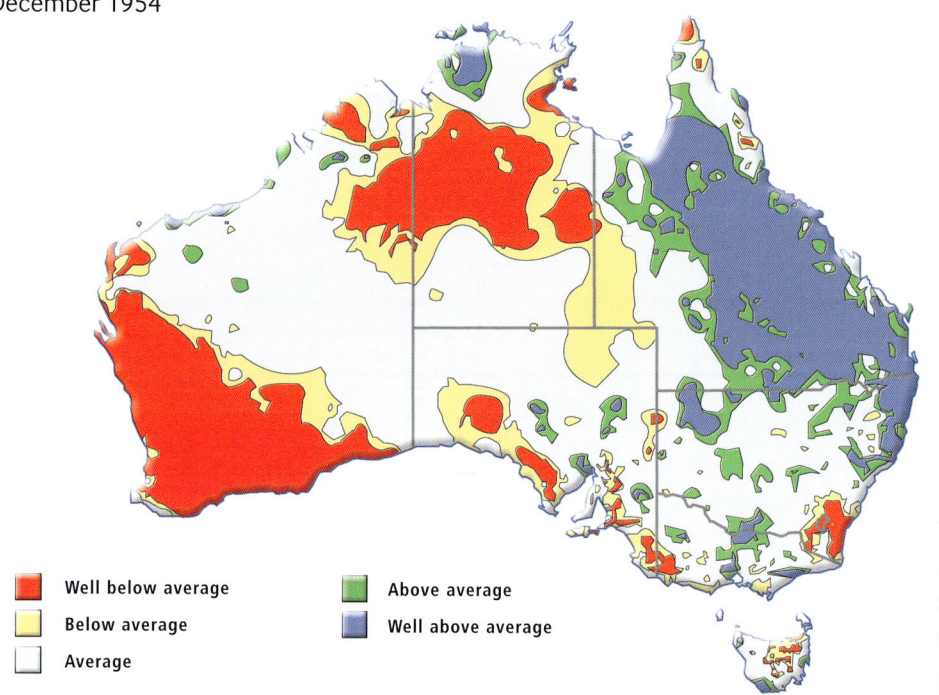

Three in a row — the years 1954, 1955 and 1956 formed one of the wettest three-consecutive-year periods in recorded history for eastern Australia. Flooding became common, with the Hunter Valley inundation of 1955 being amongst the worst ever across the area.

Rainfall Relative to Historical Records
January to December 1955

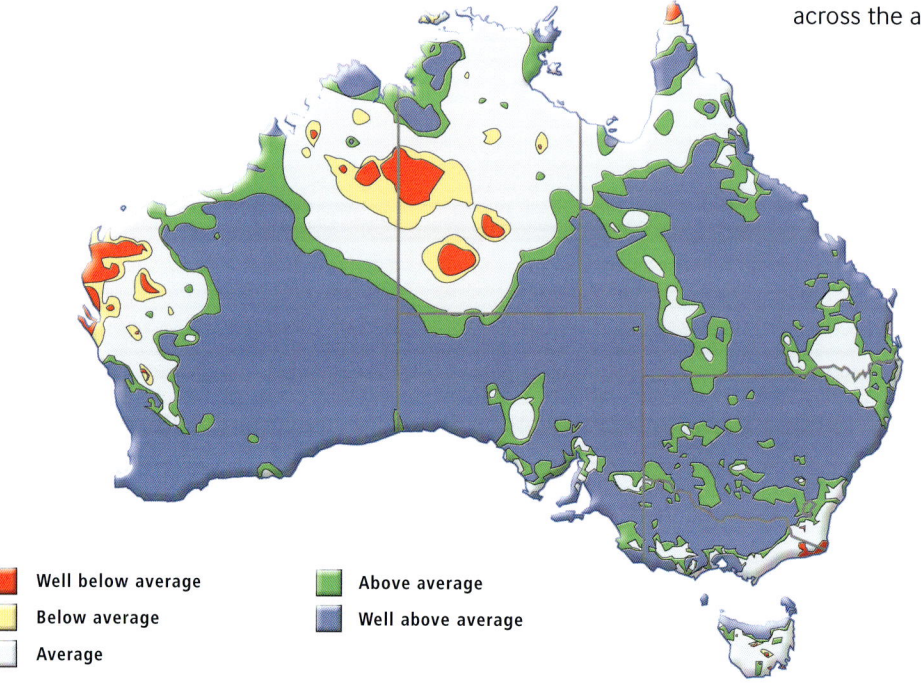

Rainfall Relative to Historical Records
January to December 1956

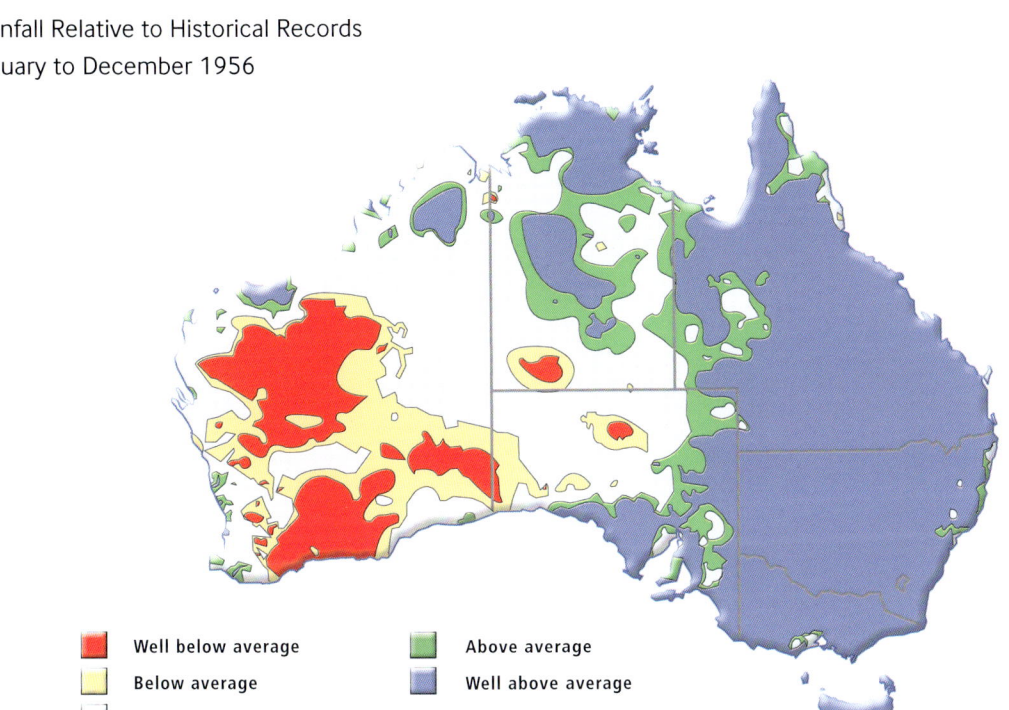

can proceed to Singleton. The Paterson River is 23 feet at Paterson. The Williams is overflowing at Dungog. The South Maitland position is gradually getting worse. Wallis Creek is rising and all residents should be prepared for ultimate evacuation. The Mayor of Singleton asks all truck drivers to report to him and all people in low-lying areas should be prepared to leave. The Mayor views the position at Singleton seriously and expects flooding this afternoon. In Maitland and the Lower Hunter all persons in any danger area are cautioned to be well on the alert and ready to leave without delay. The position in Maitland is becoming serious and before midnight all residents in threatened areas should be ready to evacuate their property. The ferries on the Williams River are not operating.

The rain continued right through 24 February and the mayor's alerts became increasingly urgent. At 10 pm the mayor's office advised:

The Mayor feels that the position has so deteriorated that it is now becoming critical. He now advises all people in the low areas that before morning it is likely that the river will overtop the banks and that the time has come for all people in these areas to leave their houses and go to higher land. This should be done as soon as possible so that it can be done in an orderly manner while there is still time …

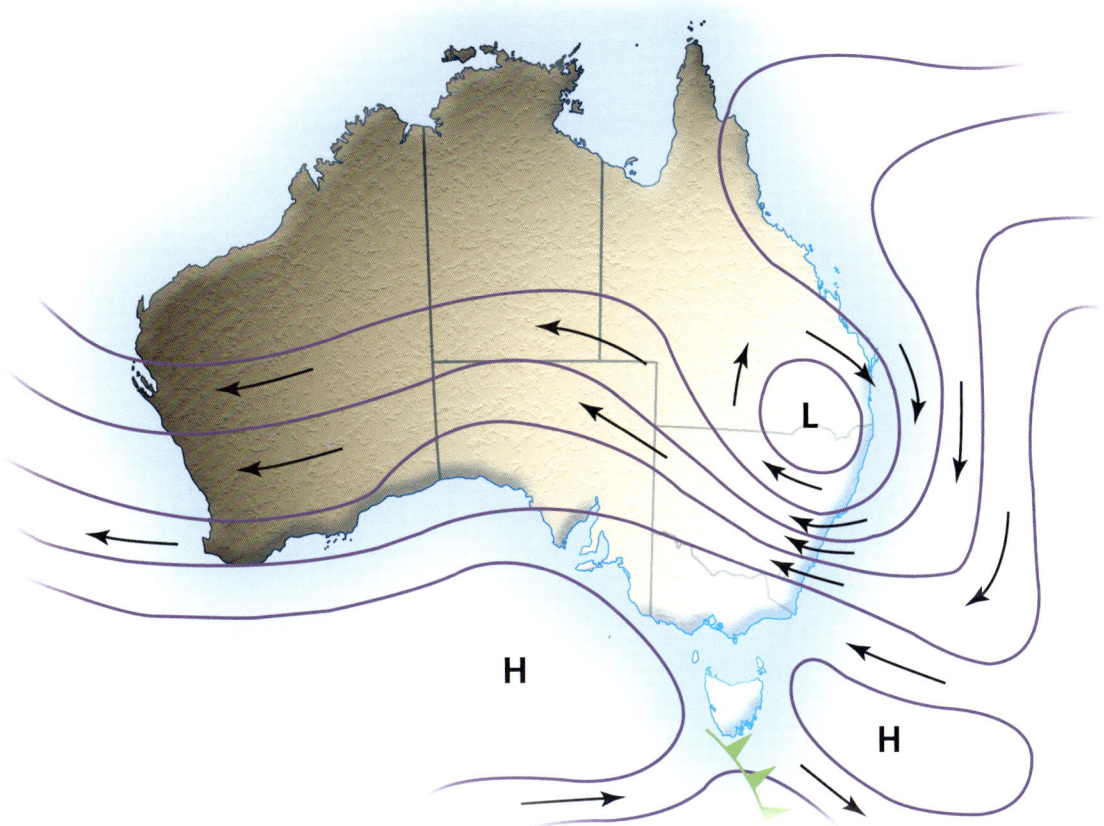

A reconstruction of the 3 pm weather map of 24 February 1955. The low-pressure cell situated over south-eastern Queensland was driving moisture-laden winds across the Hunter Valley in the direction of the arrows (i.e. from the south-east). This produced heavy rain across the area for about 48 hours.

On 25 February the full impact of the disaster struck. Large areas of Singleton and Maitland were inundated, with thousands evacuated from both townships. Floodwaters stretched across the Hunter district and extended into the central west area as well. In all, some 32 towns had been either flooded or cut off by the rising waters. Many thousands of stock had perished, and several people were known to have drowned. A family attempting to flee the floodwaters at Bulga by driving to Singleton was lost when their truck was swept off the road by raging floodwaters from the Parsons River. In their amphibious 'ducks', the army rescued hundreds of people marooned on their rooftops as water lapped the eaves. Two soldiers were electrocuted when their 'duck' struck a 64,000 volt high-tension wire near the Maitland railway bridge.

The Sydney-bound Glen Innes Express was derailed near Scone in a scene reported to *The Sydney Morning Herald* by a couple who were passengers:

A Navy helicopter rescues a man from the Maitland floodwaters. Tragically he fell to his death only a few seconds later.

We had both been ill and left our home in Manila to see a doctor in Sydney. It rained

Flood-warning System

Up until the time of the Maitland floods there was no accurate way to predict river heights during a flood. To do this was a difficult operation: for each river catchment system, a network of rain and river-height gauges would need to be established, and monitored daily. Then there was the problem of the prediction of rainfall amounts, which clearly could only be meaningfully attempted by the Bureau of Meteorology, augmented and enhanced by the incoming information from the gauge network. Also to be developed was a method for prompt dissemination of the information to relevant organisations, and this was quite difficult at the time, given the communications available.

Then there was the thorny issue of government control. Many of the operations involved were already conducted by State governments, each of which 'did things differently'. These individual modus operandi had to be integrated with the systems of the Bureau of Meteorology — a Commonwealth government entity. Some of the State organisations resented what they saw as a Commonwealth intrusion onto their turf.

The then Director of Meteorology, Len Dwyer, gradually began gathering information and decided to first set up a flood-forecasting system over the Macleay River catchment on the New South Wales north coast. This catchment had also been affected by the 1955 floods, but presented a simpler problem than the much more complex Hunter River catchment. For the first time in Australia, hydrologists sat beside meteorologists in a combined attempt to forecast river heights, and the national flood-warning system had begun. Early endeavours tried to correlate historical rainfall readings with resultant river heights and assume similar outcomes in the future.

Today this system has evolved into a 'high-tech' operation involving automated networks of gauges recording rainfall and river heights integrated with computer models of the various catchments. Hydrologists can now simulate what effect a certain fall of rain will have on a river given the current 'dryness' of the surrounding catchment. When this information is married with the meteorologists' predicted rainfall figures, a forecast of river heights is generated. When these forecasts indicate critical levels being reached, flood warnings are issued, and the whole gammut of emergency service procedures starts up.

In the event of a massive flood such as was seen in 1955, significant damage to property and infrastructure is inevitable. However, with an effective flood-warning system such as we now have, this damage can be minimised, and the threat to human life and stock is substantially reduced.

---

hard all night and the further we went, the harder it rained. Our carriage was derailed near Scone. We were tossed about backwards and forwards but escaped injury. Other people were hurt and a woman with us had a deep cut across the face. Doors of the carriage jammed and people had to climb out the windows. The engine and tender tore free and plunged into a mud hole. The side of the engine was only a foot out of the water and men could only reach it by swimming.

At 12.00 noon the next radio transmission stated that:

The position is becoming increasingly grim and from now on the broadcasts will be very brief ... We anticipate shortly that the telephone will be out of action.

Reports at Branxton indicated the phenomenal speed of the water's rise: by 9.00 am the water had reached the

1893 flood level; by 2.15 pm it was 2.13 metres above that level. By this time water was 'pouring down High Street in Maitland' to a depth of 1.52 metres and by 7 pm it was estimated that the river had reached a height of over 13.4 metres.

The rain finally began to abate during 26 and 27 February, and on 28 February the mayor issued his final broadcast:

> *Water is gradually receding in Maitland and at the Town Hall the main floor is now clear.*

The crisis was over. In all, 14 people had died, more than 10,000 houses were flooded and 30 others had been entirely swept away in Maitland, the most severely affected town. Thousand of sheep and cattle were lost and the enormous damage to bridges, roads, railways and telephone lines took months to repair.

The magnitude of the disaster was such that the government came under considerable pressure to organise a better flood-warning and response system, not just for New South Wales but on a national basis. It was out of the mud of this disaster that the Bureau of Meteorology's flood-forecasting system was born.

Maitland flood damage. Sam Hood, The State Library of New South Wales

1961

The Flight of Tango Victor Charlie

There was a violent electrical storm centred between Cronulla and Kurnell. At 7.25 pm there was a terrific flash of lightning, followed by two dull red objects falling slowly from the sky.

Eyewitness report from Penshurst at about 7.15 pm on 30 November 1961

At 7.15 pm on 30 November 1961, the scheduled Australian National Airways (ANA) flight from Sydney to Canberra began running up its engines on the east–west runway at Sydney airport. At the controls of the Vickers Viscount Series 700 aircraft, callsigned VH-TVC or Tango Victor Charlie, was Captain Stan Lindsay, assisted by First Officer Ben Costello and accompanied by flight attendants Elizabeth Hardy and Aileen Keldie.

Also aboard were 11 passengers, all but one of them Canberra residents returning home after a stay in Sydney. As the aircraft rolled into position, lightning flashed to the west and south, followed by a huge crack of thunder that shook the airport.

At 7.17 pm, Lindsay released the brakes, applied full power to the four Rolls-Royce Dart engines, and the big airliner began gathering speed along the runway. Take-off was on schedule and Tango Victor Charlie climbed quickly and soon vanished into low cloud at around 250 metres.

What happened in the next five minutes will never be precisely known, but the outcome was a watershed event that changed the course of Australian domestic aviation, and has left its mark on aircraft operating regulations today, mainly in the area of aviation radar.

Back in 1961, Sydney airport was equipped with an Air Traffic Control (ATC) radar which was designed and used almost exclusively for directing incoming and outgoing aircraft movements. Although this radar could also 'see' weather, it was not used for this purpose, and the meteorological team at the airport had no direct access to the radar display.

This photograph of the Vickers Viscount VH-TVC was taken about a year before the plane crashed. Viscounts were state of the art in the early 1960s and could carry more than 50 passengers over a distance of 1500 kilometres.

In those days, the meteorological team at any one time consisted of three forecasters from the Bureau of Meteorology – two to prepare aviation forecasts for domestic flights and one for international. Before departure, the pilot would receive a briefing and written weather forecast from the 'Met Office' (Bureau of Meteorology) and then submit a flight plan to the Senior Operations Officer (SOO) for approval. This flight plan was then passed on to the Air Traffic Control Tower so that a firm knowledge of all outbound operations was always available.

On 30 November 1961 the weather was particularly unsettled. A low-pressure trough located over central New South Wales during the morning moved steadily east during the day, triggering thunderstorms across eastern parts of the State. Late in the afternoon, thunderstorms crossed the Blue Mountains in the west and reached Sydney.

At 6.40 pm a pilot over Sylvania in the south of Sydney reported:

Thunderstorms – an Aviation Hazard

Thunderstorms have long been recognised as an aviation safety hazard. The technical term for this form of cloud is 'cumulonimbus', and in aviation circles they are known as the dreaded CBs or 'Charlie Bravos' – the monster of the cloud family. These giant clouds frequently extend 12 kilometres in height, which is much higher than Mount Everest, and contain about the same energy as a small-scale nuclear weapon. Within the cloud itself there are violent up- and downdraughts, lightning, heavy rain and often hail, producing a very aircraft-unfriendly environment. Aviation hazards produced by thunderstorms include severe turbulence, airframe icing (accretion of ice on the body of the aircraft) and possible lightning strikes, and pilots therefore avoid penetrating CBs whenever possible. When standing alone during the day, these clouds can be seen from many kilometres away and are easily avoided. But at night, hidden by surrounding clouds, and with no radar image to act as a guide, they become invisible hazards to all aviation operations.

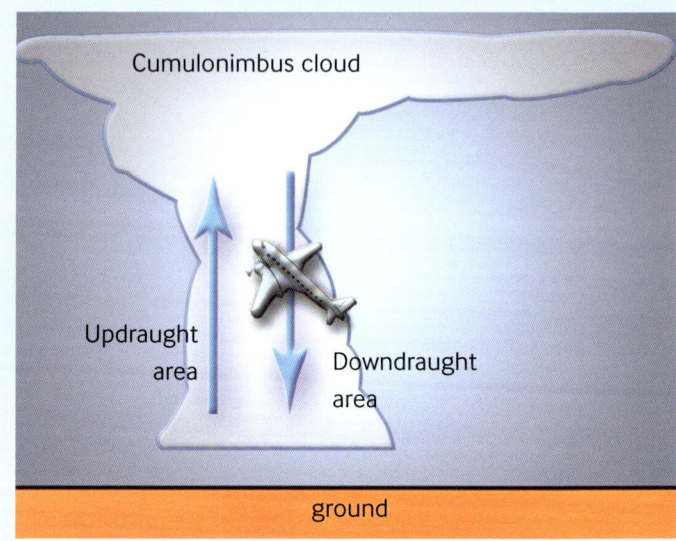

The size of the aircraft has been greatly exaggerated in this diagram; to scale Tango Victor Charlie would have been less than the size of a pinhead here. Caught in the violent downdraught area of the cloud, the pilot could loose control of the plane.

… a thunderstorm overhead, base 1200–1500 feet. There was a half mile diameter circular opening in the base. The cloud forming the base of the thunderstorm was moving towards this opening from all directions at an estimated 50 knots. Above the opening was an inverted funnel which extended a considerable distance vertically.

Numerous other reports had also been received from aircraft. One of the most telling was from Tango Victor Charlie itself, which earlier in the day had flown from Sydney to Canberra and back. On the approach to Sydney at around 5.40 pm it reported 'Severe continuous turbulence of a jolting nature in which the air speed indicator was fluctuating up to 15 knots either way'.

Captain Lindsay would have been aware of at least some of these reports, and certainly the nature of the turbulence encountered by Tango Victor Charlie would have been relayed to him before his flight began. A warning of widespread thunderstorm activity across eastern New South Wales had also been distributed by the Bureau of Meteorology to the Department of Civil Aviation (DCA), and then widely promulgated throughout the airline companies, including ANA. Captain Lindsay's formal pre-flight weather briefing at the Met Office also indicated the possibility

A typical cumulonimbus cloud formation. These clouds can reach nearly double the height of Mount Everest.

of thunderstorms and heavy turbulence en route.

Although this looked like a stand-out dangerous situation, in fact this sort of weather was not all that unusual for November in south-eastern Australia, and several similar events could generally be expected at around this time each year. And for a modern aircraft like the Viscount, which was to be flown that night, such situations were thought to be well within the limits of safe operations.

The Vickers Viscount was one of the success stories of postwar British aviation. It was a sturdy four-engined turbo-propeller-driven passenger aircraft, one of the earliest to be equipped with a fully pressurised interior. It could cruise comfortably at 8000 metres and about 510 kilometres per hour. Its windows were nearly 50 per cent larger than those in today's modern jet aircraft and allowed passengers panoramic views during the flight.

The Viscount could also carry more than 50 passengers over a range of around 1500 kilometres, and this of course meant it was ideal for the inter– capital city runs, in this case, Sydney to Canberra. This sort of performance is modest compared with that of today's aircraft, but in 1961 the Vickers Viscount was state of the art, and really had only one notable weakness. This was the lack

The wreckage of Tango Victor Charlie spread out across the floor of a Department of Civil Aviation hangar during the investigation. The extreme nature of the fragmentation points to a high impact speed with the water and shows that the aircraft was probably under full power at the time.

of an on-board radar system, which would enable the captain to precisely locate thunderstorms and to avoid them in flight.

Soon after Tango Victor Charlie entered the cloud there were several radio exchanges between the cockpit and the control tower. The aircraft was instructed to begin a long climbing left turn out over Bondi. It was then to return in the opposite direction and pass back across Botany Bay at about 2500 metres, before tracking out towards Canberra. This manoeuvre was designed to provide a safe separation distance between all the flights in the area. But it didn't take into account the massive thunderstorm that was still boiling over Botany Bay …

Abruptly, soon after 7.22 pm, all transmissions from Tango Victor Charlie ceased. The DCA declared a search and rescue operation. With all the lightning around, it was still believed that the most likely problem was a radio malfunction. But when the aircraft failed to arrive in Canberra at the expected time, it was apparent that something much more serious had occurred and the distress phase of the search and rescue operation was declared.

It wasn't until after first light the next day that some wreckage was found on the southern shore of Botany Bay. Later in the morning, the main fuselage debris was located in about 8 metres of water, in the north-eastern corner of the bay. There were no survivors. The wreckage was salvaged and taken to a hangar at the airport for analysis.

A Board of Accident Inquiry was established to determine the cause of the disaster, under the chairmanship of Mr Justice Spicer. After a very thorough investigation, the final report was made public in August 1962. This became known as the 'Spicer Report', and it was to have far-reaching implications for aviation in Australia.

Justice Spicer concluded that Tango Victor Charlie was still climbing over Botany Bay when it suddenly encountered extreme turbulence associated with the interior of a thunderstorm cell. This had caused the aircraft to descend rapidly, and in an effort to regain control, Captain Stanley had applied correctional action that resulted in severe stress on the aircraft.

At around 2000 metres, the starboard wing severely deformed and a large outer section of it broke off. Soon after, the starboard tailplane also broke off, leaving the aircraft totally out of control. With all engines still under power, the aircraft entered into a tumbling dive and struck the water at high speed, killing all on board.

Eyewitness accounts of what could have been the actual crash were also included in the report, including that quoted at the beginning of this chapter, and this one from the northern Sydney suburb of Chatswood:

… there was fairly heavy electrical storm activity with thunder and lightning at frequent intervals, and heavy rain. A heavy

Radar

RADAR is an acronym for 'radio detection and ranging' and is one of the most important tools available to both the meteorologist and the airline pilot.

Radar was originally designed to detect approaching aircraft during the Battle of Britain in the early 1940s, but it was soon noticed that radar could also detect showers and thunderstorms.

Initially this was seen as a nuisance; weather 'echoes' sometimes masked aircraft movement and made detection and monitoring of air traffic more difficult. But it became obvious that radar could also be used as a short-term weather-forecasting aid, and it was to eventually become standard equipment in meteorological offices around the world.

A weather-watch radar unit fires a radio beam out into the atmosphere and then 'listens' for a return signal. If the beam encounters rain or hail, part of it will travel through and part of it will be reflected back where it is picked up as an 'echo'. With very heavy rain or hail, more of the beam will be reflected back, and this enables an estimate of the intensity of the precipitation to be displayed.

Radar shows precisely where and how far away it is raining and is invaluable to the airline pilot for identifying and avoiding thunderstorms during a flight.

---

detonation was heard, and out at 156 degrees [that is to the southeast] the witness saw a yellow and blue–white glow lasting several seconds and descending fairly fast.

After sifting through the mountain of information, Justice Spicer concluded that all officers of the Department of Civil Aviation and Bureau of Meteorology had performed their duties correctly and as prescribed by the regulations, but that the regulations themselves needed changing.

In particular, he recommended the development of a specialised radar weather watch at Sydney airport, with formal communication to be established between ATC and the Bureau of Meteorology during times of severe weather. ATC was to take into account the position of thunderstorms in their deliberations on aircraft separation, and not just consider traffic control in isolation. Another result was the recommendation that all commercial passenger aircraft should carry on-board radar to allow the captain to be precisely aware of the position of any thunderstorms near the aircraft track. These recommendations were accepted, and eventually became part of the structure of Australian commercial aviation.

The safety record of aviation in Australia is excellent, but as with aviation all around the world, this safety has come at a price. Tragically, the flight crew and passengers of Tango Victor Charlie paid a big slice of the Australian safety bill on the night of 30 November 1961.

1967

The Apple Isle Burns

We didn't put it out. It just ran out of Tasmania.

Tasmanian fireman after the crisis was over

Hobart is one of our more picturesque capital cities, located in south-eastern Tasmania amid a series of islands and peninsulas and nestling at the foot of Mount Wellington.

Hobart's overall climate is certainly quite equable, even taking into account the cold and blustery conditions sometimes encountered in winter. Summer is normally mild, with an average maximum temperature in January of 21.5°C, which is the lowest figure of all our capital cities.

But even Hobart can experience spells of very hot weather during summer, nearly always associated with north-westerly winds building ahead of an approaching frontal system. When this happens, the mild and pleasant south-easterly sea breeze that normally blows up the Derwent River is swamped by hot winds surging across from inland Tasmania. Under such conditions, the mercury can climb well over 30°C.

This, combined with the low humidity normally associated with winds blowing from across the inland, can produce ideal bushfire conditions across south-eastern Tasmania, particularly around Hobart.

Several bushfire outbreaks had occurred in this general area over previous years, the largest being the so-called 'Great Fire' of 31 December 1897, when severe fires burned out large tracts of land to the south-west of Hobart as well as part of the Port Arthur settlement. Four people were killed – the first recorded bushfire deaths in Tasmania.

During the early spring of 1966, bountiful rain fell across much of Tasmania, and as the warmer weather arrived, thick grass and undergrowth sprouted vigorously, particularly around Hobart. But during November, the wet weather pattern abruptly ceased, and the heavy vegetation build-up of the previous two months rapidly dried out and became highly flammable.

The tragedy of bushfire is graphically revealed as this Tasmanian couple watch their home being engulfed in flames on 7 February 1967. Over 1400 houses were to be destroyed in this way.

Many landowners became concerned with this situation and began systematic summer burn-offs to reduce the load of fuel on their properties. Some graziers also lit fires to promote nutritious secondary growth for their livestock during the winter months – a long-standing practice in the area. As a consequence of these activities, over 80 small fires were burning around Hobart as Tuesday 7 February 1967 dawned.

That morning, strengthening north-westerly winds ahead of a cold front approaching from the Great Australian Bight began to blow across Tasmania. The relative humidity of the atmosphere plummeted as the air dried rapidly, temperatures soared and the strength of the wind continued to build. In Hobart, temperatures reached 39.4°C, wind gusts peaked in excess of 100 kilometres per hour and the relative humidity fell to an extremely low 12 per cent at 1 pm.

The table below is an hourly summary of these conditions, together with what is called the Fire Danger Index, which is a rating combining the weather conditions with the 'dryness' of the bushland. A rating of 100 is towards the top end of the scale and the table shows that Hobart's figure at 1300 hours (1 pm) was 96. However, it is likely that even higher figures were recorded between these hourly observations. (Note the temperature fall at 2100 hours [9 pm] after the wind had turned to the south-east following the passage of the front.)

The concurrence of all these events – heavy spring growth, land clearing using controlled burn-off, and extreme meteorological conditions – would produce a terrible conflagration many thought impossible for Tasmania.

The numerous small fires already burning rapidly united into an inferno driven at tremendous speed by the hot, dry winds. By noon, a huge pall of smoke covered Hobart. A major fire front developed to the north-west of the city and proved totally unstoppable, with reports of incredible scenes coming from the worst affected areas.

Witnesses described 'whole hillsides erupting, great balls of flames rolling ahead of the main fire, houses exploding and also huge explosions occurring some hundreds of feet above the ground'.

Severe fire whirlwinds, or tornadoes, also developed on the slopes of Mount Wellington, and the wind generated by the fire was 'strong enough to snap pole-sized timber off some twenty feet above the ground'. The progress of the fire was accompanied by

Hobart on 7 February 1967

Time	Air Temp (°C)	Relative Humidity (%)	Wind Velocity (km/hr)	Wind Direction	Fire Danger Index (0–100)
0300	21.3	49	–	–	6
0600	23.3	43	–	–	9
0900	31.7	21	11.3	NW	19
1000	33.9	18	15.3	NW	33
1100	36.1	16	41.8	NW	65
1200	38.3	14	43.5	NW	85
1300	39.2	12	44.3	WNW	96
1400	38.1	13	53.9	WNW	86
1500	36.1	15	43.5	W	72
1600	32.8	20	37	WNW	
1800	26.1	31	25.7	NW	18
2100	18.6	35	0	SE	9

Fire sweeping across a railway area sets several carriages ablaze. Areas not normally thought to be fire prone were devastated by the outbreak.

'deafening roar sounding like a continuous roll of thunder'.

Some towns and suburban areas of Hobart were overcome. The township of Snug was almost totally destroyed in apocalyptic scenes as firefighters tried in vain to halt the inferno. Students at the local primary school were saved through the heroic efforts of teachers, who moved them into a brick building as the fire engulfed the area. One of the teachers described the scene:

A scene of utter devastation is revealed after the fire raged across this neighbourhood. A boy inspects the remains of his billycart beside the burnt-out wreck of the family car. Miraculously, the fire that destroyed his father's workshop didn't reach the house.

We finally got them to the hall and there were flames everywhere. The school tractor went up with a big boom. We shut the curtains so the children couldn't see the sparks and flames. The music teacher played songs for the children to sing. The church was on fire across the road and they said if the petrol bowsers at the shop were faulty, we'd all go. So we lined the children up against the opposite wall, and we linked hands behind them so that we'd take the first blast. The music teacher played 'The Lord is my Shepherd'. I was so scared I couldn't sing.

Miraculously, the building protecting the children remained intact, despite the fact that the close surroundings were almost totally ravaged by flames.

Communications across Hobart shut down as burning trees fell across lines. At one stage only one radio station was still transmitting, greatly adding to the confusion of both emergency services and the general population. Water supplies began running out in some areas and firefighters had to resort to wet sacks and tree branches. The fire front advanced remorselessly, reaching to within a few hundred metres of the Hobart GPO and central business district. It even jumped the ocean to Bruny Island as airborne debris generated spot fires. As one firefighter later remarked, 'We didn't put it out. It just ran out of Tasmania'.

Eventually the cold front from the Great Australian Bight reached the area and conditions began to moderate. The crisis was coming to an end. In just over five hours, 62 people died, more than a quarter of a million hectares were burnt out and over 1400 dwellings were destroyed. It was estimated that more than half the area south of a line from New Norfolk to the east coast was affected by fires in various degrees of severity.

Damage to buildings, as well as agricultural losses involving stock, fencing and destruction of pasture was estimated to be around $25 million. On top of this was the considerable damage inflicted on the State's communication and electricity network. The final damage estimates varied but the true figure was probably close to $28 million – a huge figure in 1967 terms. At the time, this was the largest loss of life and property on any single day in the history of Australia.

A major investigation following the fires resulted in a significant increase in the funding of general fire-fighting resources, including the formation of several new firefighting units. One of these was the Snug Fire Brigade, which now oversees the area so severely damaged in the 1967 fires. Regulations involving the setting of controlled burns and fuel-reduction procedures were also overhauled in an effort to minimise the chance of a recurrence of this type of disaster.

However, long, hot Australian summers are often characterised by extreme weather

The historic Cascade Brewery, built in South Hobart in 1824, was totally destroyed in the fires. Some four million beer bottles were melted and fused into a gigantic heap by the heat of the flames.

conditions, and severe bushfires are part of this scene. The events around Hobart in February 1967 are a sad reminder of the need for constant vigilance, even in suburban areas not generally associated with high bushfire danger.

1967

Prime Minister Lost

The Prime Minister is missing, believed drowned. He disappeared in heavy surf off Portsea's ocean beach soon after noon yesterday and late last night had not been found.

The Age, Monday 18 December 1967

Sunday 17 December 1967 was a hot, humid and blustery Melbourne day, and many people, including the eighteenth prime minister of Australia, the Honourable Harold Holt, headed off to the numer-ous bayside beaches to escape the early summer heat.

Holt had flown into Melbourne from Canberra on the previous Friday in his VIP aircraft. After spending Saturday with friends at Portsea, he had driven his Pontiac Parisienne down to nearby Cheviot Beach with the idea of indulging in one of his favourite pastimes – snorkelling. Several friends, including Majorie Gillespie, her daughter Vyner and a young businessman, Alan Stewart, accompanied him.

Although Holt was 59 years of age, he was a fit and powerful swimmer, handicapped only slightly by a shoulder injury he had suffered as a young man. He was also handsome, and reputedly somewhat vain, with a supreme confidence in his physical abilities. He enjoyed his image as an action man and a famous photograph was widely circulated in the media showing him in a 'James Bond' pose dressed in his diving gear and surrounded by three women in bikinis. To improve his snorkelling performance, he told friends that he sometimes held his breath for extended periods during parliamentary sessions, and could in fact do so for around two minutes – very good for a man of his age.

As soon as the party arrived at Cheviot Beach, it was obvious that conditions were far from ideal. Westerly winds across Bass Strait during the previous 48 hours had resulted in rough seas at most Victorian surf

Harold Holt

The Right Honorable Harold Edward Holt was Prime Minister of Australia from 26 January 1966 to 17 December 1967. The son of two school teachers, Holt was a gifted student and talented athlete, and graduated as a lawyer in 1930.

Displaying an early interest in politics, he was elected to federal parliament in 1935 as a member for the United Australia Party — the forerunner of the Liberal Party of Australia.

He became a long-term minister of the Liberal Party under Prime Minister Robert Menzies, eventually becoming prime minister himself in 1966.

This famous photograph of Prime Minister Holt with his daughters-in-law provides a sharp contrast with the previous prime minister, the very conservative Sir Robert Menzies. Holt was a strong and fit man for his age and a powerful swimmer. However, he was overcome by the rough seas at Cheviot Beach on 17 December 1967.

beaches and that afternoon, under the influence of the continuing winds, the seas were still very rough and choppy. The local surf-lifesaving club had closed nearby Portsea Surf Beach to the public because of the adverse conditions, but Cheviot Beach was not patrolled – anyone who desired could swim there. Despite the misgivings of his companions, Holt entered the water.

The Mornington Peninsula, where Cheviot Beach is located, is an immensely picturesque area that has attracted tourists in numbers since the 1880s. The northern side fronts onto the sheltered waters of Port Phillip Bay and for the most part experiences only benign sea conditions. However, the southern side, where both Portsea Surf Beach and Cheviot Beach are located, is open to the notoriously turbulent waters of Bass Strait. It frequently experiences rough seas and heavy swells as south-westerly winds originating from Antarctic latitudes sweep across southern Victoria.

The Portseas area became world famous during the mid to late 1950s as the training camp of the legendary athletics coach

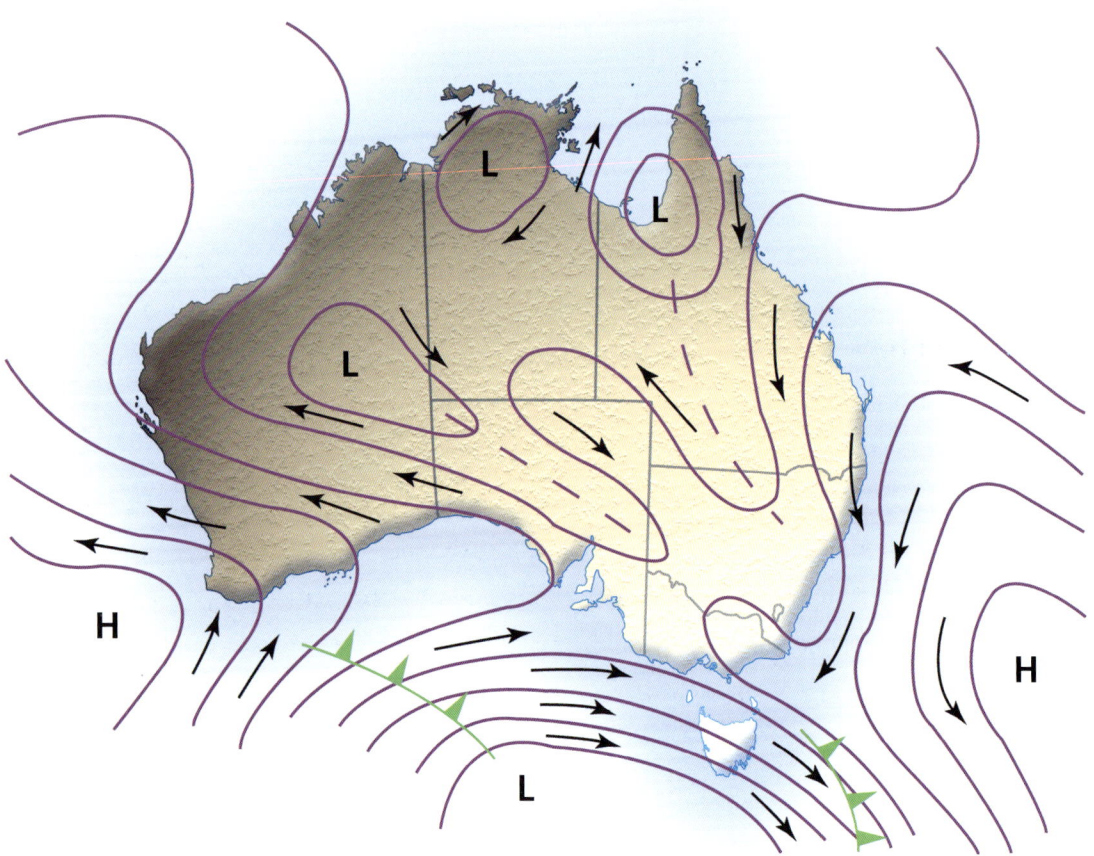

A reconstruction of the 3 pm weather map of 17 December 1967. A low-pressure area to the south-west of Tasmania was directing strong winds from the west across the Bass Strait area, as indicated by the arrows. This produced rough ocean conditions along much of the Victorian coastline.

Percy Cerutty, who demanded that his runners sprint up and down the steep sandhills as a way of improving their stamina. This unconventional training produced the world champion runner Herb Elliott, who went on to win the gold medal in the 1500-metre event at the 1960 Rome Olympic Games.

In what was perhaps a hint of things to come, Cerutty later recounted a story of how he and Herb had completed a tough training run and then jumped into the Portsea surf for a cool down. Cerutty was promptly carried out to sea in a fierce undertow. Elliott swam out and pulled him into shore. The local shoreline had a bad reputation for treacherous conditions, but Harold Holt, who snorkelled regularly in the area, claimed to friends that 'I know this beach like the back of my hand', and had no hesitation about swimming in rough conditions.

Almost as soon as Holt entered the water, things began to go horribly wrong. Alan Stewart was clearly daunted by the turbulent waters, but remarked: 'If Mr Holt can take it, I had better go in, too'. However, because of the fierce undertow he did not go out of his depth, and stayed within about 10 metres of the shoreline. But Holt plunged straight in and began swimming away from the beach.

Stewart later described to police how Holt had alternately swum and waded towards one of his favourite spear-fishing spots – a pothole described as being '30 yards by 50 yards, 40 feet deep and opening at one end in a narrow rip only 80 yards from the breakers'. He then pushed off from the rock shelf towards the centre of the pothole, and was last seen swimming strongly in the backflush of the surf bursting over the area.

His silver hair was soon lost to sight in the churning white of the foam produced by the rolling breakers. Majorie Gillespie later remarked: 'It was like a leaf being taken out. It was so quick and so final'. His companions along the shoreline became increasingly concerned as the minutes ticked by and he didn't reappear. Finally, it became apparent that something was terribly amiss and the alarm was raised.

A prime minister missing in the surf was a totally unprecedented situation and produced utter consternation in official circles. A massive search and rescue operation was immediately organised. Police and military helicopters were sent to the area, and navy frogmen plunged into the surf all along the beach.

In the meantime, the news was spreading like wildfire as radio stations suspended routine broadcasts to concentrate on the story. Large crowds had picked up the news on their portable radios at the beach and gathered in long lines along the Nepean Highway as police and military vehicles converged on the area. As hours passed and evening fell it became increasingly obvious that Holt was unlikely to be found alive in the boiling surf. Australians watched the evening television news in stunned disbelief as the events of the day were reported and they realised that their prime minister was missing, believed drowned.

The massive air, sea and land search continued for the next week until it was accepted that Harold Holt was lost. Bizarre theories abounded, including suicide, assassination and even that he had been taken aboard a Chinese submarine that was waiting off shore.

However, a joint report by Commonwealth and Victorian police submitted in January 1968 concluded that: '… there has been no indication that the disappearance of the late Mr Holt was anything other than accidental'. The report found that 'his last movements followed a routine domestic pattern, his demeanour had been normal and despite his knowledge of the beach, the turbulent conditions (high winds, rough seas and rip tides) overcame him'. Several theories were advanced to explain the failure to find his body. These included a shark attack and the possibility that he could have become wedged in one of the numerous submarine rock crevices or simply taken far out to sea.

The disappearance of a prime minister, presumably by drowning, changed the course of Australia's history, and would be one of the very few examples, if indeed any others exist, of a head of state dying in this way.

Harold Holt in 1966, preparing to go spearfishing near Portsea, Victoria

1968 & 1989

Earthquake: Meckering and Newcastle

You can no more win a war than you can win an earthquake.

Jeannette Rankin, US pacifist and politician

Earthquakes are more common in Australia than is popularly believed, but in many cases they occur in sparsely settled areas, producing minimal human impact. The largest known earthquake in Australia's history occurred at Meeberrie, Western Australia in 1941. It registered 7.1 on the Richter scale but no damage was reported because of its remote location.

But in 1968, and then again in 1989, strong earthquakes occurred across populated areas, with devastating results, including heavy damage and even loss of life.

Meckering, 1968

In the mid-morning of 14 October 1968, an earthquake registering 6.9 shook the small township of Meckering, about 140 kilometres east of Perth.

Some 11 days before, there had been signs that something untoward was happening. On 3 October, the local police constable was walking down the main street of the town when he reported that 'the ground seemed to turn to jelly' and he found it difficult to stand. Two further, more minor tremors occurred over the next hour although no significant damage was reported.

But about 7 kilometres below the surface of the ground, movement was building. An ancient fault line, part of an extensive area of seismic activity that is about 60 kilometres

wide and extends across the south-western corner of Western Australia, was becoming active once again.

Then, abruptly, on the morning of 14 October, the ground literally 'broke' as the fault thrust upwards, vertically displacing the ground surface over an area of 200 square kilometres and producing a scarp line over 35 kilometres long and over 3 metres high in some areas. Meckering, close to the epicentre, was almost destroyed, with many buildings flattened or at least heavily damaged, but amazingly, no one was killed. The effects of the quake were felt right across the southern half of Western Australia, producing minor damage in Perth and in the adjacent townships of Northam and York.

Mr Vic Edwards, the local butcher, was in his backyard just out of town when he heard what sounded like loud explosions and was knocked to the ground three times. He saw cracks opening and closing in the ground with spurts of white dust emerging. Another

Opposite: The long scarp produced by the Meckering earthquake. This scarp extended for over 35 kilometres and reached a height of 3 metres in some areas.

Above: Police and locals survey two wrecked houses in Meckering. Looking at the scale of the damage it was indeed fortunate no fatalities occurred.

witness in a nearby car park noticed the same phenomenon, accompanied also by a pungent odour similar to carbide. A man parked in a truck was amazed to see 'two distinct ground-waves' move across the main street, travelling at about 10 kilometres per hour, and with about two seconds separating the crests.

Motorists near the outskirts of town at the time of the quake also told amazing stories. Two occupants of a truck heard 'a loud noise which seemed to be moving north, and the truck suddenly thumped up and down with a sensation akin to a flat-tyre'. Looking to the side of the road they saw 'laterite pebbles jumping and bouncing as much as 50 centimetres from the ground'.

Driving out of town a little later, they saw buildings disintegrating, and were lucky to survive when their truck flew off the top of the fault line that had dropped the roadway by nearly 1.8 metres in front of them.

Another driver reported 'trees along the roadside, already agitated by wind and rain, started to whip violently and at the same time the car rocked as if a tyre had blown out'. Then, immediately in front of him 'a 2.5 metres high bump rose in the road where two seconds before none had existed'.

Meckering remained Australia's most destructive earthquake until 1989, when the record was broken spectacularly in the New South Wales city of Newcastle.

Newcastle, 1989

On 28 December 1989, Australians were enjoying the break between Christmas and New Year, with most still in holiday mode. Down in Sydney, it was a typical summer day until 10.27 am, when many people became aware of a strange general movement of the ground which was soon identified as 'an earth tremor'. Radio stations crackled with the news as listeners phoned in. One station playfully broadcast Carole King's hit 'I Feel The Earth Move' and people good-naturedly compared experiences and swapped yarns over the airwaves.

But soon after, more serious news began to trickle in from the north. Newcastle residents too had experienced the 'tremor', but they were describing it instead as an earthquake. It became apparent that Newcastle had been hit, and hit hard. Amazing stories emerged of collapsed buildings and massive damage across the city and the virtually unthinkable was fast becoming a reality – for the first time a major Australian city had been devastated by a large earthquake.

Scientific information also began to emerge. The earthquake had measured 5.6 on the Richter scale and the effects were felt in a radius of 800 kilometres from Newcastle. Buildings over 9000 square kilometres radiating out from the area were damaged to varying degrees.

On the streets of Newcastle, the enormity of the event was gradually being realised. There was extensive damage to buildings in the central business district and over 3000 residences suffered various degrees of damage. But even worse news was to follow. Reports of deaths began to be received, with many suspected casualties occurring at the Newcastle Workers Club, which had completely collapsed during the height of the quake.

Witnesses reported seeing the building fall in a cloud of dust, and it was later established that it began collapsing from the top, causing the structure to 'implode', trapping numerous workers and patrons in the wreckage. A massive search and rescue operation swung into action at the club, with emergency services personnel frantically searching through the debris for survivors.

The final death toll for the earthquake was 13 people, and more than 160 were injured. This was the first case recorded in Australia

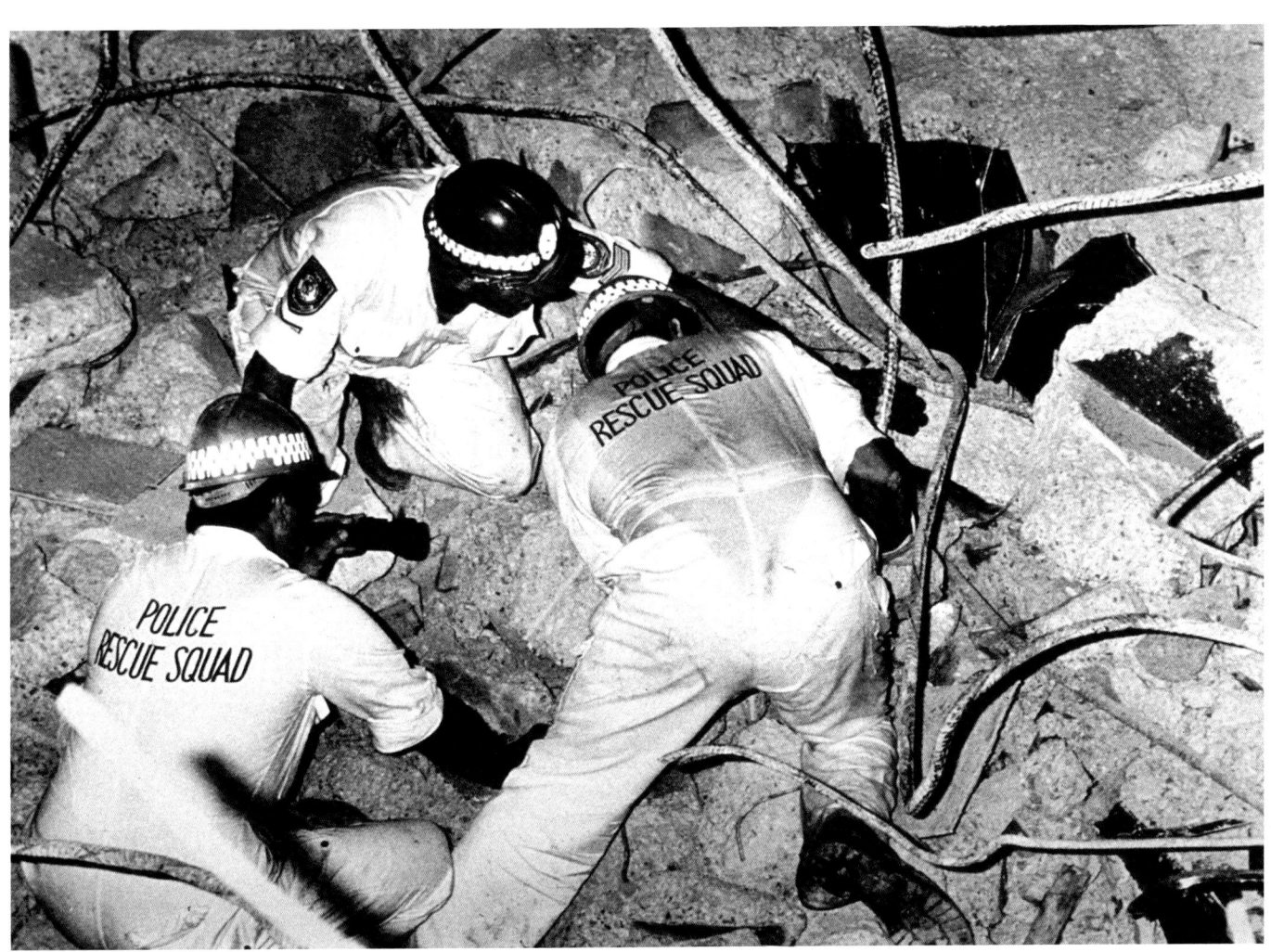

Members of the Police Rescue Squad desperately search for survivors in the rubble of the Newcastle Workers Club.

A collapsed section of the Newcastle Workers Club showing slabs of masonry and reinforcing rods that have fallen to the floor below.

Elderly patients are evacuated from a Newcastle nursing home following the earthquake.

where loss of life had resulted from an earthquake. In addition, the insurance loss was around $1 billion, which stood as the Australian record for nearly another ten years until broken by the massive Sydney hailstorm of April 1999 (see page 99).

Once and for all, the myth that earthquakes in Australia were not a serious issue was shattered and the incident had profound effects on disaster planning in New South Wales. The revelation that there was an ancient but sporadically active fault line that extended from Newcastle through Maitland, Murrurundi, Quirindi and Narrabri – called the Hunter Mooki Thrust – came as a complete surprise to most Australians. It was probably a movement along this fault that had generated the Newcastle disaster.

There were also implications for the

building code in the area. Most of the structural damage was sustained in the older style non-reinforced masonry buildings that had been erected between 1900 and 1950, with the great majority of the modern structures bearing up comparatively well.

The incident had obviously demonstrated that disaster management in Australia was not adequately prepared for a strong earthquake over a major city, and an eventual response to this was the preparation of a formal scientific study called Earthquake Risk in Newcastle and Lake Macquarie. This was the most comprehensive study ever undertaken to assess the risks of earthquake over an Australian city, and carried implications for government decision-makers, as well as the building, insurance and finance industries. The study was also relevant to the other southern capitals of Sydney, Melbourne and Adelaide, which have buildings with similar structures to those in Newcastle.

Measuring Earthquakes

Earthquakes are measured with a highly sensitive instrument called a seismograph. This normally consists of a heavy weight suspended from a horizontal rod by a cable; the weight remains vertical even when the rest of the instrument is moving from side to side in an earthquake. A pen is connected to the base of the weight and draws a line on a paper graph below, recording the intensity and duration of the disturbance.

The Richter Scale

The Richter Scale was used to measure both the Meckering and Newcastle earthquakes. This scale is a mathematical way of comparing the intensity of earthquakes and was developed in 1935 by Charles F. Richter of the California Institute of Technology. He expressed the intensity of earthquakes as 'magnitudes', rating from M1 to M9, in order of ascending severity. Today a slightly different scale is commonly used – the Moment magnitude scale – that rates the magnitude of the earthquake by a different means. It commonly uses 12 different intensities rather than the 9 of the old Richter Scale.

- M1–3: Recorded on instruments, but generally not felt by people.
- M3–4: Often felt, but no resultant building damage.
- M5: Felt widely, with slight building damage near the centre of the quake.
- M6: Damage to poorly constructed buildings and other structures within tens of kilometres from the centre of the quake.
- M7: Major earthquake, causing serious structural damage up to 100 kilometres from the centre of the quake.
- M8: Severe earthquake, generating widespread destruction and loss of life up to hundreds of kilometres away from the quake centre.
- M9: Rare great earthquake, producing major damage and loss of life over a large region reaching over 1000 kilometres from the quake centre.

1972 & 2003

Flash Floods in Melbourne

The day that cars floated in the street.

The Age, 18 February 1972

Melbourne has a reputation for being one of our wetter capital cities but in fact the statistics show that this is somewhat undeserved. The average annual rainfall for Melbourne is 648 millimetres compared with Sydney's figure of 1213 millimetres – nearly twice the amount. When it comes to the average number of days per year on which rain falls Melbourne and Sydney are quite close – 159 to 162 respectively. When it comes to the average number of days per year on which rain falls, our champion capital city is Hobart, with 160 days. Sydney is second with 148 days and Melbourne third with 143.

As far as the average sunshine hours per day are concerned, Melbourne's figure is 6.0 compared to Sydney with 6.8. Perhaps it is this somewhat gloomy statistic that gives Melbourne the reputation of having a rather bleak climate, particularly during winter.

However, the rainfall figures are more revealing. Far less rain falls in Melbourne than in Sydney, but the two cities have a similar number of wet days. This immediately tells us that Sydney's rain is generally heavier. Or, put another way, we would expect rainfall intensity in Sydney to be greater than that in Melbourne, and this is indeed the case in most circumstances.

Rainfall intensity is different to rainfall amount, because it takes into account how fast rain is falling. We are used to hearing of, say, 50 millimetres of rain falling over a 24-hour period, and this in itself is not a remarkable event. But if 50 millimetres were to fall in, say, half an hour, it would produce a vastly different effect, particularly over an urban area.

Heavy rainfall across a city can produce extreme results simply because very little of the water soaks into the ground. Instead, it runs off all the impervious surfaces, such as bitumen, concrete and tiles, and is directed into the underground drainage system. If the capacity of this system is unable to handle the amount of incoming water, it will quickly accumulate in the streets, causing flash flooding, often with spectacular results.

Because of Melbourne's normal rainfall pattern, the street drainage system does not have the same capacity as, say, Sydney or Brisbane, where higher intensity rain is common. This can readily be seen when comparing the sizes of the street gutters in the Melbourne central business district (CBD) with those in Sydney, where they are far deeper. In tropical areas, intense rainfalls are still more common and gutters in cities such as Mackay and Townsville are commensurately deeper again.

Flooding has occurred several times within the Melbourne CBD, including in 1863, when a major flood swamped the central city, even inundating the nearby Princes Bridge. Elizabeth Street is one of the lower lying areas of the central city, and because of this, appears to be one of the more vulnerable areas during heavy rain. This was to be spectacularly revealed in the late summer of 1972, when the greatest flood in living memory up until then swept through the city streets.

Flash Floods, 1972

In mid-February 1972 Melbourne was sweltering in almost tropical conditions. Several days of high temperatures, steaming humidity and afternoon thunderstorms had affected many suburbs. On both 15 and 16 February, Melbourne city recorded over 35 millimetres of rain from this thunderstorm activity.

It looked as though 17 February was going to be a re-run of the previous two days, with storm clouds again looming over the city skyline by early afternoon.

Over south-eastern Australia, thunderstorms generally come from the west, the speed being determined by the wind structure on the day. The surface wind itself has little bearing on the direction of movement of thunderstorms; winds between around 1.5 kilometres and 5.6 kilometres above the Earth's surface are the main influence. If these winds are light, thunderstorms in the area will only be slow moving.

This was the case on 17 February, as thunderstorms developed in and around Melbourne; Bureau of Meteorology forecasters were aware that the upper winds

The Structure of Wind

Wind is simply air in motion; it extends from ground level into the upper levels of the atmosphere. Interestingly, wind often changes direction with height. An observer on the ground will sometimes note that clouds are moving in a different direction from that indicated by the wind at ground level. Meteorologists use the term 'vertical wind structure' to talk about what the wind is doing at different levels of the atmosphere — upper, middle and lower.

Thunderstorms tend to be driven by the so-called 'mid-level' winds — those blowing at altitudes between 1.5 and 5.6 kilometres above the ground.

A pedestrian is marooned on a bench in Elizabeth Street as floodwaters a metre deep surge past.

over the city were only very light.

Heavy rain from a large thunderstorm cell commenced across the city centre soon after 3.30 pm and, because the system was barely moving, the rain continued in a solid downpour. Gutters began to run freely, discharging the water into the underground drainage system. But water was arriving at a much faster rate than it was getting away. Soon it was running over gutters and across roads and footpaths in a relentlessly rising torrent, and there was no sign of the situation easing at all.

Up until that day, the record one-hour fall in Melbourne was 47 millimetres, but on this day 78.5 millimetres fell during the same period. This phenomenal fall was easily the most intense rain ever seen over the central city. Later calculations revealed that an estimated 100,000 tonnes of water was dumped over a square kilometre of the CBD.

Elizabeth Street, with its low-lying geography, was particularly hard hit. The streetscape became a raging river over a metre deep. Water cascaded over cars, flooded trams and poured into shop basements along the entire southern end of the street. Large waves generated by gusty winds accompanying the storm lifted cars from the road and swept them away.

The Melbourne GPO was flooded, fruit barrows were washed away and a youth was reported manoeuvring on a surfboard in the service lane along St Kilda Road. Training for the 1972 VFL season had already commenced for some clubs, and groups of North Melbourne footballers on a training run were reported as having to wade knee deep through water in Clarendon Street.

Flooding at Flinders Street station knocked out a large chunk of the suburban train network, throwing peak-hour rail commuting into utter chaos. The Spirit of Progress rail service from Melbourne to Sydney was also delayed for nearly half an hour. This, combined with substantial dislocation of vehicular traffic about the city, produced an extended period of general transport confusion that resulted in one of the worst traffic jams in the history of Melbourne. As late as 8.30 pm traffic lights were out and intersections were clogged with traffic. Thousands of commuters arrived home hours late.

Interestingly, the whole event was highly localised and even nearby inner-city suburbs only received light and unremarkable falls. Melburnians were astonished to see the television reports and newspaper pictures the next day showing some of the incredible scenes across the city at the height of the downpour.

One of the notable aspects of the event was the remarkable series of images taken by *The Age* photographer Neville Bowler, who happened to be 'on the spot' in Elizabeth Street at the height of the deluge. They brilliantly captured the flood in full fury, although Bowler himself was terrified by the event. He was nearly swept away by the swirling waters but was saved at the last second by an amateur photographer who grabbed his arm and pulled him back to safety. For his work Neville Bowler received the 1972 Walkley Award for excellence in press photography.

The likes of this downpour were not to be seen over Melbourne again for over 30 years, and indeed it was thought by many that it was a freak event that probably would not be seen again in a lifetime.

A fantastic scene in Elizabeth Street as high-speed floodwaters engulf a parked car. This is one of the award-winning photographs taken by Neville Bowler of *The Age* newspaper.

Flash Floods Again, 2003

Almost 32 years later, history repeated itself, although in a different area of the city.

During the afternoon of Tuesday 2 December 2003, a slow-moving low-pressure trough was drifting across Victoria, generating scattered thunderstorms.

In the early hours of 3 December Melbourne was lit up by a spectacular light show, as intense lightning tore across the

night sky with the approach of a large thunderstorm. Then the rain began, heavy and unremitting, and seemingly centred on the inner-city suburbs around the west, north and east. The intensity of the rainfall was well in excess of the capacity of the drainage system, and the water began to mount inexorably.

Reports of severe flash flooding began to come through. After seeing the rising water ahead, some drivers pulled over to the side of the road only to be marooned as the flood rapidly submerged their vehicles to near rooftop level. Even four-wheel-drive vehicles could not cope, with several stalling alongside their conventional cousins as the water level rose above engine level. Motorists stranded on the roofs of their cars along the Eastern Freeway had to be rescued by boat.

Drivers stranded in Dudley Street, West Melbourne, were forced to take refuge on the roofs of their vehicles during the December 2003 downpour.

One motorist had a very lucky escape at Templestowe, when he was driving to the aid of his girlfriend who lived nearby. His four-wheel-drive plunged into deeper and deeper water, before stalling with all the electric windows rendered inoperative. Water entered the vehicle and he was unable to open the doors because of the pressure outside. He managed to call his girlfriend on a mobile telephone and she alerted the State Emergency Services (SES) by dialling 000.

Two SES workers arrived to find the vehicle floating with the motorist still trapped and the water nearly filling the inside. He was only able to breathe by tilting his head back into the remaining bubble of air.

One of the SES men scrambled on top of the car and kicked in the back window before dragging the motorist to safety. A tragedy had only been narrowly averted, thanks largely to the mobile phone.

The storm produced widespread flooding of homes and business premises and damaged many vehicles. It was estimated that the final damage bill ran up into tens of millions of dollars. The Royal Automobile Club of Victoria later warned motorists about buying flood-damaged vehicles, noting that the extent of the damage could limit the level of insurance cover available.

A later rainfall analysis revealed that some areas of the city had received over 100 millimetres of rain during a two-hour period. This was of a similar intensity to the 1972 downpour.

1974

Cyclone Tracy Flattens Darwin

For the wind passeth over it, and it is gone; and the place thereof shall know it no more.

Psalm 103:16

Darwin, Australia's northernmost capital city, is located near latitude 12°S and, as such, has a pure tropical climate with well-defined wet and dry seasons. The wet season varies in length from year to year but is normally between November and May, and corresponds with the 'cyclone season', when the northern coast of Australia is occasionally threatened by tropical cyclones.

Even during the comparatively short period of European settlement, Darwin has witnessed several disasters with substantial damage caused by tropical cyclones, including January 1878, January 1897, April 1917 and March 1937. The 1897 cyclone was, by all reports, particularly severe, with nearly all of Darwin destroyed and 28 deaths reported.

Until 1974, tropical cyclones had only passed across Darwin itself five times in the previous century, although there had been numerous 'near misses'. But Tracy was to dramatically and powerfully boost this number to six.

The tropical cyclone season of 1974–75 got off to a fairly uneventful start across the Top End of the Northern Territory. Early in December 1974, tropical cyclone Selma had approached Darwin, but had suddenly veered away when it was about 50 kilometres out and passed across Bathurst Island to the north. Many locals believed that this was because 'cyclones never hit Darwin' – the lessons of the past were all but forgotten because the previous cyclone, in 1937, was so long ago. Although Selma did produce a period of strong winds across the city, little or no damage was reported. This incident produced a feeling of general complacency, and when the first warning for Tracy was

The utter destruction of Darwin was compared to the scenes over Hiroshima following the dropping of the atomic bomb in 1945.

Tropical Cyclones

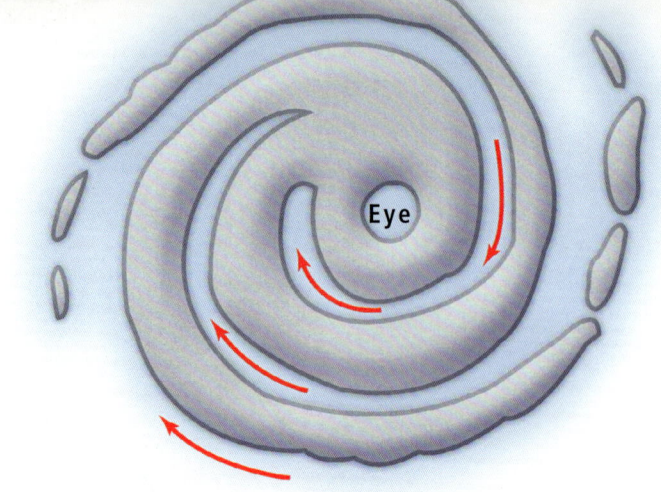

A tropical cyclone from above (top) and from the side. From above we see spiral arms of cloud converging towards a clear 'eye' at the centre of the circulation. This eye can vary considerably in size but is typically 40–50 kilometres across. The view from the side has a highly exaggerated vertical scale for explanatory purposes. Cells of rising and falling air surround the centre of the cyclone in a sort of 'honeycomb' structure.

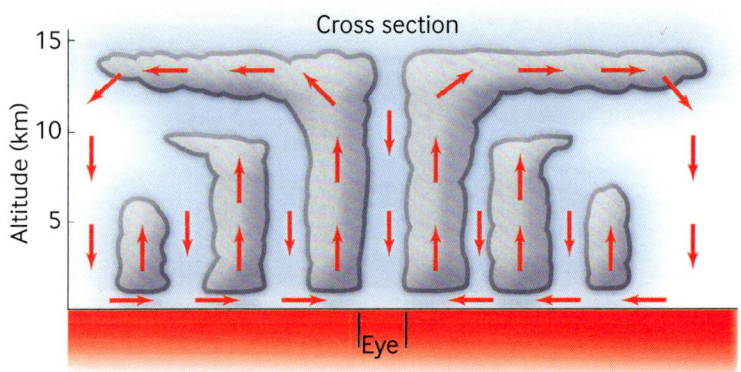

issued at 4 pm on 21 December, the community reacted with mild disinterest.

Tracy originated as a weak tropical disturbance about 700 kilometres to the north-east of Darwin on 20 December 1974. Slowly building, it moved irregularly south-west, monitored by the Bureau of Meteorology, using the satellite photography of the day. Although the technology was nowhere near the same quality and frequency as today, the cyclone was accurately tracked. Following its official naming as 'Tracy' on 21 December, regular updates were issued over the next three days as the system moved from north-east to south-west towards the north of the Top End.

Early on 24 December, the situation began to deteriorate rapidly. Tracy changed direction, moved around the south-western corner of Bathurst Island and abruptly headed straight for Darwin. By this time radar tracking was also possible, and the automatic weather station located at Cape Fourcroy on Bathurst Island began to register strong winds.

At 12.30 pm on 24 December the Bureau of Meteorology issued Flash Warning Number 16, which noted the change in direction of the cyclone, and forecast 'very destructive winds in the Darwin area tonight and tomorrow'. Further periodic warnings were issued until 2.30 am on Christmas Day, when the bureau noted that 'Tropical Cyclone Tracy was 18 kilometres from Darwin and

Major damage occurred at the Darwin Sailing Club. Many boats were driven ashore by the ferocity of the winds.

that the eye was expected to move over Darwin soon'.

Community reaction to all these warnings was far from ideal. Office Christmas parties were in full swing and the general atmosphere of goodwill easily overrode the unwanted negativity of the cyclone warnings. Alan Stretton, in his book *The Furious Days*, recalled that: 'On Christmas Eve, pubs were full of cheerful people discussing the cyclone forecasts. They were laughing and joking, and even singing how cyclones never hit Darwin.'

However, soon after the bureau's last warning, Tracy began to move slowly across the city, producing sustained winds of over 200 kilometres per hour. Because the cyclone moved slowly, the city was subjected to these ferocious blasts for several hours. Power failed completely at around 3.30 am and the city was plunged into darkness, adding to the general fear and confusion.

Residents huddled in terror as their houses were ripped apart around them, and families found themselves in total darkness amid a shrieking tempest and pelting rain.

Cyclone Categories

CATEGORY 1

Wind gusts 90–125 km/h – gale-force winds

Typical effects:

Minor damage to houses – roof tiles displaced, small tree branches down.

CATEGORY 2

Wind gusts 126–164 km/h – Destructive winds

Typical effects:

Some house damage – wooden fences down, small trees blown over.

CATEGORY 3

Wind gusts 165–224 km/h – very destructive winds

Typical effects:

House roofs lose tiles and shutters, power failures and big trees down.

CATEGORY 4

Wind gusts 225–279 km/h – highly destructive winds

Typical effects:

Roofs torn off, many trees down, widespread power failure, dangerous airborne debris thrown great distances.

CATEGORY 5

Wind gusts more than 280 km/h – extremely destructive winds

Typical effects:

Widespread destruction of houses, devastating damage across a wide area.

The eye of the cyclone passed across the devastated city at around 4 am, bringing with it a deathly quiet. Many residents erroneously assumed that the storm had passed and emerged from the ruins to take stock of the situation.

However, after the eye had passed, the winds returned with similar ferocity from the other direction, inflicting another round of devastation on those structures still standing. Several people were caught in the open at this time and injured; at least one was killed by flying debris.

Many eyewitness accounts provide an insight into that night of fury. One woman described how she was awakened 'by the house beginning to creak and groan'. She and her husband ran outside with their two young daughters and huddled in an outside toilet. She recalled: 'We could hear roofs being ripped around us as though they were made of paper. It was like bombs going off. In minutes our home was blown apart … We spent four hours inside the toilet … we prayed … God knows how we survived.'

Conditions at last began to moderate just before dawn on Christmas Day, and Darwin residents were able to see the extent of the damage for the first time. A Darwin ham radio operator described the scene: 'It looks as though an atom bomb has hit. There's not a tree with a branch left on it. There is no food, no power and no water …' The main streets in the central business district resembled battle zones; mountains of debris

At the airport, light aircraft were thrown about like toys.

were scattered throughout the thoroughfares, rendering most impassable.

The airport was in chaos. Aircraft had been thrown together and flung upside down many metres from where they originally stood. Eerily, there were no flies or mosquitoes about. They too were gone with the wind.

The officer commanding the Darwin RAAF base, Group Captain Hitchins, who had been in Japan after the dropping of the atomic bomb, likened the appearance of Darwin to Hiroshima, confirming the description of the ham radio operator.

The destruction was enormous. Most buildings in the city were either levelled or badly damaged. Sixty-five people were dead, either killed in the city or drowned at sea. The devastation was so bad that it was even suggested that the Australian government cut its losses and not bother rebuilding the city.

The main question everyone was asking was 'How strong were the winds that produced such devastation?', and here an interesting story emerged. The Bureau of Meteorology maintained a wind-recording device – called an anemograph – at Darwin airport, which showed a peak gust of 117 knots (217 kilometres per hour) at about 3 am on Christmas Day. However, this instrument was damaged by the ferocious

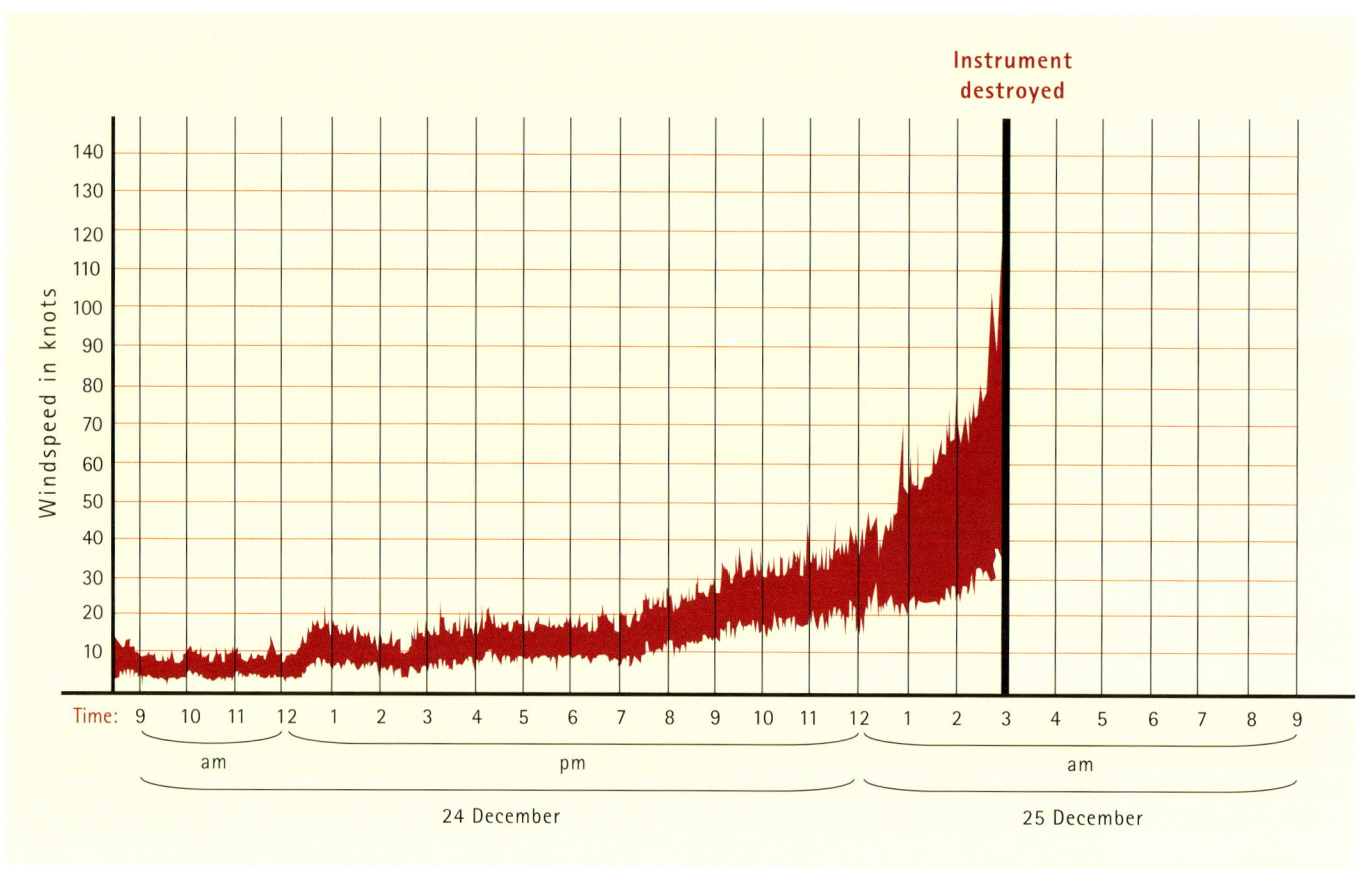

A reconstruction of the anemograph (wind) record from Darwin airport showed a peak gust of 117 knots (217 kilometres per hour) at 3 am on Christmas Day. Winds may have been higher than this but were not recorded because of instrument failure.

winds and became inoperative soon after. Theoretical calculations based on the central pressure of the cyclone suggested that gusts could have been stronger with a possible peak of 240 kilometres per hour, making it a category 4 cyclone.

The political aftermath of the cyclone was scarcely less dramatic than the actual event. A large percentage of Darwin's population was airlifted to the southern states to avoid an epidemic. The Director General of the National Disasters Organisation (now known as Emergency Management Australia), Major General Alan Stretton, made sensational allegations of official mismanagement which were eventually denied in parliament by the Prime Minister himself, Mr Malcolm Fraser.

Cyclone Tracy remains a tragic example of how a destructive event was made worse by a lack of concerted community response to the warning system in place. While there would have been no way at the time to prevent the colossal structural damage, the high death toll may have been reduced by a proper response to the timely cyclone warnings issued during the lead-up period. Only a repetition will reveal how much we have actually learned from this disaster.

1983

Dust Storms and Bushfires Sweep Victoria

*On the runs to the west of the Dingo Scrub there was drought, and ruin, and death,
And the sandstorm came from the dread northeast with the blast of a furnace breath.*

'The Bush Fire', Henry Lawson

During 1981 and 1982, south-eastern Australia was experiencing severe, widespread drought; 1982 was the driest year on record for much of Victoria and New South Wales. When strong wind is superimposed across such a dry landscape there are two usual outcomes – dust storms and fire – and both of these were to sweep across Victoria during the savage February of 1983.

A Wall of Dust

In particular, with virtually no surviving vegetation, Victoria's Mallee and Wimmera areas had become a 'dust bowl'. And when hot, strong northerly winds swept across Victoria ahead of a cold front on 8 February 1983 – the so-called 'dry change' – they picked up a wall of dust from the Mallee-Wimmera area and rolled it south-east towards Melbourne.

Conditions in the city were very hot and windy that afternoon, with the temperature nudging above 43°C soon after midday. Just before 3 pm, Melburnians were astonished to see a huge mountain of dust towering some 300 metres over the city, dwarfing the skyline of the central business district.

As the dust hit, the sky turned abruptly black. Visibility plunged to less than 100 metres in a matter of seconds. The dust was followed by a gale-force wind change that blew the roofs off some 50 houses as it rampaged across the metropolitan area, and caused temperatures to plummet. After about an hour, the wind abated, leaving much of Melbourne coated with a talcum-powder-fine cover of red dust that infiltrated every nook and cranny.

A moving mountain of dust descends on Melbourne. It was later estimated that about 1000 tonnes of soil were dumped on the city from this dust storm.

Rainfall Relative to Historical Records
January to December 1982

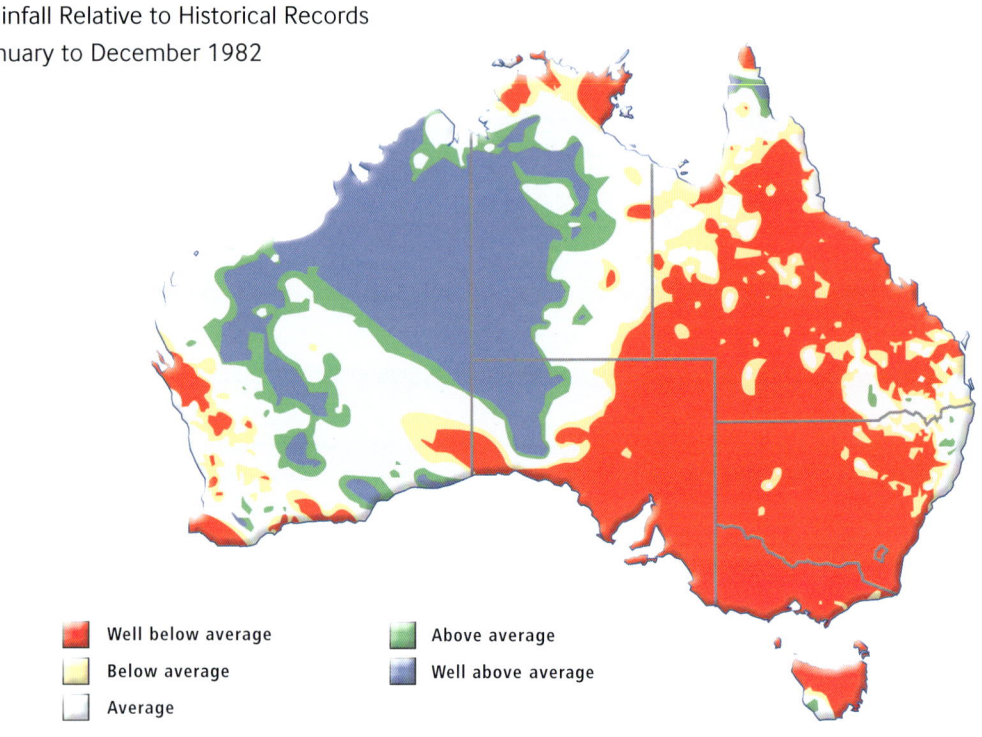

The rainfall pattern in 1982 shows the extent of the drought across eastern Australia that was a lead-up the disastrous fires early in 1983.

Post-storm analysis revealed its full extent. It was estimated that around mid-afternoon, the dust extended across the entire width of Victoria and reached heights of over 2000 metres. Some 50,000 tonnes of topsoil were stripped from the Mallee-Wimmera area, about 1000 tonnes of which were dumped on Melbourne.

Barely a week later, the drought produced a far more deadly effect – fire.

Ash Wednesday

It's unusual for severe bushfires to hit the same area twice in a single lifetime. Unfortunately, this often means that the general public forgets the lessons of the past, and it therefore becomes one of the main duties of government to retain a 'memory' of past events to ensure that we do, in fact, learn from the lessons of history.

The dreadful conflagration that affected much of Victoria in January 1939 (see page 88) was believed by many to have been a freak event that was unlikely to ever occur again across the State. In the 40-year period following this tragedy there had been numerous bushfire outbreaks across Victoria, but none with anywhere near the ferocity and widespread devastation of 'Black Friday' – 13 January 1939.

Weather forecasting, particularly in relation to bushfires, had improved considerably during this period, as had the structure and coordination of the various emergency services and fire authorities.

Firefighters battle the blaze at Dales Creek, about 70 kilometres to the west of Melbourne.

It was widely considered that no bushfire would ever be able to reach the scale of 1939 again because of all these improvements in the fire-prevention and firefighting infrastructure.

In January 1983, bush conditions were tinder dry across much of Victoria. Numerous small bushfires were reported, some of which were in inaccessible country and could not be extinguished.

On 16 February, as in 1939, an approaching cold front generated the type of weather most dreaded by firefighters – skyrocketing temperatures, strengthening northerly winds and plummeting relative humidity. Temperatures edged over 40°C across much of South Australia and Victoria, with Melbourne eventually peaking at 43°C, which was only about three degrees less than the 1939 record.

Gigantic fires erupted into unstoppable infernos across large tracts of south-eastern Australia; some of the worst affected areas included South Australia's Mount Lofty Ranges and the Dandenong Ranges – Macedon area of Victoria. As the conflagration raged, increasingly weary firefighters eagerly awaited the arrival of the cold front, which was expected to produce a desperately needed easing of the weather

Opposite: A menacing pall of smoke towers over Melbourne as the Ash Wednesday fires rage around the city.

Above: Twelve firefighters tragically lost their lives in Upper Beaconsfield when their truck became trapped by the fire and flames overwhelmed the area.

conditions and a slowing of the various fire fronts. But instead, a nasty surprise was developing.

Cold fronts that pass across south-eastern Australia are somewhat like human fingerprints – they all contain similar general features but no two are the same. Nearly all produce a temperature drop of some magnitude, but not all result in rain. Nearly all generate a change in wind direction and wind speed, and some, but not all, result in a rise in humidity. But each front produces its own unique combination of all these factors, and it is this uniqueness that makes the job of the weather forecaster so difficult.

As the cold front approached the fire-ravaged areas of south-eastern Australia, weather forecasters grappled with the problem of predicting how this particular change would affect the behaviour of the fires. A drop in wind, a fall in temperature and a rise in humidity would produce conditions resulting in a slowing of the fire spread, aided by any rain that followed. But a fall in temperature alone may not help.

In this case the wind was expected to change from northerly to westerly, and while this was almost certain to produce a drop in temperature, it also had the potential to create its own set of problems.

Bushfires fanned by strong northerly

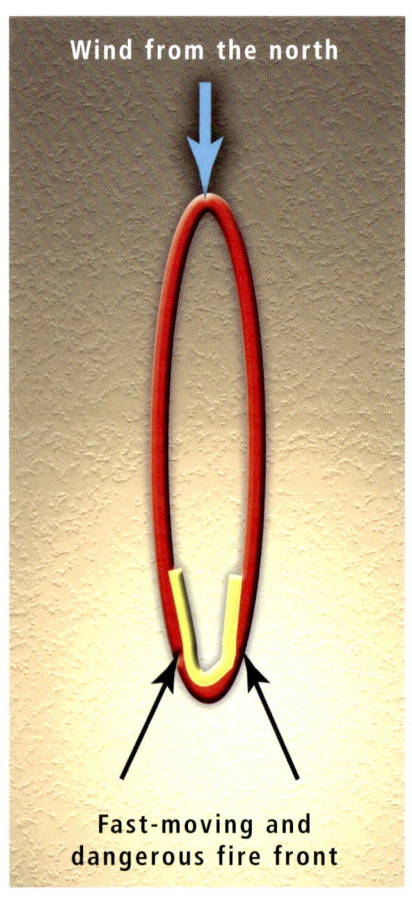

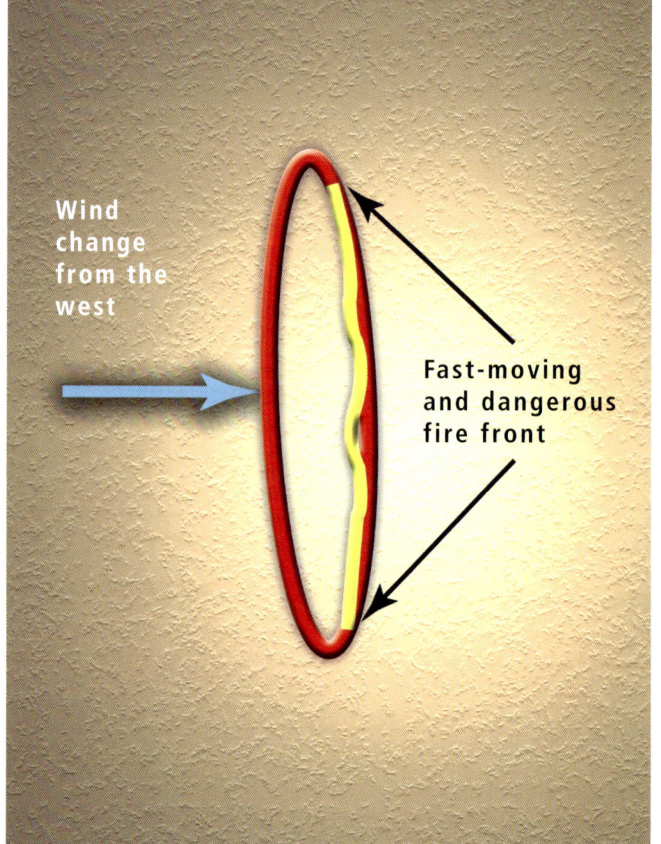

Left: A change in wind direction can cause a huge increase in the size of a fast-moving fire front.

Opposite: Eighty-three people spent a whole day huddled in a tunnel, while above, flames destroyed their small country town.

Much awarded opera singer Dame Joan Hammond (1912–96) lost her house at Anglesea (shown here), along with all records of her musical career. Sifting through the debris, she said: 'It is as though I have never lived.' The almost complete destruction of vegetation bears witness to the ferocity of the blaze.

winds tend to run in long 'corridors' that are oriented north to south, with the dangerous, fast-moving fire front located at the southern end. The arrival of a westerly wind without rain will cause the eastern flank of the fire to become the fast-moving sector, and this is normally many times longer than the old southern fire front.

Although there is usually a temperature drop in such a situation, this may not have a significant impact on the fire.

The long-awaited change began moving quickly across South Australia and Victoria as a 'dry front', producing low humidity instead of rain, and gale-force westerly winds with gusts in excess of 100 kilometres per hour.

Huge new fire fronts now rampaged from west to east, catching fire crews by surprise, and beginning a whole new cycle of destruction.

Over the next 12 hours, the winds gradually moderated; only then did fires begin to ease. Blazes persisted across the area for several days.

The fires had been truly devastating. Seventy-five people had died and about 2500 houses were destroyed. Several Victorian townships, including Cockatoo, Aireys Inlet and Macedon, were almost totally razed and some major forests in both Victoria and south-eastern South Australia were burnt to the ground.

As a result of the official inquiry that

The Ash Wednesday fires devastated some of the small Victorian townships, including Cockatoo, shown here. This man and his son leave the remains of their home, carrying their dog and few possessions.

followed the disaster, changes were made to the nature of meteorological briefings issued to fire control headquarters. In particular, more-detailed information regarding wind changes was to be provided. This process has been greatly assisted over the intervening years by the proliferation of automatic weather stations (AWSs) across much of Australia.

Automatic Weather Stations (AWSs)

Automatic weather stations are located in areas that the bureau considers to be important to the national weather observation network. They can be solar powered or hooked up to mains electricity, and provide a continuous stream of measured data, including temperature, wind speed and direction and humidity, which is transmitted to the various offices of the Bureau of Meteorology virtually instantaneously. This vastly improved data base has resulted in far more detailed weather information being available to both weather forecasters and firefighting authorities.

Whilst AWSs do not require human assistance to record their data, they do need regular maintenance to ensure proper performance. The AWS pictured is at Marion Reef off the north Queensland coast.

1939 vs 1983

It's interesting to compare the figures for the 1939 fires with those of 1983. The tragic death tolls were similar: in 1939 71 people died compared to 75 in 1983. But the 1939 fires consumed a far greater area of forest: 2,000,000 hectares compared to the 1983 fires with 418,000 hectares.

It is tempting to therefore conclude that the 1939 fires were more severe; but comparisons of this type can be misleading. Firefighting capabilities in 1939 were far less than those of 44 years later and the fires were able to take hold and consume larger areas of forest before they could be tackled.

One of the main differences between the two fire outbreaks was the nature of the weather changes that affected the fires. A southerly change produced a gradual moderation of the 1939 fires; a westerly change produced an explosive intensification of the Ash Wednesday fires. In fact, subsequent analysis indicated that more loss of life and damage was sustained in the hour following the strong westerly change than during the hot northerly wind period preceding it. The tragic deaths of 12 firefighters in Upper Beaconsfield in 1983 were associated with the change; they became trapped by the sudden shift in direction of the fire.

1985

Huge Hail Hits Brisbane

And the Lord cast down great stones from heaven, upon them unto Azekah, and they died: they were more which died with hailstones than they whom the children of Israel slew with the sword.

Joshua 10.11

Afternoon summer thunderstorm activity is no stranger to Brisbane. Thunderstorms, occasionally accompanied by hail, strong winds and heavy rain, have been recorded across south-eastern Queensland ever since formal records began. In fact, Brisbane is Australia's second most thunderstorm-prone capital city, with an average of 30 thunderstorms per year (Darwin gets 88). December is the peak of the Brisbane thunderstorm season, followed by November and January, with a sharp drop in frequency during winter.

Friday 18 January 1985 in Brisbane began as a hot, humid summer's day. But a late southerly change, with likely showers and thunderstorms, was forecast in the wake of a cold front that was moving up the east coast.

During the early afternoon, cloud began to increase from the west, and the Bureau of Meteorology's Brisbane radar began picking up thunderstorm 'echoes' to the south-west of the city. South-westerly winds were pushing the storms directly towards the city.

As the afternoon wore on, a large area of thunderstorm activity entered the mature phase to the south-west, but one thunderstorm cell towered above the rest, reaching to around 18 kilometres above the ground. To meteorologists watching on the radar, it was becoming obvious that a 'supercell' (see page 96) was advancing on Brisbane. Soon after 4.40 pm, it was approaching the central business district.

This was particularly unfortunate timing. Many office workers were finishing up for the day, looking forward to the weekend ahead

Workers battle to lay tarpaulins across the heavily damaged roof of Brisbane's Chermside Hospital in the wake of the Brisbane storm.

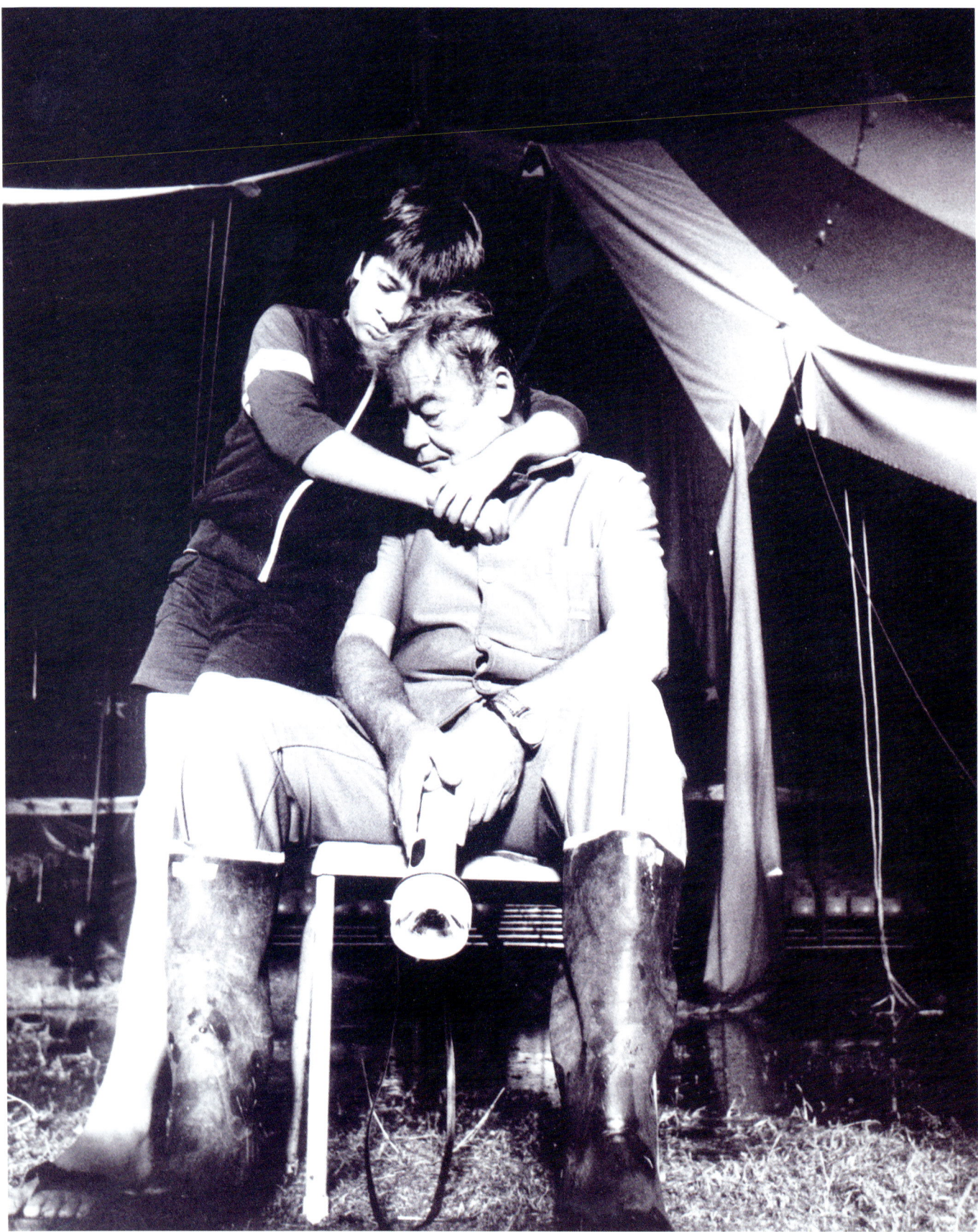

and beginning the afternoon drive home. Afternoon peak hour was almost in full swing when, with a roar, the supercell unleashed its full fury across the city.

Cutting a swathe of destruction from south-west to north-east, the storm produced torrential rain and billiard ball-sized hail. Raging winds drove the hail almost horizontally, turning it into a deadly and destructive missile attack. A record wind gust of 185 kilometres per hour ripped across Brisbane Airport, where the pluviograph recorded 57 millimetres of rain in only 15 minutes – close to Brisbane's average monthly rainfall for July.

Not surprisingly, there were numerous reports of intense flash-flooding across the city, particularly affecting those areas near creeks and watercourses. Shortly after 5 pm, parts of the city and suburbs were under nearly 2 metres of water, and a metre of water lay on the railway track in the tunnel between Brunswick Street and Central stations.

The devastating combination of large hail and intense wind gusts wreaked havoc on vehicles caught in peak-hour traffic and also on suburban housing. The ice pummelled thousands of grid-locked cars, smashing windscreens and pulverising body panels. Many thousands of house windows were smashed, and roofs were ripped off in cyclonic winds. It was later estimated that power was cut to about 80,000 homes during the late afternoon and early evening. Terrified residents hid under mattresses as their houses were battered by ice, water and wind. Many people were injured, mainly by flying debris and hail.

Trains ground to a halt, many with windows smashed by the hail. Some light aircraft were also damaged, and Brisbane airport was closed to all flights.

The four major metropolitan hospitals were damaged. A large section of the roof of the Prince Charles was peeled away by the rampaging winds. Patients were immediately shifted to other wards to escape the rain and hail that pelted through. At the Royal Children's Hospital, staff battled to mop up after the hail had smashed dozens of windows, and at the Women's and Royal Brisbane hospitals, tarpaulins were used to cover gaping holes in the roof.

As well as battling the elements, these hospitals also had to cope with a multitude of injured people. Patients were arriving at the Royal Brisbane Hospital every minute after the storm finally ceased soon after 5 pm. So many people arrived in so short a period of time that patients were double parked in the aisles waiting for the overworked staff to treat them. Injuries included broken limbs, lacerations, bruising from hailstone impact and trauma from motor vehicle accidents. Multiple cuts from flying glass and roofing

Opposite: The owner of Silver's Circus, Tommy Hanlon Junior, slumps exhausted into a chair after the storm destroyed the circus big-top tent at suburban Windsor.

iron were common, both among those caught out in the open and others showered with broken shards indoors. People were also injured whilst cleaning up after the storm. Hospital staff also noted that many people who had been outside when the storm struck were deeply shocked and frightened by the ferocity of the event.

In the final count it was estimated that 20 per cent of the vehicles in the city were hail damaged, over 20,000 buildings sustained at least some damage and 80,000 premises were blacked out. During the height of the storm it was estimated that damage was accumulating at the rate of about $5.5 million per minute. The total bill for the storm was estimated to be in excess of $300 million, making it one of the worst natural disasters in the history of Brisbane.

1990

The Big Wet in the East

And every creek a banker ran,
And dams filled overtop
'We'll all be rooned' said Hanrahan
'If this rain doesn't stop'.

'Said Hanrahan', John O'Brien

Australia is a dry continent. More than half its land area is desert, and less than 30 per cent receives sufficient rainfall to support general agriculture. A large proportion of the mainland receives an average annual rainfall of less than 300 millimetres. Bountiful, reliable falls occur only in areas within about 200 kilometres of the coast across eastern and northern Australia and even these parts are subject to drought on occasion.

But the other remarkable feature of Australian rainfall is its extremely high variability. Sometimes soaking rains cover huge areas of the inland and the desert produces spectacular displays of flowers for many thousands of square kilometres. One such event took place in the summer of 1973–74, when heavy rain fell over large areas of western Queensland. The water from these falls flowed down the Cooper Creek and Diamantina River before emptying into Lake Eyre, producing a gigantic inland sea and the highest ever recorded water level in the lake.

This great variability was evident again during the 1980s, and in particular in 1982, which was an exceptionally dry year across much of eastern Australia (see page 169).

The year 1990 began on an encouraging note over inland areas of Queensland. Good rain during March and April produced local, but not severe, flooding. But the rain saturated the soil across several inland catchments, meaning that any substantial subsequent rainfall would result in water run-off into the rivers.

Ominously, on 18 April, a low-pressure

Rainfall Relative to Historical Records
January to December 1990

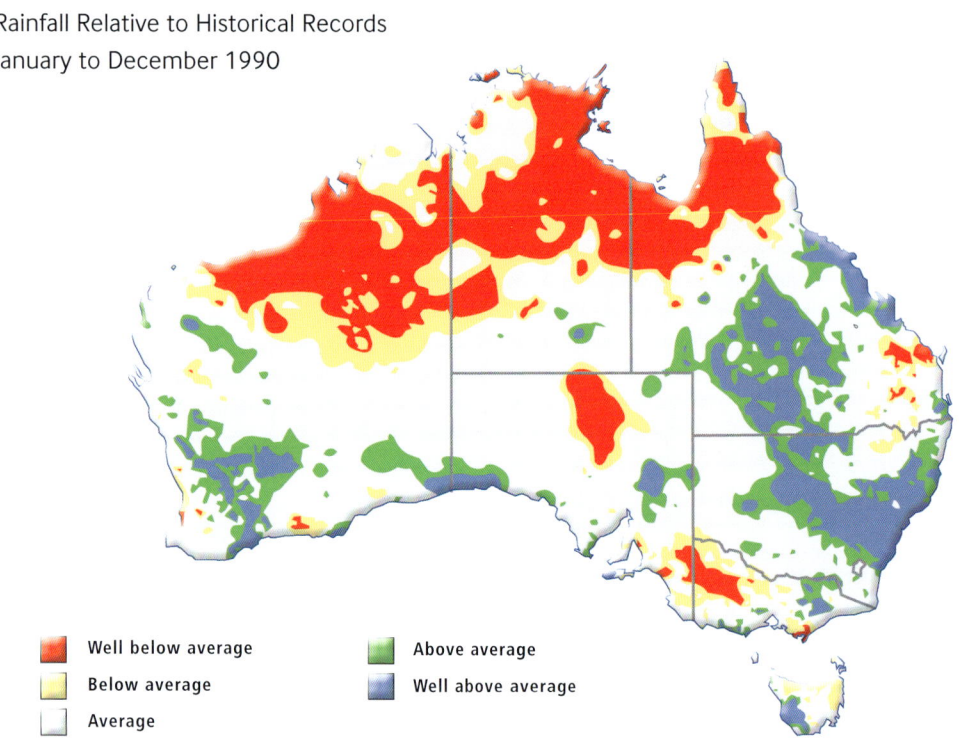

The annual rainfall map for 1990 shows the rainfall 'footprint' of the floods. Large areas of inland New South Wales, Queensland and eastern Victoria experienced well above average rainfall for the year, much of this falling during the month of April.

system developed in the upper atmosphere over eastern Australia. Systems of this type often produce heavy rain across inland areas. 'Upper lows' that move rapidly or even steadily can produce significant good rain, but usually the rain clears as they move away. But this particular system was barely moving, and forecasters at the Bureau of Meteorology in Queensland and New South Wales were worried.

Rain began falling across large areas of central Queensland and continued virtually unabated for the next three days. This would have been a serious enough situation in itself, but in view of the fact that much of the affected area was already saturated from the previous rain, the only possible outcome was flooding. It was a question of where and how much.

Between 18 and 21 April large tracts of inland Queensland received over 150 millimetres of rain, with local pockets reeling under falls of over 300 millimetres. This was far more water than the local catchments could handle, and soon floodwaters were surging along the major Warrego and Maranoa river systems, as well

A truck is stranded on the Mitchell Highway, damaged by flooding, near Nyngan.

as numerous smaller rivers and creeks across the area. The towns of Alpha and Jericho, about halfway between Emerald and Longreach experienced record flooding and part of the Longreach railway track was washed away.

The city of Charleville lies on the Warrego River in the heart of Queensland's so-called 'mulga country' and is the largest town in the State's south-west outback region. During 20 and 21 April the river rose rapidly, fed by the huge rainfall to the north.

Early on 21 April the river was 'running a banker' through the town and still rising rapidly. At one stage, the water rose an estimated 2 metres in just three hours. Soon the water broke over the levees and spread in all directions, forcing many residents to either flee or climb onto their rooftops. The river continued to rise during the day, peaking at 8.5 metres, about 1.5 metres above the previous record.

In what became Australia's biggest mass evacuation since Cyclone Tracy, the entire

Below: Floodwaters over a metre deep surge past the Nyngan Post Office the morning after the flood peaked.

Opposite: The Air Force at work preparing a load of bedding for air dispatch to Charleville from Brisbane. The C130 Hercules aircraft, such as the one in the background, is ideal for flood-relief work as it is capable of carrying very heavy payloads.

Above: Food is provided for people rendered homeless by the floods in Charleville.

Opposite: Army field ambulance team members assist flood victims to evacuate to Brisbane.

population of Charleville was transported to the airport. They were joined sporadically by groups of people who had been rescued from their rooftops by helicopter or boat. An estimated 4000 people huddled in makeshift shelters or tents around the airport, lighting small campfires in an attempt to keep warm. Many retreated to the Royal Flying Doctor Service hangar, trying to rest on the floor in sleeping bags. Some people openly wept as they recounted the terrible scenes of Friday night and Saturday morning, when floods engulfed the area.

The flood peak then surged further down the river towards Cunnamulla, but fortunately remained just below the top of the levee banks there, with the town only narrowly escaping inundation. This was due in no small way to the laying of thousands of sandbags around the town over the previous 24-hour period.

But the weather situation was still evolving. A low-pressure cell developed in the lower layers of the atmosphere and moved to the south-east, changing the rainfall focus from Queensland to inland New South Wales. Close to 48 hours of nearly continuous rain triggered major flooding along the Lachlan, Macquarie and Castlereagh rivers, as well as in the nearby Macquarie marshes.

The Bogan River runs roughly parallel with the Macquarie and forms the lifeblood of Nyngan, a township of about 2500 people located close to the geographical centre of New South Wales. The river runs to the west of the town centre and forms a pleasant backdrop to the local golf course.

The Bogan began rising alarmingly during 22 and 23 April. Over 200,000 sandbags were laid in a frantic effort to raise the existing levee banks, but the river rose even faster, reaching record levels. The levees were eventually overtopped, resulting in massive inundation of the town. One resident described how she watched the water rise from the street outside to her front door in a matter of seconds.

People were forced to spend a cold and sleepless night on their roofs as the water rose to the top of the walls. Fast-flowing muddy water surged through the town, irresistibly carrying with it all forms of pollution, including sewage, petrol and household debris. Many people camped overnight on the platform of Nyngan Railway Station, one of the few dry areas left in the town.

Nearly the entire population of Nyngan was finally evacuated by helicopter to Dubbo to await the abating of the floodwaters.

After this new round of devastation, the low-pressure cell continued to rampage to the south-east, eventually tracking across the east coast of Victoria. It dropped torrential rain across the Gippsland area, flooding many of the local river systems and some 150 homes. Finally the weather improved as the low gradually moved away from the mainland, and the great tri-state flood began to recede.

The extent of the damage was huge. Two major towns had been severely flooded, large numbers of sheep and cattle drowned, roads and bridges knocked out and thousands of people left homeless. Tragically, seven people had died in the deluge. The total estimated cost of the floods was around $415 million, and this did not include the clean-up bill, which was borne largely by the residents of the affected areas.

In Nyngan itself, the height of the levees was increased by 1 metre all along the river in an attempt to prevent a recurrence of the disaster.

1992

Twisters, Wind and Hail across Queensland

It's snowing! This is Queensland, isn't it?

Peter Roebuck, cricket commentator, 29 November 1992

For much of eastern Australia, November is the early part of the thunderstorm season that sometimes continues into March or April. Rising humidity, warmer surface temperatures, and periodic bursts of colder air moving through in the upper atmosphere provide the ideal recipe for thunderstorm development and occasionally this activity can become severe and destructive.

On Sunday 29 November 1992, a series of thunderstorms erupted over south-eastern Queensland, producing huge hailstones, strong wings and flash flooding, along with one of the most powerful tornadoes ever observed across mainland Australia.

The day began in a very unsettled way. Early morning thunderstorms, with frequent, intense bursts of lightning, rumbled across much of the area, including Brisbane. For a short while the sky cleared, but later in the morning, as the hot and humid conditions persisted, cloud again increased and, just before noon, thunderstorms began to develop to the north-west of Brisbane. The echoes picked up by the Bureau of Meteorology radar indicated the possibility of hail, and a Severe Thunderstorm Warning was issued for the area between Brisbane and the Sunshine Coast.

The main thunderstorm cell in this cluster appeared to split into two distinct cells, with the northern one heading for Maroochydore, and the southern one for Brisbane.

At the Brisbane Cricket Ground (the 'Gabba'), the First Test was in progress between Australia and the West Indies. Just after 1.15 pm, amid intense lightning and thunder, marble-sized hail began falling across the ground, interrupting play. Spectators scattered for cover, with many conveniently huddling below The Hill bar, where some of the more seasoned drank on, unperturbed by the violence of nature's display.

Groundsmen battled to put the covers on the wicket, assisted by twelfth man Dean Jones, who brought several batting helmets out onto the ground for their protection.

Soon the Gabba looked like a snowfield, to the great astonishment of some of the West Indian players who had never seen hail of this type before.

But ABC radio commentator Neville Oliver knew what was happening. He said: 'Last night I saw the performance of *Jesus Christ Superstar*, and now, here I am getting stoned at the Gabba'. After about two hours, when the storm cell had moved away, play resumed.

But the northern cell continued to intensify, and developed into a so-called 'supercell' – a very severe type of thunderstorm capable of lasting several hours (see page 96). This storm tracked across the Maroochydore area, producing a phenomenal hailstorm with some stones 8–10 centimetres in diameter – larger than the average orange.

Roofs of some 80 houses, as well as numerous parked aircraft at the local airport, were severely damaged. Several swimmers were injured by hailstones at the nearby beach, and hundreds of cars were dented by

Amid a falling curtain of marble-sized hail, Dean Jones offers batting helmets to the ground staff who were trying to cover the wicket during the First Test against the West Indies.

hail. Destructive wind squalls capsized several yachts and caused further damage to houses already pummelled by hail.

But worse was to come. A tornado – the most feared and extreme phenomenon associated with severe thunderstorms – was about to make a dramatic appearance.

Meteorologists were tracking on the radar the progress of another powerful supercell that developed near Maryborough. At about 2.30 pm, reports of a tornado began to come through, and several eyewitness accounts graphically described its fury. One local recounted: '… it was like ten freight trains all at once; this big spiral of rubbish, leaves, bits of tin flying around everywhere …'

Despite its severity, because this twister was mainly confined to a rural area it destroyed only one house, although several others were damaged as it rampaged across the countryside, also cutting a swathe through a pine forest. Even more damaging than the tornado was another burst of giant hail which, hurled almost horizontally by fierce winds, smashed hundreds of windows.

Later it was estimated that the winds involved were in the range of 240–270 kilometres per hour, meaning it was likely an EF 4 tornado. Although this was one of the most powerful observed in Australia up until

The Bucca tornado of 29 November 1992 is the only F4 tornado to be officially reported in Australia. The tornado tore a 10-kilometre swathe, destroying everything in its path north of Bundaberg.

that time, another, stronger yet, was building.

Soon after 2.30 pm, another massive supercell developed to the south-west of Bundaberg. Growing in intensity, it moved north-east, firing a barrage of cricket ball-sized hail that caused widespread damage around the Bucca and Bullyard areas to the west of Bundaberg.

Then came the tornado, smashing nine houses in the Kola–Bucca area and killing 20 cattle. It was so intense that stones were embedded in trees, a picture frame was driven into the wall of a room, a small tree was driven through five walls of a house, a refrigerator was swept away never to be seen again, and a 3-tonne truck body was carried 300 metres across the ground. Had the tornado occurred over a more densely populated area it would surely have produced more catastrophic results.

A Bureau of Meteorology severe weather team examined the wreckage trail of this twister and concluded it may have been even stronger than the first one – perhaps a higher-end EF 4 at 250–280 kilometres per hour. This is one of the strongest tornadoes in Australia's recorded history

And the incredible events of 29 November 1992 were not entirely finished with the Bucca tornado. Soon after 3 pm, yet another supercell developed further north, and golf ball-sized hail tore across the Gladstone area, causing widespread damage to crops, but no significant property damage.

This outbreak of severe thunderstorms across south-eastern Queensland was one of the most widespread recorded. It demonstrates how, in suitable meteorological conditions, tornadoes can certainly occur in Australia. There is little doubt that had these tracked across a suburban area, substantial loss of life would have occurred.

1997

The Thredbo Landslide

I have found in this report that the landslide was triggered when water from a leaking water main saturated the south-west corner of the landslide in the embankment of Alpine Way, setting off the first stage of the landslide.

Derrick Hand, New South Wales Coroner

Although not normally as dangerous as an earthquake, a landslide can still be lethal. In Australia, both of these are unusual; large-scale snow avalanches such as those experienced in Europe and North America are almost unknown, mainly because we lack the heavy snow and large areas of steep alpine terrain common to those countries.

Landslides are also unusual in Australia, but they do sometimes occur on steep hillsides when heavy rain loosens the earth, causing it to slide downhill. But rainfall is not the only triggering mechanism – running water from leaking pipes can also produce the same result.

A tragic example of this occurred in 1997 at the alpine village of Thredbo in the middle of the New South Wales snowfields.

The 1997 snow season had begun slowly in New South Wales and the snow depth across the ski fields was only quite light. However, the 'old hands' were not particularly worried as they knew that maximum snow depth normally occurs during August or September, depending on altitude. After this, spring rains and rising temperatures begin to melt the snow.

The early hours of Thursday 31 July 1997 were quiet across Thredbo with only a few people about, mostly returning to their lodges after partying late in the traditionally active social scene of the ski fields.

Suddenly a rumbling roar erupted across

the valley, later described by a witness as 'like ten express trains passing through a station at one time', and many in the sleeping village were abruptly jolted from their sleep. As the last thunderous echoes faded, several people appeared from their houses to locate the source of the disturbance. What they discovered was wildly beyond anyone's imagination, and before long the news services across the country were buzzing with the story.

A huge slab of earth below the Alpine Way had broken away and cascaded down the steep slope into the valley, carrying all before it. Two ski lodges directly in the path of the landslide, the Carinya and the Bimbadeen, were almost completely flattened and buried in the river of rock and soil.

Soon after sunrise, emergency crews began arriving and made a hurried assessment of the situation. Some 19 people were missing, all thought to be guests in either Carinya or Bimbadeen. The wreckage of these two buildings, partly covered in rock and soil, was perched on a potentially unstable hillside where further slippage was likely.

The problems facing the rescuers were virtually unprecedented in Australia. To bring in heavy equipment was risky – it could crush any survivors below and possibly also generate another landslip. The steep slope of the hillside was also difficult for any machinery, and the rapidly changing local

The view along Thredbo Valley showing the steep terrain and the area of the landslip in the foreground.

weather became an important issue. Further heavy rain or snow would not only hamper the rescuers, but could also trigger further ground movements over the obviously unstable hillside.

Increasing numbers of emergency workers converged on the site, including teams from the Australian Capital Territory, Victoria and even Queensland. There was also a rising media presence, with a 'direct broadcast' eventually being established by a television network. Australia watched in apprehension as the wreckage was slowly cleared, and body after body was recovered. Overnight the scene became somewhat ethereal, with the hillside eerily lit by special globes as the work continued around the clock.

The hope of finding any survivors began to fade, and it was increasingly felt that the rescue work was really becoming a body recovery operation.

Then something quite remarkable happened. Early on Saturday morning, more than 48 hours after the collapse, a New South Wales Fire Brigade officer thought he detected a sound from below the debris. He immediately signalled to the other workers nearby for quiet, and called out, barely expecting a response. From far below came a muffled answer: 'I can hear you.'

A huge national television audience watched the unfolding drama 'live' as rescue workers frantically tunnelled through a pile of rubble, including a massive concrete slab, to finally rescue Stuart Diver some 12 hours later. He turned out to be the only survivor – the other 18 people had perished in what was, by far, the greatest single disaster in the history of the Australian ski fields.

A coronial inquiry was held under the direction of Coroner Derrick Hand; his findings were released to the public nearly three years later. He was critical of the role of both the National Parks and Wildlife Service and the New South Wales Roads and Traffic Authority with respect to the construction and maintenance of the Alpine Way, the road adjacent to the site of the landslide. Mr Hand stated:

I have found in this report that the landslide was triggered when water from a leaking water main saturated the south-west corner of the landslide in the embankment of Alpine Way, setting off the first stage of the landslide.

Bob Debus, the New South Wales Environment Minister later stated to parliament:

Mr Speaker, as Coroner Hand's investigations over

the past three years have made plain, the history of development at Thredbo over the past 39 years contrasts sharply with modern standards of planning, development control and engineering practice.

The coroner went on to recommend that an independent committee be established to 'assess the ability and appropriateness of the National Parks and Wildlife Service retaining responsibility for managing urban communities and road maintenance inside national parks'. This recommendation was accepted by the minister.

Following the tragedy, the New South Wales government spent nearly $50 million upgrading the Alpine Way, and today visitors enjoy a safer journey and accommodation than before. It is sad to reflect that it often takes a disaster to produce progress.

The rescue of Stuart Diver, some two days after the collapse, was broadcast 'live' to a huge national television audience.

1998

Disaster Strikes the Sydney to Hobart Yacht Race

With sloping masts and dipping prow
As who pursued with yell and blow
Still treads the shadow of his foe,
And forward bends his head,
The ship drove fast, loud roar'd the blast
And southward aye we fled

The Rime of the Ancient Mariner, Samuel Taylor Coleridge

At 1 pm sharp on 26 December 1998 the starter's gun boomed across Sydney Harbour. One hundred and fifteen yachts began the Sydney to Hobart Yacht Race in sparkling summer conditions and a gusty north-easterly sea breeze. Followed by the large spectator fleet that traditionally accompanies the racing yachts as far as the heads, some 1135 sailors began the 1000-kilometre ocean race to Hobart, recognised as one of the world's blue-water classics. The race follows the New South Wales coastline down to the Victorian border near Gabo Island, then out across the notoriously changeable waters of Bass Strait, down the east coast of Tasmania and finally up the Derwent River into Hobart.

The weather at this time of the year across the race area can be highly variable. North-easterly sea breezes are common during the afternoon along the New South Wales coast, and these have sometimes held for much of the race, allowing for a fast, prolonged spinnaker run southwards. But this is also the time of the famous 'southerly buster', a squally southerly change that originates over the east coast of Victoria, then flies northwards up the New South Wales coast, often generating winds of 30 to 40 knots. Southerly busters have played a key role in

The amazing sight of the start of a Sydney to Hobart Yacht Race. In 1998, 115 racing yachts, accompanied by hundreds of spectator craft, streamed out of Sydney Harbour and turned right towards Hobart. The race was heading straight for a tragic climax when the yachts entered Bass Strait about 24 hours later.

deciding many race results, with tactics that best incorporated the timing and intensity of the change often proving decisive. Ironically, races have sometimes ended with yachts being becalmed in the Derwent River almost within sight of the finishing line.

The race fleet's demand for weather-forecast information is therefore hardly surprising. Traditionally, a close relationship has existed between the Bureau of Meteorology and the Race Organising Committee at the Cruising Yacht Club of Australia (CYCA) in Sydney. For the previous 20 years or so, a meteorologist from the bureau would conduct a pre-race weather briefing around 24 December for all the crews, usually at the club's Rushcutters Bay premises. Special meteorological support was also arranged for the race – daily or twice daily weather forecasts and warnings were issued and transmitted to the fleet.

This arrangement was still in place on 24 December 1998, when some 250 sailors converged on the CYCA clubrooms at 9 am to hear the latest on the weather. This was not the issue of a formal race forecast as such – the first of these would be prepared two days later, on the morning of race day itself. Rather, it was a general 'weather outlook' and it indicated that the race should begin on Saturday in light conditions, but that a strong southerly change was possible late in the day.

Towards the end of the race briefing, the bureau spokesperson mentioned that one of the simulations operated by the European Centre for Medium Range Weather Forecasts (ECMWF) was indicating the possible development of a low-pressure cell to the south-east of Gabo Island sometime on day two of the race. This would be worth watching in the run-up to the start.

Race day dawned and soon after 9 am the official race forecast was issued to the fleet. The southerly change mentioned at the briefing two days before was still current but

Numerical Weather Simulations

Much of the information provided for the pre-race weather briefing was based on 'numerical weather simulations', a major area of progress in meteorology over the last 30 years. Mathematical equations that describe the motion of the atmosphere are combined with thousands of weather observations from around the world and fed into supercomputers to produce a simulation of the weather, normally up to a week in advance. The accuracy of these simulations is normally highest for the period 24 hours ahead, reducing to the lowest accuracy seven days ahead.

Many countries have produced their own national weather simulations and these are freely exchanged in the interests of improving weather forecasts globally. The Bureau of Meteorology in Australia has developed its own excellent weather simulation that is routinely used in all weather forecasts. In addition, the bureau has access to simulations from international sources including the USA, UK, Japan and Europe. Each simulation has its own biases and individual 'quirks', and comparing the output from each is very valuable for the meteorologist. If all the simulations are indicating similar outcomes, then the meteorologist becomes more confident of the forecast. If not, confidence is reduced and forecasts can be constructed to reflect this.

was now expected to be stronger than initially indicated and was predicted to reach Jervis Bay between midnight and 2 am on Sunday. A gale warning had been issued for all New South Wales coastal waters south from Broken Bay to cover the passage of this change, and it was with this knowledge that the fleet finally set out to sea.

However, soon after the start, high drama was emerging back at the bureau offices in Sydney's Elizabeth Street. Some of the simulations, including the bureau's high-resolution version that became available soon after race start, were now indicating that a strong low-pressure cell was likely to develop to the south over the next 24 hours. In particular, the bureau's simulation was indicating explosive development of an intense low-pressure cell during Sunday, virtually on the race route just to the east of Bass Strait.

Poring over this new data, the race meteorologists became increasingly concerned. For the first time in race history they prepared a storm warning. A storm warning is the highest category warning issued for waters in these latitudes and is only surpassed by a hurricane warning, which is used in the event of a strong tropical cyclone. The race was about two hours old when the storm warning was issued and distributed to all the relevant authorities.

As the yachts moved southwards down the coast the weather progressively deteriorated, with the wind and sea steadily rising. The leading yachts began to encounter storm conditions about 18 hours into the race, with winds averaging around 50 knots and gusting to as high as 75 knots. Conditions peaked across eastern Bass Strait during Sunday as the low-pressure cell predicted by the simulation intensified and tracked right through the fleet, creating havoc and destruction.

For many competitors, racing was forgotten as they fought for survival in the

Computer modelling plays a huge part in weather forecasting today. Mathematical simulations of the weather to come can be displayed on computer screens, along with imagery from radars and meteorological satellites.

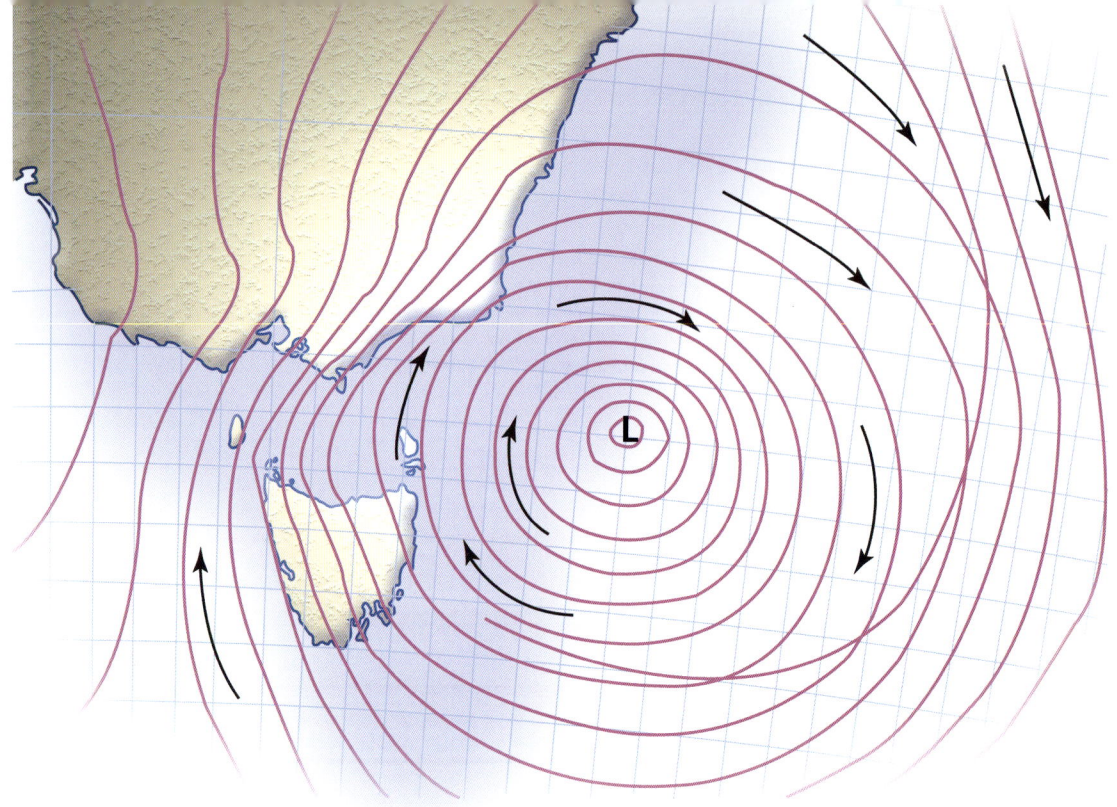

A reproduction of the Bureau of Meteorology's predicted chart for 10 pm on Sunday 27 December. This was produced by a supercomputer and became available soon after the race start. It shows the development of an intense low-pressure cell just to the east of Bass Strait.

mountainous seas and shrieking tempest. Many sailors had never seen seas like it. The scene aboard the yacht *Standaside* is described by Debbie Whitmont in her book *An Extreme Event*:

> *Mike Marshman does feel it. Like Clark, he's up on deck and sees the wave just before it hits. Marshman thinks it looks 30 metres high, a green wall towering over* Standaside's *mast like a ten-storey building. Where the top floors would be there are two metres of white, breaking water. Marshman feels* Standaside *being sucked into the bottom of the wave and flying up to the top of it. When the boat gets near the crest, a blast of wind knocks him over. Next he feels the hull crash into breaking water. Then he doesn't know what happens. All he knows is the boat's upside down and he's in the water, in the middle of Bass Strait, still hooked on by his lifeline.*

Many sailors remarked later on the wind:

> *The wind howls; a horrible unearthly wail that isn't coming from the rigging but from the core of the air itself. Seamen who've survived the worst storms nature can dish out talk about that howl. Some say it's like no other sound on earth.*

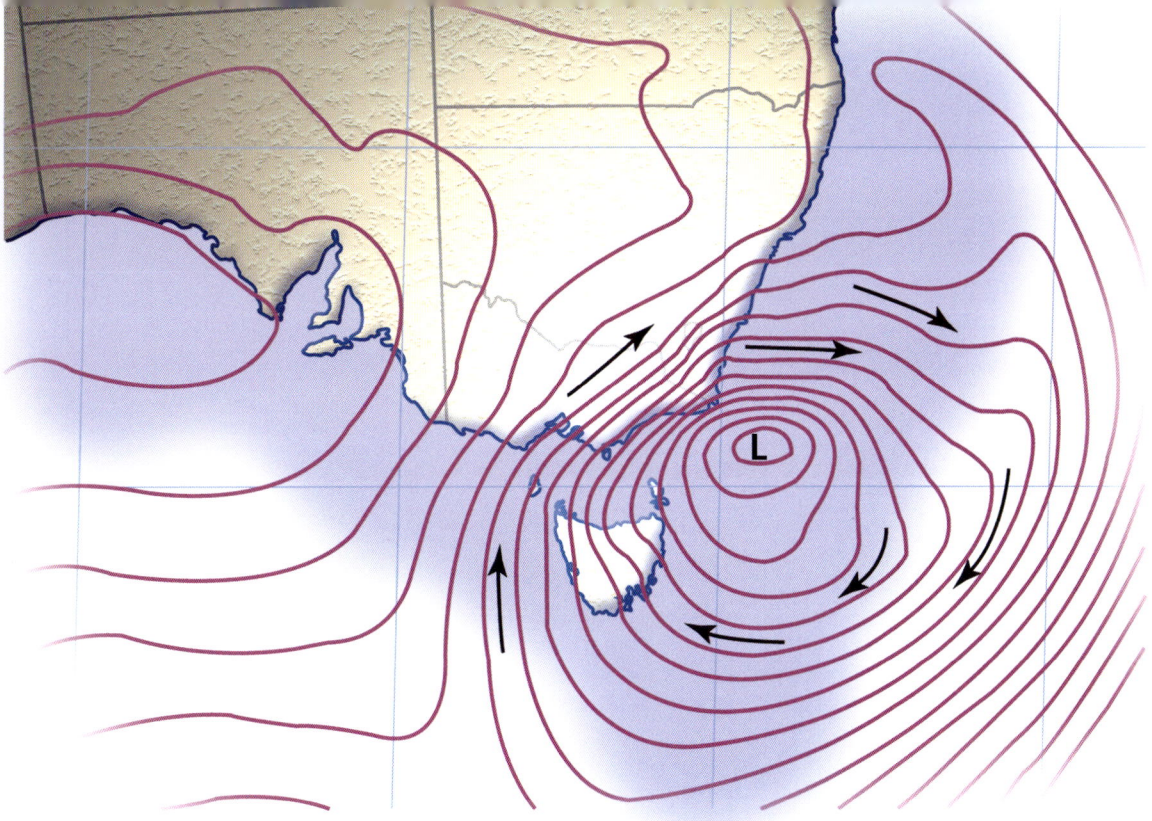

This reproduction of the actual chart for 9 pm on 27 December shows how the situation eventuated. A comparison with the computer-predicted chart on the previous page shows a good match.

Many yachts were forced to retire and several crew members were injured after being flung about their vessels. Ultimately, 55 sailors were saved from the mountainous seas through a huge rescue operation involving the Australian Maritime Safety Authority, the navy and the air force. Particularly heroic efforts were performed by helicopter pilots, who winched sailors to safety in the incredibly dangerous flying conditions. In the end, five boats had sunk, 66 retired and only 44 made it to the finish line. Most tragically, six crew members had died in the maelstrom.

A lengthy coronial inquiry was held and the findings were finally released in

Wind Classification for Warning Purposes

Strong wind
Average winds of 26–33 knots

Gale-force wind
Average winds of 34–47 knots

Storm-force wind
Average winds of 48–63 knots

Hurricane-force wind
Average winds of 64 knots or more

Above: The dismasted *Sword of Orion* is battered by huge seas and storm-force winds. It was eventually abandoned by the crew.

Opposite: An exhausted crew member from the sunken yacht *Winston Churchill* arrives in Malacoota after being airlifted to safety. Six sailors lost their lives in the mountainous seas.

December 2000. The coroner, John Abernethy, was critical of certain aspects of the conduct of the CYCA's Race Organising Committee and also recommended changes to a range of safety gear to be carried aboard yachts in future races.

As far as the weather services were concerned, he recommended changes to the wording of forecasts that would incorporate information on the upper levels of wind gusts and wave heights in addition to the average figures expected.

This increased level of detail is now part of all the forecasts issued by the bureau in support of the race.

1999

A Deadly Sleep – The Snowboarder Tragedy

I can only say that it would be prudent for snow cavers to always ensure that some type of aperture to the open air is kept, even if this means maintaining a 'watch' throughout the night.

Mr John Abernethy, New South Wales Coroner

On the morning of Saturday 7 August 1999, four young men carrying large packs and snowboards began a journey at the Thredbo chairlift in the New South Wales ski fields. It was intended to be an exciting three-day cross-country adventure involving camping out in the snow and then snowboarding on remote trails in powder snow – every boarder's dream trip.

Dean Pincini, Timothy Friend and brothers Scott and Paul Beardsmore, all in their mid-20s, had previous experience on similar snowboarding trips. They were carrying plenty of food and Scott had left a map with his sister showing their intended route and schedule, with instructions that if she did not hear from him on Monday then she should notify the police.

On the surface, this should have been a safe trip. The men were young, fit and well provisioned. They had some snow experience and they had acted responsibly by drawing up a plan and schedule that could be used as the basis for a search should the need arise.

The one negative was that the weather forecast was not great. The Bureau of Meteorology had predicted a deterioration into blizzard conditions over the following 24-hour period as a cold front moved across the area. Contrary to popular belief, the most suitable wind direction for a good snow-dump in the New South Wales ski fields is from the north-west rather than the south-west, provided temperatures are low enough, and this was the expected condition for Sunday.

Sniffer dogs were brought in by police in a fruitless search for the missing snowboarders.

However, the men did not see this as a problem as they intended to hike about 10 kilometres from the top of the Thredbo chairlift and then dig a snow cave to shelter from the expected blizzard. After the blizzard had eased they would emerge and board the pristine powder snow on the nearby slopes.

But after travelling only about 2 kilometres, the weather closed in, the wind rose and heavy snow began to fall. The men decided to bunker down and selected a snow bank a little distance away from the main walking track. Taking out their snow shovels, they dug a large snow cave, leaving a hole at the entrance to allow sufficient ventilation. Secure from the raging blizzard outside, they settled in for the night.

On Monday morning, Scott Beardsmore's sister waited for the prearranged call from her brother. Increasingly worried, she waited until later that night before notifying the Jindabyne police, who organised a search to begin at first light next morning.

When their initial efforts failed to reveal the whereabouts of the group, the police, too, became increasingly worried and called for assistance. The scale of the operation then increased steadily as more and more people joined in, and soon large numbers of official and volunteer searchers were on the ground, going over the area in fine detail.

The search, which became one of the largest operations in the history of the Snowy Mountains, involving large parties from both New South Wales and Victoria as well as over-snow vehicles and aircraft, continued daily for the rest of the month. Special heat-seeking instruments were used on the aircraft in an attempt to locate human body warmth, but despite all these endeavours, no trace of the young men was found. Reluctantly, the search was scaled down late in the month, and it was assumed that the answer to the mystery would not be found until the snow melted in spring.

On 16 November, with the snow melt now well advanced, a navy helicopter pilot flying over the area noticed a black hole in a melting snowdrift and landed nearby to investigate. He found the bodies of the missing men in the remnants of a snow cave, together with their food and equipment, all perfectly preserved in the ice. The mystery had been solved, with the expected, but devastating outcome finally confirmed.

But what had caused the tragedy? Expert advice was called in and it eventually became clear what had happened.

The men had basically done everything right, except for one vital mistake.

Family members of the missing men congregate around Seamans Hut, a structure that was used as a command post during the search.

Prevailing winds can create a slow but inexorable build-up of snow across the entrance of a snow cave. It is imperative that this entrance be kept clear to allow for interior ventilation.

The airhole they had constructed in the side of their snow cave was located away from the wind on the leeside of the snow bank. This would be the instinctive thing to do as it placed the hole on the sheltered side – away from the direct wind. However, they did not know of an insidious phenomenon. Snow tends to accumulate in areas of light wind that often occur on the leeward side of obstacles such as snow banks. In this case, as the men slept, the snow quietly but inexorably built up on the outside of their cave and eventually blocked their airhole. They died quietly of suffocation in their sleep.

Although there was no coronial inquiry, the coroner, Mr John Abernethy, did issue a statement. He said:

> *I can only say that it would be prudent for snow cavers to always ensure that some type of aperture to the open air is kept, even if this means maintaining a 'watch' throughout the night.*

The widespread publicity generated by the incident produced extensive discussion within the ski fields community, and hopefully the knowledge gained from the tragedy will substantially reduce the likelihood of a repetition.

Opposite: The tragic aftermath: the bodies of the snowboarders were eventually found in the spring thaw. Here a snowboard is taken from the site of the snow cave.

2002

The Millennium Drought

You almost heard the surface bake, and saw the gum leaves turn –
You could have watched the grass scorch brown had there been grass to burn.
In such a drought the strongest heart might well grow faint and weak –
'Twould frighten Satan to his home – not far from Dingo Creek.

'Marshall's Mate', Henry Lawson

Australia is, sadly, accustomed to drought. During the 1902 so-called 'Federation Drought' (see page 34), people were so desperate and had not seen rain for so long that they thought it would never rain again. The great dry of 1982 culminated in the disastrous 'Ash Wednesday' bushfires in February 1983 (see page 169). And in an eerie repetition of history, the 2002 drought, dubbed 'The Millennium Drought' by some media sources, was followed by unprecedented fires across Canberra in January 2003 (see page 229). And like the other droughts, this one was also associated with El Niño.

After some useful rains in February 2002, climatologists became increasingly concerned with the telltale build-up of warm water across the eastern Pacific during the autumn months. It became increasingly obvious that El Niño was forming. From March onwards, rainfall reduced dramatically and widespread drought settled across the continent. There have been many El Niño occasions where one large sector of the continent has been drought affected, but other parts have received normal or even above average rain. But the 2002 drought was unusual in terms of both severity and extent, with most of eastern and south-western Australia severely drought affected.

A view from space of the massive dust storm that crossed eastern Australia on 23 October 2002.

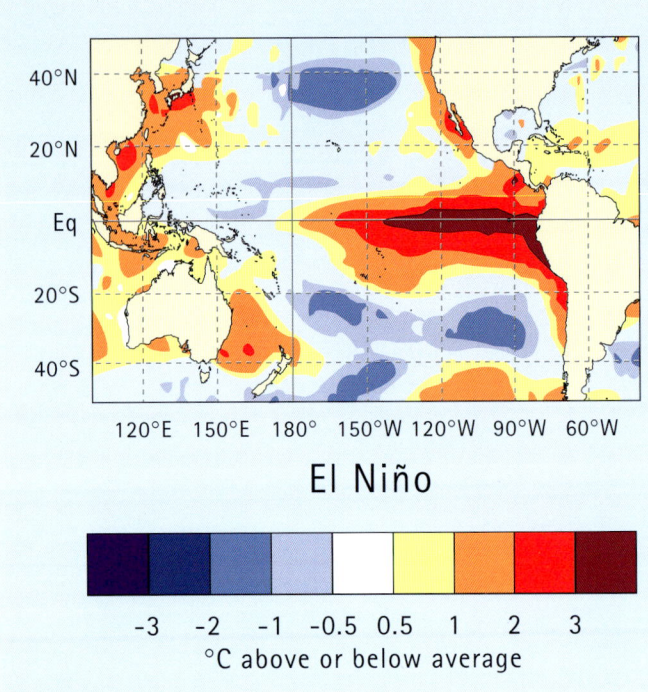

El Niño

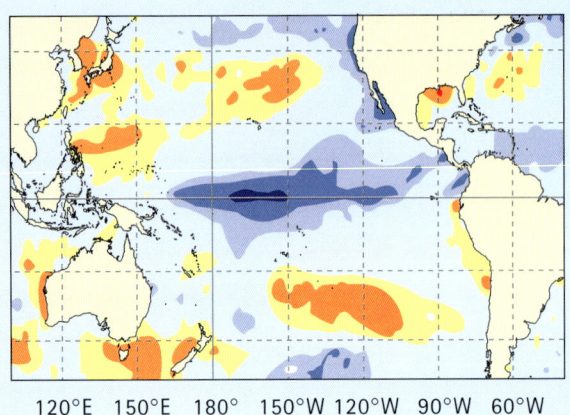

La Niña

The large red area in the left-hand map shows the warmer water associated with El Niño. The corresponding area in the right-hand map is blue, indicating the cooler water of La Niña.

Many droughts in Australia can be linked to the so-called El-Niño phenomenon. El Niño is associated with a warming of the ocean along the north coast of South America, frequently around Christmas time, that particularly affects coastal parts of Peru. El Niño is Spanish for 'boy child' — a reference to the Christ child of Christmas.

Local Peruvians have been familiar with this phenomenon since ancient times, because the influx of warm water results in a decimation of the population of anchovy fish — traditionally an important local food source. But only in recent times was it discovered that El Niño was far more than just a local warming of the ocean off the coast of South America. In reality it is a massive 'piling up' of warm water over the entire eastern Pacific, which is also associated with a weakening of the trade wind regime across the area and changes to the normal vertical wind structure. All of this tends to produce a marked drop in rainfall across much of Australia.

It has also been discovered that there is a 'reverse' situation, called La Niña (girl child), when cooler than average ocean temperatures develop over the central and eastern Pacific, and this has frequently been associated with above-average rain over parts of Australia.

By the end of 2002 only two significant areas of the mainland in remote parts of Western Australia had received above-average rainfall. All the prime agricultural areas across the country had been devastated. Parts of South Australia, northern New South Wales and Queensland received their lowest annual rainfall on record. To make matters worse, the mean Australian rainfall for the vital March to December period, when many crops should have been reaching maturity, was also the driest on record.

In its annual climate summary, the Bureau of Meteorology calculated that for Australia as a whole, 2002 was the fourth

Rainfall Relative to Historical Records
January to December 2002

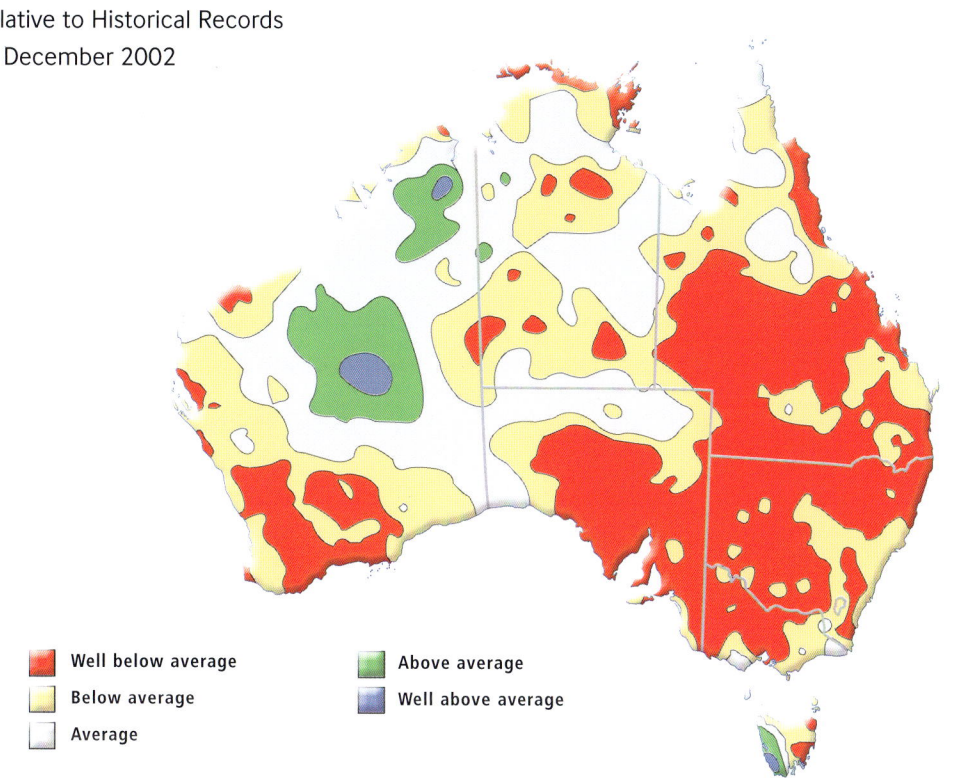

The rainfall pattern for 2002 reveals massive areas of drought, not only across eastern Australia but also across large areas of the south-west as well.

driest year since 1900, with the national average rainfall being only 339 millimetres, compared to the 'normal' figure of 472 millimetres.

Abnormally high daytime temperatures were also recorded in 2002. Australia's annual mean maximum temperature was 1.22°C above normal, the highest anomaly on record up until that time. And taking into account minimum temperatures as well, 2002 was Australia's fifth warmest year since 1910, again, up until that time.

Rural Australia was devastated. Vast areas of previously fertile farmland became dustbowls, producing widespread crop failures and stock losses. Reservoir levels dropped alarmingly, including capital city water supplies, prompting the review of water-usage patterns in urban areas.

The economic impact was no less severe. Cotton and rice production fell dramatically and the winter grain crop yield dropped to the lowest level since 1982–83, when the last widespread drought hit grain-growing areas. The situation was compounded by the fact that both eastern Australian and Western Australian grain-growing areas were hit simultaneously.

The political fallout was also considerable. A report released by the World Wide Fund for Nature (Australia) and two academics from Melbourne's Monash University in January 2003 linked the severity of the drought with human-induced global

By September 2002, conditions across much of New South Wales had become so dry that the Darling River had stopped flowing in some areas and become a chain of billabongs.

During September 2003, the level of Warragamba Dam to the west of Sydney had dropped well below capacity.
Here, Sydney Catchment Authority officers are checking the water level by boat.

Farmhand Foundation

The rural situation became so extreme in 2002 that, in addition to the normal government assistance, a large-scale private enterprise endeavour, called the 'Farmhand Foundation', was launched in October. Involving several prominent Australian businessmen, it was intended to provide immediate financial relief to those suffering the effects of the drought, and also to promote discussions of long-term strategies to help in the operation of Australian agriculture.

The CEO of the Farmhand Foundation, Mr Bob Mansfield, said:
Australians have long lived with the harsh effects of drought. The impact of the current dry has left thousands of Australians struggling to sustain themselves and their families in the face of failing crops, distressed stock, high feed prices and of course a lack of water. All this even before the start of the long, hot months of summer ...

The people who live on the land know how to make the most of the hand that nature deals them. But Australia in drought is a harsh place. Farmhand is about coming together to help out. Please give all you can.

Farmhand immediately produced results and, in conjunction with the Australian Red Cross, distributed large sums of money to rural families in the form of 'helping hand' grants.

warming. This report, called *Global Warming Contributes to Australia's Worst Drought*, compared the 2002 drought with four other major droughts since 1950 and concluded that the rising temperature trend over this period 'could not be explained by natural climate variability alone'.

One of the co-authors, Professor David Karoly, noted that the actual trend in Australian temperature since 1950 now matches the climate model predictions of how temperatures respond to increased greenhouse gases in the atmosphere. The 2002 drought was 'the first drought in Australia where the impact of human-induced global warming can be clearly observed. Most of this warming is likely due to the increase in greenhouse gases in the atmosphere from human activity such as burning fossil fuels for electricity and transport and from land clearing'.

The report was widely publicised and attracted the attention of the New South Wales Premier, Mr Bob Carr, who published a letter of response in *The Sydney Morning Herald* of 22 August 2003. He noted that human-induced global warming had the potential to produce more-severe droughts as well as more-intense bushfires,

The town of Burragorang was flooded back in 1960 with the construction of the Warragamba Dam. As the drought tightened its grip across the area in the second half of 2002, remnants of the old town emerged ghost-like from the waters once again. Here, an old water tank, posts and a bathtub have emerged from the bottom of the dam and grass has begun to grow around them.

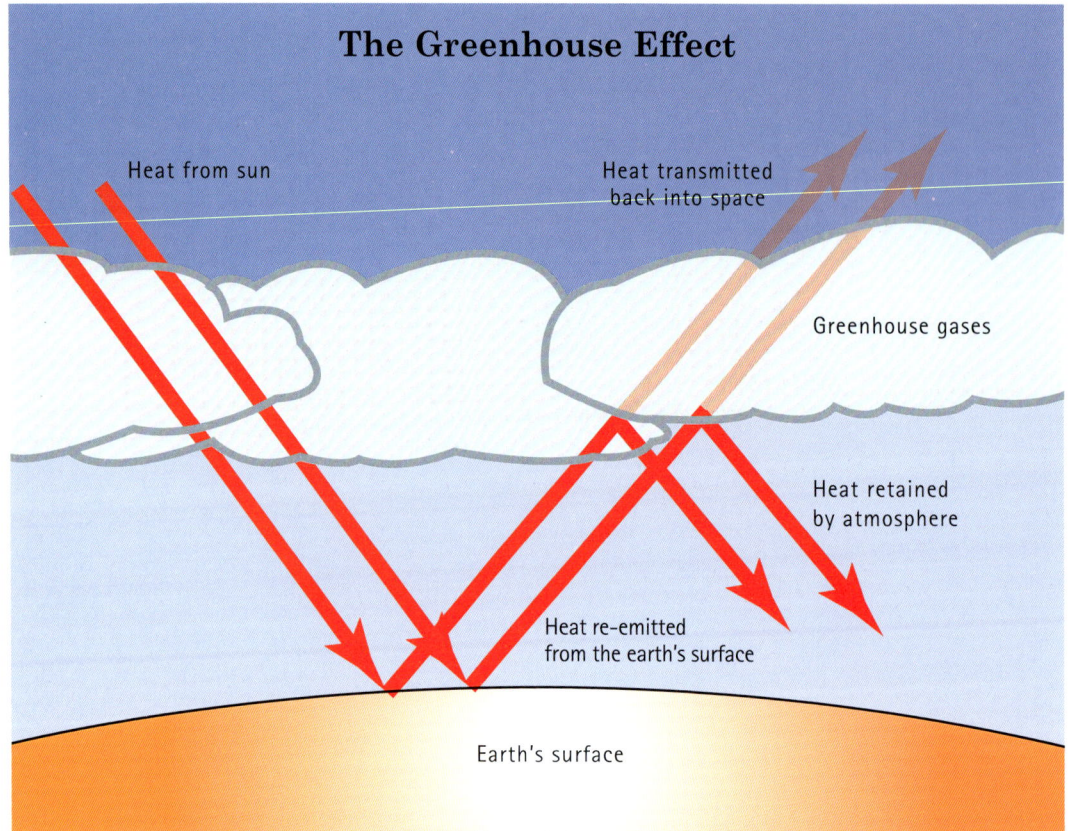

About 88 per cent of the sun's heat reflected back from the Earth's crust is kept within the atmosphere by the greenhouse gases, which include water vapour (H_2O) and carbon dioxide (CO_2). The remainder (12 per cent) escapes back into space.

Earth's atmosphere contains a unique 'cocktail' of gases that enable life — at least as we know it — to survive. Nitrogen and oxygen are the most common but other important gases, known as the 'greenhouse gases', occur in lesser amounts. These include carbon dioxide, methane, water vapour and nitrous oxide. They all let heat from the sun in, but block some of it from escaping — like a sort of one-way valve in the atmosphere — and help maintain a stable temperature at the Earth's surface that is much warmer than would be the case without them. This is the 'greenhouse effect'.

However, the worry is that human activity is increasing the concentrations of these gases — particularly carbon dioxide — through the increased burning of fossil fuels such as petrol and coal. Many scientists now believe this is producing increased global temperatures, rising sea levels, altered rainfall patterns and increased frequency of extreme weather such as drought and flood — the so-called 'enhanced greenhouse effect'.

thunderstorms and flash floods.

In December 2002 some useful rain fell across eastern Australia, but this was by no means a 'drought breaker'. Early 2003 remained dry, but after March a more normal rainfall pattern was gradually re-established over much of the southern half of the mainland. However, the so-called Millennium Drought maintained its grip over eastern New South Wales and much of Victoria throughout 2004 and into 2005, resulting in a tightening of water restrictions in Sydney and Melbourne.

2003

Canberra Burns

The drought-fiend lapped with thirsty sun-parched tongue
Each spring and tank, and sucked with ghoul-like lips
The very life-blood from the cracking soil;
Fire came to blacken earth and mar the sky
With charred and sable tokens of his wrath, –
Undimmed by miles of smoke his savage eyes
Gleamed like the outposts of the hosts of hell.

'A Bush Idyll', J. A. K. MacKay, 1888

The year 2003 began remarkably like the summer of 1983, which was hot and tinder dry as a result of the devastating 1982 drought. For much of eastern Australia, 1982 was the driest year on record. During January and February 1983, the dry weather persisted until the inevitable happened: on 16 February disastrous bushfires swept across parts of South Australia and Victoria – the notorious Ash Wednesday fires (see page 169).

The parallels with 2003 were obvious. Much of the country had been in the grip of a disastrous drought since autumn of 2002, which also turned out to be one of the warmest years in Australia's history. As the new year dawned, it was obvious to all the experts that a time of considerable bushfire danger was emerging.

During mid-January, lightning strikes ignited several fires in rugged country across the Kosciuszko and Namadgi national parks. Fanned by periodic bursts of strong winds, these fires gradually built in intensity and advanced on Canberra.

The situation built to a climax with frightening speed on Saturday 18 January. Gale-force westerly winds belted across south-eastern Australia. The temperature skyrocketed and the humidity dropped.

Rainfall Relative to Historical Records
July to December 2002

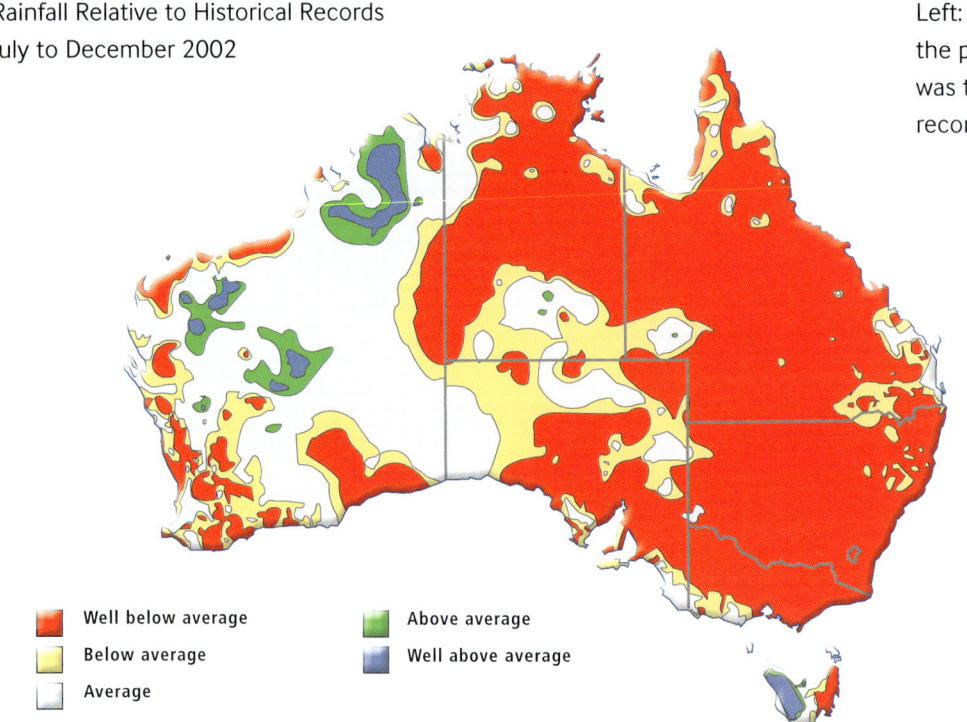

Left: For some areas of eastern Australia the period from July to December 2002 was the driest seven-month period recorded up until that time.

Opposite: This view from a NASA satellite shows a huge plume of smoke blowing eastwards across the Tasman Sea on 18 January 2003. By 21 January, the smoke had reached beyond New Zealand.

Fire Tornadoes

The intense heat of bushfires produces columns of rapidly rising air above the fire. The collision of these columns with the prevailing winds flowing over the fire – which are usually strong during intense fire conditions – can create violently rotating vortices called 'fire tornadoes' that are capable of producing highly destructive winds, as well as bursts of intense heat as flames are sucked up into the vortex. These madly spinning funnels of flame can last for several seconds and whip rapidly across the ground.

At 3 pm the temperature at Canberra airport was 36.9°C, with a relative humidity of only 8 per cent. By 5 pm the humidity had dropped to only 5 per cent. Such 'dry' air, in combination with high temperatures and winds, greatly increases the speed at which fires spread.

A vast ocean of flame surged towards the capital and burst upon the western residential areas of Chapman, Cook, Duffy, Hawker, Higgins, Kambah and Rivett with unprecedented fury. Almost surreal scenes followed as the fires created their own wind environment, considerably amplifying the already gale-force 'meteorological' wind.

Witnesses reported seeing 'fire tornadoes' that ripped out trees, destroyed roofs and sounded like 'a jumbo jet flying down the street'. Houses burst into flames – not only those near forested areas, but those in normal suburban settings – lit by flying sparks. Even neatly mown lawns burned savagely in the tremendous heat. Television crews filmed graphic images of the inferno sweeping through the streets, fanned by tremendous

winds against an almost totally black sky.

The Bureau of Meteorology confirmed that such an intense blaze could have generated fire tornadoes. Geoff Crane, acting Regional Director of the New South Wales Bureau of Meteorology, had viewed the damage trail of one of these tornadoes and remarked that 'The physical effects are the same; tornadoes in the bushfires could have been rotating at up to 300 kilometres per hour. The fires were burning with such ferocity they would generate their own local environment.'

Firefighters fought desperately to hold the front but were powerless in the face of the size and ferocity of the blaze. Control could only be re-established with a moderation in the weather conditions. Finally, overnight the wind eased and the temperature dropped. It was time to count the cost.

No one could have guessed the extent of the devastation. Aerial views across the suburbs next day showed street after street of gutted houses and huge areas of burnt forest. Five hundred and seven houses had been totally destroyed and a further 800 substantially damaged. Some 300 cars were incinerated, as was the historic 70-year-old Mount Stromlo Observatory. The total insurance bill was later calculated to be close to $350 million. But most tragically, four people died in the inferno. Although Canberra had experienced major bushfires

Pine trees exploding in flame near the Mountain Creek Road to the north of Canberra during the January 2003 fires. The sharp angle of the flames indicates that strong winds were blowing from right to left in this photograph.

An aerial view over Chapman, one of the hardest hit suburbs of Canberra, six months after the fire. Although most of the wreckage from burnt-out houses had been cleared, not much rebuilding had commenced at this time.

in the past, notably in 1926, 1939 and 1952, none of these came close to the 2003 disaster in terms of the huge insurance loss.

How did the fire attain such a degree of intensity that even the suburbs were invaded in this manner? Fire experts calculated that the blaze would have been generating about 50,000 kilowatts of energy per linear metre, whereas a firefighting crew equipped with a tanker and bulldozer can only contain blazes producing 3500 kilowatts per metre. There was therefore no way the fire could have been controlled at its peak by fire crews on the ground alone. The temperature of the flames was estimated to have reached 1100°C near the centre of the blaze, which is hot enough to melt copper.

As with most disasters, a bushfire is an intensely political event. Almost as soon as the ashes of the Canberra disaster had cooled, controversy erupted as to whether the warning services had been adequate, whether enough back-burning had been done in the run-up to the fire season, and whether or not the firefighting effort was properly coordinated.

Considerable comment was made about the length of time the fires originally started by lightning had been allowed to burn in the first place. Critics argued that more energetic efforts to extinguish them before they built in intensity and surged out

The historic Mount Stromlo Observatory was destroyed by the fires.

of control on 18 January could have averted the disaster. The old debate about fires in national parks also re-remerged. It was proposed that fires in national parks are far more severe than those over agricultural land and that the Canberra fires had in fact originated in national parks. This argument was used to advance the proposition that Australia has 'too many national parks'.

There was criticism, too, about the command and control structure used in the fighting of the fires, and in particular the distribution of resources. Because of the unexpectedly rapid movement of the blaze, a large force of volunteer firefighters that had been assembled from all over New South Wales the previous week was allegedly not in Canberra on the critical day.

One of the major issues raised was the presence of commercial pine forests close to the city. Pine trees contain turpentine, which produces very different burning characteristics to the vegetation normally found in Australian bush. Plantation radiata pines have a very high fuel load and fire can move from treetop to treetop much faster than in a eucalypt forest. Their intense burning characteristics also generate powerful updraughts and downdraughts that produce strong surface winds in adjacent areas.

The Canberra fires of 2003 were a shock occurrence that changed the way many people thought about fires. They showed that our national capital is located in a highly bushfire-prone area of Australia and that under extreme conditions fires can invade even suburban areas. Nothing would ever be quite the same again.

2007

The *Pasha Bulker* Storm

'Advice is least heeded when most needed.'

English proverb

From the time recorded maritime history began along the New South Wales coast in the late eighteenth century, it became apparent that sudden severe storms were a weather feature in the area.

On occasion storm-force winds would suddenly ramp up with seemingly no warning, generating mountainous seas and heavy rain, sometimes producing disastrous consequences for shipping in the area. A notorious example involved the sinking of the passenger ship *Dunbar* at the entrance to Sydney Harbour in August 1857, with the loss of 121 passengers and crew – still one of the worst maritime disasters in Australian history (see page 13).

As our knowledge of the local weather grew, it was discovered that the culprits in these incidents were what were later called east coast lows, or ECLs: fast developing low-pressure cells that formed off the coast of New South Wales. These systems were generated when warm humid air from the Coral Sea clashed with cold air moving up from the south triggering the explosive development of low-pressure cells. These systems were difficult for meteorologists to predict because of their speed of development, and the fact that they often ramped up overnight, when the frequency of weather observations decreased and less information was available.

A classic example occurred on 26 May 1974 when an ECL developed explosively just to the north of Sydney, producing wind gusts to 171 kilometres per hour, as recorded at Nobbys Head near Newcastle. Ocean-swell waves to 17 metres in height were generated at the entrance to Newcastle Harbour. These extreme conditions drove the Norwegian bulk carrier *Sygna* ashore on nearby Stockton Beach, where it was totally wrecked.

Pasha Bulker washed ashore on Nobby's Beach, Newcastle.

This became known as the *Sygna* storm.

However, steady progress in predicting ECLs was made from the 1980s onwards, assisted by the development of radar, satellite imagery and computer simulations of the weather. By the time we had moved into the first decade of the twenty-first century it was generally possible for the Bureau of Meteorology to accurately predict the development of an ECL four days ahead. This enabled the issuing of warnings to shipping well in advance of the bad weather, enhancing the safety of east coast maritime activities.

Then, on 8 June 2007, another powerful east coast low developed rapidly, in a position close to the *Sygna* storm system of May 1974. However, this time the Bureau of Meteorology's computer simulation had picked up the development some four days before and warnings of the impending storm were issued to shipping on a regular basis.

Early on the morning of 8 June, Newcastle Port Corporation transmitted a radio weather warning to the 56 carrier ships that were waiting outside Newcastle Harbour to load coal, advising them to put to sea because of the impending storm. Of those ships, 46 heeded the advice and cleared the shore before the weather began deteriorating. One that stayed was the *Pasha Bulker*, a massive 77,000 tonne bulk carrier, whose captain believed that the vessel was capable of riding out the storm in safety. By the time he realised that the ship was in trouble it was too late.

As the ECL continued to intensify, witnesses on the shore started to realise that the giant ship was labouring in the conditions and reported that massive seas were crashing over the top of the vessel, and that it was being blown side on to the wind, parallel to the beach. The captain tried reversing the engines, in an attempt to pull it away from the shoreline, but the winds and seas opposing it were too strong.

A growing crowd of onlookers watched the unfolding drama from the adjacent beach, all transfixed by the massive spectacle and the accompanying noise. Above the shrieking gale the huge booms of massive waves hitting the steel sides of the ship were plainly audible, as well as tremendous buckling sounds from deforming metal. At this stage many thought the ship would break up. Instead, it ran aground on Nobbys Beach, a location some 8 kilometres south of Stockton Beach, the site of the *Sygna* disaster. The *Pasha Bulker* was stuck fast in the sand about 30 metres from the shore and the 22 crew members were evacuated from the deck by helicopter, as it was impossible to get a boat anywhere near it in the huge seas.

At the height of the storm wind gusts to 130 kilometres per hour were recorded at Nobbys Head and maximum wave heights of 14 metres were registered by the Sydney Waverider buoy, around 60 kilometres to the south. The storm had also produced widespread destruction along the coast between Newcastle and Sydney, including the deaths of nine people and significant damage to thousands of houses.

The authorities were concerned that the vessel might break apart, and as it was heavily loaded with fuel oil this would have created an environmental disaster. As a result of these concerns the focus turned to salvage, but all attempts were frustrated by continuing rough weather, with further ECL development following intermittently over the next three weeks. It was a prolonged period of stormy conditions that saw the ship becoming more deeply wedged in the sand with each burst of wind and wave action.

In the meantime, the incredible sight of such a massive vessel stuck in the sand so close to the shoreline of a major Australian city quickly gained national attention and it became somewhat of a tourist attraction, with large crowds coming up from Sydney to view the spectacle.

The Danish heavy-duty salvage company Svitzer was contracted to refloat the vessel, and after establishing that the hull was not irreparably damaged, it was successfully pulled off the beach on 2 July, 24 days after the initial storm.

A New South Wales Maritime report into the incident later concluded that 'horrendous weather conditions' were the first cause of the incident, together with an inappropriate response from the ship's captain. It was also noted that he did not appear to realise the potential impact of the predicted weather, even though wind warnings had been issued by the Bureau of Meteorology some five days before the onset of the storm.

2009

The Black Saturday Fires

'Black Saturday is an Australian tragedy. It is a day that has redefined the way we consider living alongside fire.'

Chloe Hooper, author of *The Arsonist: A Mind on Fire*

On 'Black Saturday', 7 February 2009, the deadliest bushfires in the history of Australia cut a blazing swathe of destruction across the state of Victoria. 173 people lost their lives, over 2000 homes were razed and communities from all over Australia were stunned by the enormity of the catastrophe.

A similar bushfire disaster had occurred 70 years before, on Friday 13 January 1939, when massive blazes surged across central and north-eastern Victoria (see page 88). These 'Black Friday' fires burned out some 20,000 square kilometres, destroyed 650 houses and killed 71 people. At the time it was generally believed that we were unlikely to see fires of this extent and ferocity again, but this was all to change in 2009.

Much of Victoria has experienced a decline in rainfall since the 1970s, and many areas, including those close to Melbourne, have experienced below-average annual rainfall for an extended period, often resulting in tinder-dry summers. However, the summer of 2008–09 began on an optimistic note with good rains falling over much of Victoria and South Australia in December 2008. This encouraged a growth spurt in vegetation across the area.

But then the rain abruptly stopped in January, temperatures rose and much of south-eastern Australia, including Victoria, found itself in the grip of a rolling heatwave that persisted across the area from mid-January. This event was to generate widespread record high temperatures that progressively dried out the vegetation and primed conditions for a bushfire outbreak. Unlike many other notable heatwaves of the past, there was little respite. After two weeks of these temperatures and no rain, Victoria was tinder dry, with the recent December growth producing an increase in the available bushfire fuel.

Numerous temperature records were broken across Victoria, with many centres recording their highest ever figures between 28 and 30 January. Over the five consecutive days from 27 to 31 January maximum temperatures were 12–15°C above average across much of Victoria – a very rare event made far worse by the lack of rain.

On Tuesday 3 February, the computer simulations began predicting what both meteorologists and firefighters feared most: a strong cold front was forecast to move across south-eastern Australia on Saturday 7 February, preceded by hot, dry and gusty north-west winds and extreme temperatures, followed by a south-westerly change. This would bring together all the ingredients of a major fire: abundant dry fuel, low humidity, strong winds, high temperatures and a marked wind change. The stage was set for disaster.

As the front approached Victoria on the morning of the 7th, rising north-west winds sent temperatures skyrocketing and the humidity plunging, fanning existing fires into infernos that rapidly jumped containment lines. Burning embers were carried aloft and transported kilometres downwind only to fall to ground and start new fires in the tinder-dry scrub.

Large tracts of central Victoria became raging firestorms that devoured everything

Devastation on the road to Lake Mountain ski resort after 2009 Black Saturday bushfires near Marysville, Victoria, Australia

in their path as temperatures again reached, and then surpassed, the records set only a few days before.

Two of the major blazes within the outbreak occurred around Kinglake and Marysville, with the change in wind direction, following the passage of the front, producing a major effect. Following this wind change these two fires merged and then surged towards the north-east as a massive conflagration, completely out of control.

Disastrous blazes impacted Kinglake, Toolangi, Hazledene, Broadford and Flowerdale, resulting in 120 deaths and 1200 homes destroyed in this area alone. Narbethong and Marysville were heavily damaged. Smaller, but highly destructive fires struck across other areas, including

Beechworth, Bendigo, Redesdale, Bunyip Park, Central Gippsland, the Dandenong Ranges and Horsham. The extent and speed of the fires was frightening and left firefighters with virtually no chance of stopping or even restricting the blazes in any way.

Melbourne's temperature peaked at 46.4°C, well above the longstanding record of 45.6°C set on Black Friday in 1939. Some 400 individual fires were recorded on Saturday 7 February, and in one of the great tragedies in our history, 173 people lost their lives, by far the deadliest death toll in an Australian bushfire.

A total of around 4500 square kilometres were burned, and fire danger indices reached unprecedented levels. The associated smoke plume streamed out across the Tasman Sea and reached New Zealand's South Island the next day, and the smoke was plainly visible from meteorological satellites.

The situation remained completely beyond control until temperatures fell overnight and the winds began easing. It was only then that the total devastation produced by the fires began to be understood.

The causes of the disaster were closely investigated and shown to be various. These included sparks from a power cable, lightning, discarded cigarette butts, the operation of power tools and what everyone feared – arson. Several arrests followed.

The disaster was so extensive and tragic that a Royal Commission was ordered to investigate all aspects of the fires and to recommend any improvements that should be made to prevent a recurrence. Chaired by former supreme court judge Bernard Teague, the commission reviewed several key aspects of the fires, including the 'stay or go' policy that attempted to assist homeowners threatened by a bushfire to reach the best decision in a realistic time frame.

There was a total of 67 recommendations in the final report, covering a wide range of factors, that essentially redesigned Victoria's Bushfire Safety Policy. The commissioners called for a comprehensive approach to evacuation including the potential for emergency evacuations when doing so would provide a greater level of protection. The report also called for designated community refuges in areas of high bushfire risk and recommended that the government significantly increase the amount of controlled burning it undertakes on a yearly basis. It also recommended parts of Victoria's ageing electricity infrastructure be upgraded to reduce the risk of fires from downed or clashing electricity cables. The report also flagged a program of voluntary acquisition of homes in high-risk areas.

Like Black Friday in 1939, Black Saturday in 2009 soon passed into the history books, but the lessons learned were not forgotten. Many of these were put to good use in the summer of 2019–20, when south-eastern Australia was once again under a massive bushfire threat.

2009

The Eastern Australian Dust Storms

'It was like waking up on Mars.'

Sydney resident Marcus Schappi in an email to Wired.com

As day began over Sydney on the morning of Wednesday 23 September 2009, the population was astonished to wake to an eerie red and brown dawn with visibility falling to less than 100 metres in some areas. The switchboards of radio and television channels lit up like Christmas trees as people rang in to report the amazing scenes, with many concerned that Sydney was on fire or being attacked by some strange enemy force.

However, the invasion was being produced by a natural phenomenon, one seen often over inland Australia, but most unusual at this intensity along the east coast. It was dust, and the massive wall that engulfed Sydney had moved from inland parts of New South Wales overnight and silently rolled in across the city in the early hours of 23 September.

Dusts storms of this nature have occurred in Melbourne before, notably on 8 February 1983 when a wall of dust swept across the city in the afternoon (see page 171). But many Sydneysiders had never seen a dust storm before and the amazing scenes that emerged caused mass consternation across the city.

This strange episode was the culmination of a series of events that all came together at that time. It had been an extreme year for much of south-east Australia with Victoria still reeling from the catastrophic Black Saturday fires of early February. For New South Wales, August had been dry across much of the state with below average rainfall dominating. In addition, maximum temperatures across most parts had been classified as 'very much above average'.

This resulted in a dry landscape coming in to the second half of September, and a powerful cold front, moving across south-east Australia on the 22nd, began picking up dust from northern parts of South Australia and western New South Wales. This dust gathered into a rolling line that moved inexorably eastwards, picking up more dust along the way and continuing to grow in size.

It struck Canberra on 22 September, an intense event that was notable and attracted massive news coverage. However, forecasters were not all that concerned about Sydney because inland dust storms are not unusual for New South Wales. In the vast majority of cases they are prevented from reaching the coast in any quantity by the massive wall of the Great Dividing Range, which acts as an impenetrable shield protecting the coast from any such invasion.

On the morning of the 23rd the meteorological situation was very different to 'normal'. The distribution of the winds from the surface to the upper levels, combined with the vertical temperature variation of the surrounding atmosphere and the strength of the front itself combined to produce an ideal 'lifting' environment for the dust.

Instead of being stalled by the Great Dividing Range, it went 'up and over', reaching nearly 3000 metres above the ground, and then descended on Sydney in the early hours, producing amazing scenes right across the city.

The dust consisted of very fine particles and the CSIRO later estimated that 75,000 tonnes were dumped over Sydney. This created havoc with swimming pools and air conditioners but turned out to be great news for commercial car washes that were run off their feet across the next two weeks or so. The dust also infiltrated houses, even those that had been closed up, coating the interiors with a fine layer that penetrated all nooks and crannies.

The social disruption that followed was extensive, with traffic on the roads forced to reduce speed, ferry services on the harbour shut down for the morning and building sites closed. In a very rare event, the scheduled horseracing at Canterbury Racecourse was cancelled for the day. The dust also played havoc with airline flight schedules, with several incoming international flights having to divert to Melbourne and Brisbane because of poor visibility and domestic flights also disrupted. In addition, there was a significant health impact, with a peak in hospital admissions for asthma-related presentations, as well as other respiratory problems.

The event was observable on satellite images, and during the daytime hours of the 23rd the dust cloud grew to around 1500 kilometres in length and 200 kilometres across while continuing to move east. It then rolled across Brisbane later on the 23rd,

Sydney dust storm.

Dust storms cover Brisbane, Queensland.

having crossed two other capital cities over the previous 24 hours. The dust reached northern Queensland in the evening with reduced visibility reported at Rockhampton, Mackay, Cairns and as far north as the Gulf of Carpentaria. However, it was losing intensity by this time and its effects were less noticeable.

Continuing off the coast it then tracked over the Tasman Sea, reaching the North Island of New Zealand, including Auckland and Taranaki on the 25th.

In a repeat performance, some three days later, another dust storm took much the same track, but this system was less powerful and the overall impact was much less than that of the first event.

Further investigation into the history of dust storms in Sydney confirmed the initial view that the 2009 event was rare in terms of its intensity, although three similar storms were recorded in October, November and December of 1944. During this time widespread bushfires were also raging across south-eastern Australia. It was also discovered that the dust storm triggered a significant increase of microscopic phytoplankton in the waters of Sydney Harbour, indicating that storms of this type are important in enriching the oxygen content of the oceans.

Scientists investigating the long-term frequency of dust storms over the east coast of Australia have discovered valuable information stored in sediment layers on the bed of the Tasman Sea. By taking core samples and investigating the layers contained in them scientists can build up a picture of significant dust storms of the past and relate this to climate change across the area.

2010 & 2011

Queensland floods

La Niña is Spanish for 'The Little Girl' – a distribution of sea surface temperatures across the equatorial Pacific Ocean that often promotes heavy rain over eastern Australia.

The years 2010 and 2011 were notable in Australian meteorological history as times where widespread flooding occurred across both mainland Australia and Tasmania over two consecutive years. It was the most significant event of this type since that of 1973 and 1974, where similar areas suffered major inundation.

The first cause of these disastrous floods was the La Niña phenomenon, when waters across the central and eastern equatorial Pacific Ocean cool, and warmer ocean areas gather closer to north-east Australia. Rain tends to cluster around the warmest parts of the ocean because the warmth produces rising air, and this in turn generates cloud and rain.

La Niñas are usually associated with enhanced rainfall over eastern Australia with moist tropical air often extending down from Queensland well into the southern states, even as far south as Tasmania, where flooding occurred during the second week in January 2011. This is opposite to the El Niño phase, where warmer waters gather on the South American side of the Pacific and eastern Australia will often lapse into below average rainfall patterns (see page 222).

During 2009 and the first half of 2010 a below average rainfall pattern was largely dictated by a an El Niño of moderate strength but this abruptly flipped into a strong La Niña phase in May of 2010. This brought with it bursts of heavy rain across the second half of the year, and then into 2011.

A rising crescendo of major rainfall events followed that rolled across Queensland from September 2010 onwards. Catchments right across the state became increasingly saturated as one rainfall event followed another. Queensland rainfall records began to tumble, with the spring of 2010 the wettest for the state since 1900 and

A car is submerged in deep floodwater in Kangaroo Point, Brisbane.

December 2010 was the wettest on record up until that time.

By the end of 2010 most of the catchments across south-eastern Queensland were totally saturated and any additional rainfall would then just run off into the adjacent river systems – a critical situation to be in during the initial stages of the Australian tropical wet season. This disaster-in-waiting then cut loose early in the new year.

Catastrophic flash flooding erupted through Toowoomba on Monday 10 January 2011, after 160 millimetres fell in just 36 hours, across an already saturated catchment in the Lockyer Valley. These falls were generated by a line of thunderstorms moving through the area and produced a situation where rain was entering the catchment at a much faster rate than the local waterways could take it away. These burst their banks and amid surreal scenes a wall of high-speed water swept through the city centre of Toowoomba carrying all before it.

The nearby town of Grantham was utterly devastated by the torrent, with the height of the water surge estimated to have been around 7 metres as it entered the town. Houses were swept away in scenes later described by the Queensland Premier, Anna Bligh as 'an inland tsunami'. Most tragically, nine people died in the Lockyer Valley event.

Major flooding then burst across much of south-east Queensland on 11 and 12 January with Brisbane itself inundated as the Brisbane River burst its banks and rose to levels just short of the 1974 flood. The degree of flooding in the area placed the disaster in the top three of floods, alongside 1893 and 1974 (see page 25).

The streets of Brisbane were covered with kilometres of mud, and some 20,000 houses were flooded. Massive flooding also resulted across Ipswich, about 30 kilometres south-west of Brisbane, and it was estimated that nearly one-third of the city was underwater, with the central business district, along with 3000 nearby houses, flooded out.

Great controversy surrounded this event as massive water releases were conducted from the Wivenhoe Dam on 11 January in an attempt to get water levels down, but it was alleged that this also was a major contributor to the Brisbane River flooding over the next two days. It was also claimed the releases played a big part in the flooding of the Bremer River that produced widespread inundation in surrounding areas, including Ipswich. Legal action surrounding these floods was launched in 2014 alleging 'negligence and nuisance' in the way that the Wivenhoe and other dams had been managed during the disaster.

In addition, there was major flooding along the Fitzroy and Balonne rivers, and there was also extensive inundations around the Condamine and Mary River catchments. This disaster was responsible for 33 deaths with a damage bill estimated to have been around $2.39 billion. In addition, an estimated 20,000 people were affected in many significant ways, including the loss or extensive damage of homes and property, and with forced relocation the result.

Several Queensland coal mines were flooded, as well as the associated railway tracks, and this severely impacted on the state's coal production. These facilities only slowly recovered and it would be nearly six months before normal production was resumed.

Thousands of volunteers banded together to help clean up Brisbane streets, attracting praise from the Prime Minister, Julia Gillard. These combined with personnel from the Defence Force and the State Emergency Service to assist with the giant operation, with help also coming from military and civil defence teams from New Zealand.

Prime Minister Julia Gillard announced that a flood levy would be imposed on Australian taxpayers, in order to conduct the extensive reconstruction works.

On 17 January 2011 a Commission of Enquiry was established with wide terms of reference to investigate all aspects of the disaster and make recommendations as to how the prediction and responses could have been improved.

The event was of great interest to meteorologists. It was unusual to flip from an El Niño to a La Niña so abruptly, and then for such incredibly wet weather to last for an extended period thereafter. The El Niño/La Niña phenomena march to an irregular beat but have always been a big part of Australia's climate, often producing drought and floods along the way. As Dorothea MacKellar wrote in her poem 'My Country', we live in a land of 'droughts and flooding rains' and these rainfall extremes were well illustrated in the disastrous events of 2010 and 2011.

2011

Tropical Cyclone Yasi

*'I think people were prepared but I don't think we really understood
the magnitude of what was about to happen.'*

Local resident June Perkins

Tropical cyclones are intense low-pressure cells that develop over tropical oceans and then often move in erratic paths. They are capable of generating tremendously strong winds and heavy rain across a large area and do most of their damage when moving across the coast from the sea. In addition, there is the storm surge – coastal flooding produced when the ocean is literally blown inland by the extreme winds (see page 54).

These three effects – destructive winds, heavy rain and storm surge – have produced incredible property damage and tragic death tolls in Australia since formal records began. A great deal of effort has gone into identifying and then trying to predict the movement of these systems so that effective warnings can be given well in advance.

At the centre of a tropical cyclone is what is called the eye: a clear area of light winds surrounded by raging tempests that can produce wind gusts up to 300 kilometres per hour. The eye is normally around 50 kilometres across but can be larger or smaller depending on the nature of the cyclone. The eye is surrounded by towering walls of cloud that extend up to 15 kilometres into the sky (see page 164).

Tropical cyclones are categorised according to their intensity, which relates directly to the strength of the winds they generate. Five categories are used in Australia (1 to 5) with category 1 the weakest end of the spectrum. Cyclones of category 3 or above are termed severe tropical cyclones. At the top of the tree is category 5 – wind gusts in excess of 280 kilometres per hour (see page 166).

Tropical cyclones often move in highly erratic paths that present real challenges to meteorologists trying to predict their movement and intensity. After crossing a coastline, a tropical cyclone will generally weaken considerably as a result of increased frictional forces between the air and the land below but it can still dump huge quantities of rain over the surrounding countryside as it weakens. The resulting floods can be just as deadly as the high winds produced in the coastal crossing.

Australia has experienced numerous tropical cyclones that have caused massive damage and large death tolls. The deadliest cyclone in Australia's history was the so-called Bathurst Bay cyclone in north Queensland on 4 March 1899. An estimated 407 people died, including nearly all the sailors aboard a pearling fleet anchored in Bathurst Bay.

The prediction of the movement of tropical cyclones had improved substantially by the first decade of the twenty-first century with computer simulations providing increasingly better advice as to the future path a particular cyclone would take. This was of tremendous value in the issue of warnings, both to shipping and land-based areas in the path of an approaching storm.

A good example was tropical cyclone Anthony that threatened the north Queensland coast from 23 to 31 January 2011. After its formation it had led forecasters on a merry dance as it gyrated across the ocean in the area. The computer simulations predicted that it would move

On 2 February 2011 the MODIS instrument on NASA's Aqua satellite captured this visible image of Cyclone Yasi making landfall in Queensland, Australia. The eye of the cyclone is very clear and indicative of the power of this tropical cyclone.

southeast, before reversing direction and heading back towards the coastline. And this is precisely what happened, with the highly erratic path accurately predicted by Queensland meteorologists.

Then, hot on the heels of Anthony, there was Yasi, a far more dangerous system that would occupy a great deal of the forecasters' time over the following week.

Yasi began as a tropical low-pressure cell north of Vanuatu on 30 January and was named by the Fiji Meteorological Service. It started moving west to south-west and intensifying over the next 48 hours. Yasi was classified as a very large and upper-end category 4 system, very close to category 5, on 1 February, and started to charge towards the Queensland coast soon after. Tracked precisely by the Queensland tropical cyclone team and aided by very accurate computer simulations, it crossed the coast just to the south of Innisfail in the early hours of 3 February, with the eye itself passing directly over Dunk Island and Tully.

The cyclone generated wind gusts in excess of 250 kilometres per hour but it is likely that higher gusts, up around 285 kilometres per hour were produced, meaning that it could well have reached category 5 status close to the time of coastal crossing. Driven by these extreme winds a massive storm surge pushed some 300 metres inland, destroying several coastal structures and inundating the surrounding land with salt water. A 5-metre storm surge was recorded by the tide gauge at Cardwell and there was extensive oceanic flooding along the coast between Cairns and Alva Beach.

Torrential rain and massive storm surges followed Yasi inland, producing an immense damage trail right across the area. Rainfall totals between 200 and 300 millimetres were recorded between Cairns and Ayr in the 24-hour period ending at 9 am on Thursday the 3rd, with 471 millimetres the highest total at South Mission Beach.

The devastation produced was immense. In Tully 30 per cent of the houses were destroyed and extensive tracts of the local banana and sugar crops were flattened by the wind and rain. In total around 1000 people were directly affected by significant damage to their homes and power was lost to thousands of properties. In addition, cars were carried considerable distances from their original parking positions and boats were found piled up along the shoreline.

As the cyclone moved inland and weakened it generated a huge band of rain that produced widespread falls over central Australia, South Australia and further southwards into north-west Victoria. Even Melbourne felt the impact when Lyndhurst, a south-eastern suburb, recorded 180 millimetres of rain in a 24-hour period.

The estimated damage bill of the cyclone was $3.6 billion, making Yasi one of the costliest natural disasters in Australian history.

An interesting feature of the storm was the death toll. Only one fatality was reported, a surprising statistic considering the size and ferocity of the storm. The highly accurate weather predictions issued by the Bureau of Meteorology were likely a major factor, assisted by the computer simulations that scientifically indicated the most likely path that the cyclone would take.

2019–2020

Blazing Summer – The East-Coast Bushfires

'What matters most is how well you walk through the fire'.

Charles Bukowski, American writer

Bushfires across eastern Australia burned through massive areas of the mainland and Tasmania from October 2019 and then across the summer months of 2020. In term of intensity, longevity and extent the fires were unprecedented in Australia's recorded bushfire history.

Although fires of a greater area occurred in 1974–75, these were essentially grass and scrubland fires over inland Australia, and mainly over unpopulated areas. They were of much lower intensity compared to the giant forest fires of 2019–20, where 3500 homes were destroyed and 34 people lost their lives.

In December 2019, NSW Rural Fire Services Commissioner Shane Fitzsimmons said it was 'absolutely' the worst bushfire season on record. In January 2020, the President of the Australian Academy of Science, Professor John Shine, stated 'the scale of these bushfires is unprecedented anywhere in the world'.

The toll on wildlife was catastrophic with the Australian Academy of Science's Professor Chris Dickman estimating that Australia has lost at least a billion birds, mammals and reptiles during the period of the bushfires.

The extraordinary longevity of the fires was a standout with major blazes continuing to flare over several weeks, in contrast to the short, sharp fire disasters of Black Friday in 1939 (see page 88), Ash Wednesday in 1983 (see page 169) and Black Saturday in 2009 (see page 238) These latter fires were short-term in comparison, with the worst of the blazes lasting around 48 hours, whereas the 2019–20 fires were to alternately smoulder and flare across an extended period of three to four months in some areas.

The impact of the fires was also pronounced over all our eastern capital cities – Brisbane, Sydney, Melbourne, Canberra and Hobart – where thick smoke settled for extended periods. This produced poor air quality and health issues, particularly for those with existing respiratory problems such as asthma. With something like 43 per cent of the population of Australia exposed to smoke in some way during the time of the fires – that is more than 10 million people based on 2018 population figures – the social impact of the fires was massive, even for those not directly impacted.

And the smoke had an international effect as well. Massive palls rolled across the Tasman Sea with skies across New Zealand turning yellow and glaciers tinted brown from the smoke and dust that had travelled some 2000 kilometres. Satellite data obtained by NASA later showed that the smoke had actually circumnavigated the entire globe by mid-January.

As well as the longevity of the forest fires, their geographic extent was also remarkable. Fires stretched from southern Queensland, southwards into New South Wales and then the Gippsland area of Victoria. Large fires also cut through the Adelaide Hills, an area north of Perth, and even parts of the east coast of Tasmania.

Existing fires continued to spread and enlarge from early October 2019, with record low rainfall and high temperatures

On 19 January 2003, satellites captured a series of images of the fires in south-east Australia and the plume of smoke wafting thousands of kilometres out over the Pacific Ocean.

The erratic nature of fire leaves pockets of untouched bush in among totally razed areas and those already recovering with little green leaves. Blue Mountains, New South Wales.

exacerbating the situation. Fires that were dormant became reactivated each time there was a spike in wind and temperature and they continued to grow in size. The sheer extent of the blazes meant that it was never going to be possible to extinguish them using human intervention.

Several of the fires devastated towns across the south coast of New South Wales and eastern Victoria including Batemans Bay, Balmoral, Lake Conjola, Mogo, Cobargo, Mallacoota and across large swathes of the East Gippsland area. These were all tragic events producing loss of life and catastrophic property damage, including hundreds of houses, and forced thousands of people to relocate and seek shelter in other areas.

In South Australia, a large part of Kangaroo Island was burned out with a fast-moving blaze that tragically took the lives of two men who were caught in their car.

Some of the individual blazes within this big picture were also remarkable. The Gospers Mountain fire, near the New South Wales Central Coast, started in late October – likely through a lightning strike – and continued to burn for weeks after, growing on a daily basis. It soon assumed proportions that proved far too large for firefighters to extinguish and became a 'fire reservoir' that burst across the surrounding countryside with every surge of wind and temperature. The only control possible was around the fringes of the fire using aerial bombing.

Experts believed that this blaze was the largest single ignition point forest fire in

Australia and was larger than any single Californian or Mediterranean forest fire.

It was not only the highly flammable eucalyptus forests that were burned. Areas of subtropical rainforest, not normally susceptible to bushfires because of their perpetually damp growth pattern, also experienced extensive blazes. This included the unique and World Heritage Listed Gondwana rainforests of north-east New South Wales and south-east Queensland, considered to be the last living links with the ancient continent of Gondwanaland. This was the Southern Hemisphere supercontinent, that broke apart under the influence of continental drift some 180 million years ago.

The fires also threatened the ancient Wollemi Pine, whose survival was only discovered in 1994 when a few stands were found in a remote and rugged area 150 kilometres to the north-west of Sydney. This area became part of the Gospers Mountain fire.

The fire management itself was very well conducted, with timely evacuations launched from many areas well before the fires hit. The public generally responded well to the wishes of the authorities and this was at least partly the result of the public education campaigns previously conducted by the various fire commands.

Saturation media coverage kept public awareness high for an extended period and helped generate considerable debate about the connection between climate change and bushfires. This debate had a polarising effect across the country with a great deal of direct attention moving away from the fires towards discussions and debates about climate change. Bushfires often become political events and this was certainly the case here.

There was also lengthy discussion about using the military in some role in the firefighting process, either as personnel on the ground or involved in the logistical chain as providers of transport, rations, field kitchens and general supplies. Early in January there was increasing involvement of the military, in particular the Army Reserve and the Navy, and this proved to be of considerable assistance.

The economic impact of the fires was immense, from several different standpoints. The summer tourist industry, the backbone of many of the small coastal townships in both New South Wales and Victoria, was devastated with cancellations. The insurance bill ran up over $600 million, with national premiums affected as a result. The actual damage bill was significantly higher as many property owners were underinsured or carried no insurance at all.

Rain at last arrived across some of the fire grounds in mid-January and then continued with major rain events developing across Queensland, New South Wales and Victoria during February and March. By mid-March the fires were out and the crisis was over.

2020

After the Fire Came the Flood

'No matter the natural disaster I've covered, whether it's a wildfire or flood, I always come back with a much greater perspective.'

Ginger Zee, American television presenter

The late spring and early summer of 2019 and 2020 were times of devastating drought, with 2019 officially declared to be the hottest and driest year in Australia's recorded history.

A strong positive Indian Ocean Dipole (IOD) – a configuration of sea surface temperatures across the Indian Ocean that suppresses rainfall over much of mainland Australia – produced widespread drought that was exacerbated by record high temperatures across 2019. This set the scene for the catastrophic forest fires across the period, blazes that produced massive media coverage, both national and international (see page 251).

Then, abruptly, in the second half of January 2020, the IOD weakened and the weather flipped over into a high rainfall mode for eastern Australia. During the first two weeks of February some of the highest rainfall seen for years was recorded along the New South Wales Central Coast, and with Sydney also receiving a solid drenching.

The transition from drought to flood was as abrupt as it was astonishing, with flood warnings quickly replacing the fire weather warnings, dust and smoke of late spring and early summer. This transition began with the arrival of the wet season over the tropical north – in this case it was a rapid and well-defined onset rather than a gradual process. Tropical cyclones Claudia and Blake developed in early January and delivered heavy falls to the Top End and northern parts of Western Australia and this high humidity air then began to track south during the second half of January.

Severe thunderstorms ignited across south-eastern Australia between 15 and 20

Floods at Carrara sports precinct, Gold Coast, with Metricon Stadium reflecting into flood damaged waters.

Opposite: Weeks of rainfall pounded Queensland in January and February 2019, causing destructive flooding in the region.

January, producing flash flooding across New South Wales and Queensland as well as destructive hail over Canberra and the south-eastern suburbs of Melbourne. Heavy rain fell across parts of Victoria during the last week of January, and for some locations it turned out to be the wettest January on record.

The first two weeks of February continued on this wet trend with much of eastern Australia soaked, and this was greeted with great enthusiasm as rain fell in some of the worst of the drought-affected areas. It also began falling on the fire grounds of the previous month, with several blazes slowed and some even extinguished as the rain persisted.

Moderate to heavy falls continued along the New South Wales coast and in south-east Queensland during the first two weeks of February, with Sydney recording a 24-hour fall of 176 millimetres on the 10th. This then developed into a massive four-day event when 392 millimetres fell from the 7th to the 10th – the highest such total for Sydney since 1990. The February total for Sydney ended up at 441.6 millimetres, the wettest February since 1990 when 630.6 millimetres fell.

Widespread coastal flooding resulted, with flood warnings issued for Sydney, Wollongong, Newcastle and south-east Queensland. Despite all the problems associated with flooding, this was judged to be more good news than bad, with the fire areas continuing to dwindle – the first time that any real progress in halting the blazes had been achieved since late spring. And by the end of February all fires were finally under control in New South Wales, Victoria and Tasmania, to the massive relief of

exhausted firefighting crews who had been in continuous action for more than three months.

And the rain kept coming – this time with heavier falls in the eastern inland areas in addition to the coastal fringe. In early March the remnants of tropical cyclone Esther took over, generating large rainfall totals over inland areas of Queensland, New South Wales and Victoria, bringing some big falls to those areas that had missed out in January and February. A massive pulse of tropical moisture associated with Esther surged right across Australia from the north-west parts of Western Australia, down through the Red Centre, into central New South Wales and the ACT and then into Victoria.

This was a real game changer with widespread inland flooding resulting, closing roads in Central Australia and south-west Queensland, and eventually extending as far south as Tasmania. Canberra received 72.4 millimetres of rain from 4 to 6 March, the highest consecutive three-day total since June 2016.

Victoria received a statewide drenching on 4 and 5 March with Melbourne recording 54.6 millimetres in a 24-hour period, the highest daily March rainfall since 1929. This produced widespread flash flooding across the city with trees down and train and tram tracks flooded, causing significant delays in public transport.

One of the most important functions of science is to look at what has happened and then attempt to explain why. If this can be achieved it helps us identify similar situations in the future, and hopefully predict their onset.

During 2019–20 perhaps the most remarkable feature of the whole meteorological situation was the speed of transition. The weather moved from extremely hot and dry to tropical and wet in a well-defined and rapid change that began in mid-January. The most obvious cause was the demise of the positive IOD that had resulted in widespread drought over much of eastern Australia. As these sea surface temperatures adopted a more normal pattern the IOD returned to what is called a neutral phase, with immediate effect on the weather patterns across much of Australia.

Other indicators that climate scientists use to monitor the Australian seasons – the El Niño/Southern Oscillation pattern (ENSO) and the Southern Annular Mode (SAM) also assumed neutral configurations. This meant that other climate drivers assumed more importance as the seasons progressed into autumn and winter.

The incredible meteorology of 2019–20 will form the basis of numerous case studies for climate scientists in their attempt to understand and predict our seasons. It will also be part of the much bigger picture of climate change and its likely impact for Australia in the years to come.

Glossary

automatic weather station
An instrument that automatically measures and records meteorological variables such as temperature, rainfall, wind speed and direction and humidity.

barometer
An instrument that measures atmospheric pressure.

barometric pressure
The atmospheric pressure at a given time. In Australia the common unit used is the hectopascal, which has the abbreviation hPa.

cirrus
A high cloud formation that looks like fine filaments of hair. Cirrus is a Latin word meaning 'wisp of hair'.

climate change
The alteration in the long-term state of the atmosphere, usually relating to temperature and rainfall patterns.

cold front
The line between an existing mass of 'warm' air and an invading mass of 'cold' air.

cumulonimbus
A cloud formation that produces thunderstorms. Can extend to altitudes of around 14 kilometres.

cumulus
A fluffy, 'bubbly' cloud formation that can produce showers. Cumulus is a Latin word meaning 'heap'.

deep low-pressure cell
An intense low-pressure circulation in the atmosphere. Normally used to describe low-pressure cells with a central barometric pressure less than 1000 hectopascals.

depression
An area of low pressure in the atmosphere. May or may not develop into a closed rotating low-pressure cell.

downdraughts
Areas of downward motion in the atmosphere. Commonly encountered in thunderstorms and mountain waves (see pages 75 and 97).

echoes
Radar signals reflected back from precipitation areas. Used to pinpoint the location and intensity of thunderstorms.

El Niño/La Niña
Areas of anomalously warm or cool waters across the Pacific Ocean that have a marked effect on the climate of Australia.

frogmen
Swimmers specially equipped for underwater operation, usually with wetsuit, flippers and aqualung.

front
The line between air masses of different temperatures (see **cold front**).

frontal system
See **front**.

greenhouse effect
The warming of the atmosphere produced by certain gases that allow heat in but prevent part of it from escaping back into space.

hectopascal
See **barometric pressure**.

high pressure
An area of the atmosphere that has higher barometric pressure than the surroundings. Can take the form of an anticlockwise-rotating eddy that is normally associated with settled weather conditions.

humidity
A measure of the moisture content of the surrounding air.

hydrologist
A scientist whose speciality is the study of rivers or underground water flows.

isohyet
A line on a map that joins areas that have received the same amount of rainfall over a given period.

low pressure
An area of the atmosphere that has lower barometric pressure than the surroundings. Can take the form of a clockwise-rotating eddy that is normally associated with unsettled weather conditions.

low-pressure cell
A clockwise-rotating eddy in the atmosphere that is normally associated with unsettled weather conditions.

mammilated
A cloud formation that consists of rounded protuberances hanging from part of the cloud.

meteorologist
A scientist who specialises in studying the state of the Earth's atmosphere, particularly in relation to weather and climate.

monsoonal rains
Rains that have tropical origins and normally occur during the so-called 'wet season'.

monsoon trough
An area of low pressure that extends from tropical areas towards higher latitudes.

offshore wind
A wind that blows from the land towards the sea.

pluviograph/pluviometer
Instruments that measure the amount and intensity of rainfall over a given location.

radar
An acronym for radio detection and ranging. Also describes an electronic instrument that locates and measures the intensity of atmospheric precipitation.

rain depression
A zone of low pressure that is generating rain.

rainsqualls
Areas of rain accompanied by strong and gusty winds.

Richter scale
A scale designed to rate the intensity of earthquakes. It ranges from magnitudes 1 to 9 in ascending order of severity.

scarp line
A steep cut in or elevation of the Earth stretched out in the form of a ragged line.

squall
A sudden gust or burst of wind, sometimes associated with showers.

storm surge
An abnormally high ocean tide produced by strong onshore winds pushing seawater towards the land. Normally associated with tropical cyclones crossing coastal areas.

stratus
A low, layered cloud formation. It sometimes covers and obscures land features such as mountains or hills and on occasion, even tall buildings.

supercell
A type of intense thunderstorm in which the updraughts and downdraughts achieve a balance. Can last for extended periods and produce severe weather such as large hail, heavy rain, strong winds and even tornadoes.

surface low-pressure system
A low-pressure system that exists at or near ground level.

synoptic weather chart
More popularly known as the 'weather map', this is a display that shows the position of the various weather systems such as high- and low-pressure cells and fronts over a certain area at a given time. Synoptic weather charts are shown in most daily newspapers.

tropopause
The level in the upper atmosphere between the troposphere and stratosphere, typically at around 10 kilometres in altitude, although this can vary considerably.

trough
An elongated area of low pressure.

turbulence
Irregular motion of air in the atmosphere. Can cause bumping and jolting sensations for aircraft passengers.

updraughts
Areas of ascending air in the atmosphere. Common in and around thunderstorms.

upper low-pressure system
A low-pressure cell located in the upper layers of the atmosphere.

wind structure
Refers to how the wind changes its speed and direction with height.

Metric Conversions

1 inch = 25 mm	1 mile = 1.61 km
1 foot = 30.5 cm	1 knot = 1.85 km/h

Bibliography

Abernethy, John, 2000, *Report of the NSW State Coroner into the 1998 Sydney to Hobart Yacht Race*, NSW Coronial Enquiry, 12 December.

Bissett, Sir James, 1959, *Tramps and Ladies*, Angus & Robertson, Sydney.

Brown, Ian, 2003, 'Deadly White Blanket', *Outdoor Australia Magazine*, March 2003.

Bureau of Meteorology, 1967, *Report on the Meteorological Aspects of the Catastrophic Bushfires in South-eastern Tasmania on 7 February 1967*, Australian Government Publishing Service, Canberra.

Bureau of Meteorology, 1974, *Brisbane Floods, January 1974*, Australian Government Publishing Service, Canberra.

Bureau of Meteorology, 1975, *Technical Report 14, Cyclone Tracy*, Australian Government Publishing Service, Canberra.

Bureau of Meteorology, 1991, *Report Into the Sydney Thunderstorm of 21st January 1991*, Sydney.

Chambers, James, http://members.ozemail.com.au/~jamestorm/. I obtained valuable information concerning the storm described in chapter 28 from an article on this website.

Geoscience Australia 2002, *Earthquake Risk in Newcastle and Lake Macquarie*, CD with hard copy overview booklet.

Gordon, F. R. and Lewis, J. D., 1980, 'The Meckering and Calingiri Earthquakes October 1968 and March 1970', *Western Australia Geological Survey Bulletin 126*, 229 pp.

Hand, Derrick, 2000, *Report of the Inquest Into the Deaths Arising From the Thredbo Landslide*, NSW Coronial Enquiry, 29 June.

Job, Macarthur, 1991, *Air Crash 1*, Aerospace Publications, Canberra.

Job, Macarthur, 1992, *Air Crash 2*, Aerospace Publications, Canberra.

McArthur, A.G., 1967, *The Tasmanian Bushfires of 7th February 1967 and Associated Fire Behaviour Characteristics*. Report for the Forestry Commission of Tasmania, Hobart.

Newman, B.W., 1947, *Phenomenal Hailstorm with Thunderstorm, Sydney 1st January 1947*, Bureau of Meteorology, Sydney.

O'Reilly, Bernard, 1958, *Green Mountains and Cullenbenbong*, W.R. Smith and Paterson Pty Ltd, Brisbane.

Stretton, Alan, 1976, *The Furious Days*, William Collins, Sydney.

Whitmont, Debbie, 1999, *An Extreme Event*, Random House, Sydney.

Index

Page numbers in *italics* refer to photographs and diagrams.

Abernethy, John 212, 219
Adelaide
    heatwaves 88–9
    storms 105–9
Adelaide Tempest *10–11*, 105–9
air traffic control 127
air waves, mountain 75–6
aircraft
    communication with 67, 70, 73, 84
    navigation 84, 87
Aireys Inlet 180
Alpha 190
'Ash Wednesday' bushfires 172–81
athletics races 40–4
atmospheric circulation 79
Australian National Airways (ANA) 67, 70
automatic weather stations 181
aviation, meteorological services 68, 76, 127–8, 133
aviation accidents
    inquiries 132–3
    Kyeema 83–7
    Southern Cloud 66–71
    Stinson 72–6
    survivors 75
    Tango Victor Charlie 126–33
aviation safety 76, 84, 128, 133
Avro 10 (aircraft) 67–9
Beardsmore, Scott and Paul 214–19
Binstead, Joe 75
Bissett, James 105
'Black Friday' bushfires 88–92, 174, 181
Bogan River 192, 194
Bondi 77–82
Bowler, Neville 159

Boyden, Rex 72
Branxton 125
Brighton 58–9
Brisbane
    floods 25–33
    hailstorms 182–6, 197–8
    storms 182
Brisbane Cricket Ground 197–8
Bucca 198–200
Bureau of Meteorology
    cyclone warning system 53
    East Coast Low prediction 236–7
    flood warning system 124
    storm investigation 50
    storm tracking 48
Burragorang *226–7*
Burrinjuck Dam 38
bushfires
    Canberra 10, 229–34
    east coast 251–4
    Tasmania 134–41
    time scale 9
    Victoria 88–92, 169–81, 238–40
Camm, Harold 68–9
Canberra
    bushfires 10, 229–34
    rainfall 118
Carr, Bob 226, 228
caves, snow 215–19
Cerutty, Percy 145
Chapman 233
Charleville 190, 192
Cheviot Beach 142, 144–5
Cockatoo 180
cold fronts 67, 68, 176
Costello, Ben 126
Crane, Geoff 232
Cunnamulla 192
Cyclone
    Conroy 110

    Selma 164
    Tracy 9–10, 162–8
    Wanda 30
    Yasi 248–9
cyclones *164*
    categories 166
    East Coast 110–17
    forecasting 51–3, 112
    Mackay 51–6
    naming 110–11
    warning system 117
Darling River *224*
Darwin 162–8
DC2 (aircraft) 85
derailments, train 124
Derby, Tas. 63
disaster management 9–12
Diver, Stuart 204
downbursts *49*
droughts
    2019–20 255
    breaking 36–7
    droughtproofing 37–8
    Federation 34–9
    forecasting 12
    Millennium 220–8
    time scale 9
Dunbar (ship) 13–18
dust storms
    eastern Australia 241–3
    Narrandera *38–9*
    Victoria 169–72
Dwyer, Len 124
earthquakes
    measuring 155
    Meckering 149–50
    Meeberrie 147
    Newcastle 150–5
    time scale 9
East Coast Lows 235–6
Edwards, Vic 150
El Niño phenomenon 220, 222, 245, 247, 258

Elliott, Herb 145
Farmhand Foundation 224
Fire Danger Index 136
fire tornadoes 230, 232
floods
    Branxton 125
    Brisbane 25–33
    eastern Australia 187–94, 255–8
    Lismore 113, *114–15*
    Mackay 51–6
    Maitland 118–25
    Melbourne 156–61
    Murwillumbah 117
    Queensland 188–92, 245–7
    Rockhampton 56, *111, 112, 113*
    Singleton 123
    Tasmania 62–5
    time scales 9
    warning system 124
forecasting, weather *see* weather forecasting
Friend, Timothy 214–19
fronts, cold 67, 68, 176
Fujita Scale 59, 61
Gillespie, Marjorie 142, 145
Glenelg Jetty 106–9
global warming 226
Goyder, George Woodroffe 19–24
Goyder's Line 19–24
Green, James 14
greenhouse effect 228
hail guns 36
hailstorms
    Brisbane 182–6, 197–8
    Queensland 195–200
    Sydney 93–104
Hammond, Joan 179
Hand, Derrick 204
Hanlon, Tommy Jnr *184*
Hardy, Elizabeth 126

heatwaves
    Adelaide 88–9
    Melbourne 89
helicopter rescue 122, 212
Hercules C130 (aircraft) 191
Hitchins, Group Capt. 167
Hobart 42–3
    climate 134
    fire 134–41
    rainfall 156
Holt, Harold 142–6
Humphreys, Col 117
Hunter Valley 119
irrigation 38
Jericho 190
Johnson, James 16–18
Jones, Dean 196–7
Karoly, David 226
Keldie, Aileen 126
Kyeema (DC2 aircraft) 84, 85–7
Kyogle 113
La Niña phenomenon 222, 245, 247
Lacey, H. 96
landslides, Thredbo 201–5
Launceston 64–5
lifesavers, surf 79–82
Lindfield 46–7
Lindsay, Stan 126
Lismore 113, *114–15*
McDonald, A.S. 119
Macedon 180
Mackay 51–6
Maitland 118–25
Mansfield, Bob 224
Marshman, Mike 210–11
Matlock 90
Meckering 149–50
Meeberrie 147
Melbourne
    climate 156
    dust storm *170–1*, 172
    floods 156–61
    heatwaves 89
    rainfall 156, 158
Menzies, Edna 96
meteorological services, aviation 68, 76, 127–8, 133

Mount Stromlo Observatory 234
Mount Wellington 40–4
mountain air waves 75–6
Murrumbidgee Irrigation Scheme 38
Murwillumbah 117
Narrandera *38–9*
natural disasters
    public awareness 10
    time scales 8–9
Newcastle 150–5
Newman, B.H. 112
Noojee 90
Nyngan *190,* 192, 194
ocean swells 78, 105–6
Oliver, Neville 198
O'Reilly, Bernard 37, 74–6
Pasha Bulker (ship) 235–7
Pincini, Dean 214–19
plane crashes *see* aviation accidents
Portsea 145
prime minister, missing 142–6
Proud, John 75
Pudney, Archibald 109
Queensland
    floods 188–92
    hailstorms 195–200
    storms 195–200
races
    athletics 40–4
    Sydney to Hobart yacht race 10
radar 127, 133
Radford, George 44
radio broadcasts, flood warning 119–21
rainfall
    Australia 118, 156, 187
    intensity 157
    prayers for 34–5
    year 1902 *35*
    year 1982 172
    year 1990 188
    year 2002 223, 230
    years 1954–1956 120–1
Richards, Mark 44
Richmond River *116*
Richter Scale 155

Rockhampton 56, *111, 112, 113*
Rose Bay *95*
Royal Commissions, Victorian bushfires 92
running races, Mount Wellington 40–4
Sandon 60–1
shipwrecks
    Dunbar 13–18
    survivors 16
Shortridge, Travis 66
Singleton 123
Smith, Charles Kingsford 67
snow caves 215–19
Snug 136–7, 140–1
South Australia, farming land 19–24
Southern Cloud (Avro 10 aircraft) 66–71
Spicer, Justice 132–3
Standaside (yacht) 210–11
Stewart, Alan 142, 145
Stiger Vortex Gun 36
Stinson (tri-motor airliner) 72, *73*
storm surges *54,* 106, 108
storm warnings 209–10
storms
    Adelaide 105–9
    aviation hazard 128
    Brisbane 182
    forecasting 12
    phases 96–7
    Queensland 195–200
    Sydney 45–50, 93–104
    time scales 9
    warning 48
Stretton, Alan 9–10, 166, 168
Stretton, Leonard 92
supercells 96–7
surf rescues, Bondi 77–82
Sword of Orion (yacht) 212
Sydney
    hailstorms 93–104
    rainfall 118, 156
    storms 45–50, 93–104
    tornadoes 46, 50
Sydney to Hobart yacht race 10, 206–13

Tango Victor Charlie (Vickers Viscount) 126–33
Tasmania
    bushfires 134–41
    floods 62–5
    weather 63
Thredbo 201–5, 214–15
thunderstorms *see* storms
time scales, natural disasters 8–9
tornadoes
    Brighton 58–9
    Bucca 198–200
    classification 61
    Sandon 60–1
    Sydney 46, 50
    Victoria 57–61
train derailments 124
tropical cyclones *see* cyclones
Turramurra Uniting Church *48*
twisters *see* tornadoes
Vickers Viscount (aircraft) 132
Victoria
    bushfires 88–92, 169–81
    dust storms 169–72
    tornadoes 57–61
Warragamba Dam *225*
Warrego River 190
Watsons Bay 17, 46
waves, ocean 78
weather forecasting 9–12, 98, *209,* 235–6
weather simulations 208–9
weather stations, automatic 181
weather warnings 9–12, 53, 98
Webb, A.C. 85, 87
Westray, Jim 75
Whitmont, Debbie 210
wind 157, 211
Wragge, Clement 36, *37,* 110
yacht races
    meteorological support 208
    Sydney to Hobart 10, 206–13
Yatina 22–4

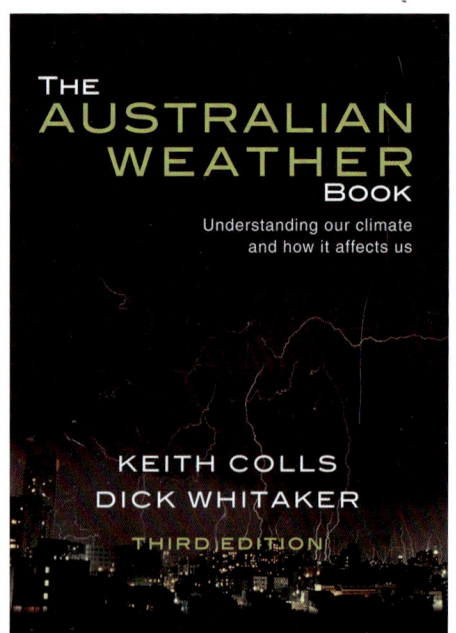

Fully revised and updated, the second edition of this fascinating book describes Australia's climate and weather in a lively and readable way. It gives full information on the following topics:

Do you know how to protect yourself and your home from a bushfire?

- How the weather affects us in our day-to-day living.
- An explanation of Australia's climate – rainfall, temperature, drought, flood, El Niño, the Southern Oscillation Index and weather extremes.
- Climate change and the effect of human activity on climate, including the greenhouse effect and ozone depletion.
- How and why the atmosphere works – details of wind circulations including the southerly buster and Spillane eddy.
- Clouds – how they form and the different types.
- Instruments used to measure weather phenomena – from barometers and thermometers to radar and Automatic Weather Stations.
- Well-known disasters – Cyclone Tracy, the two great Sydney hailstorms, the Ash Wednesday bushfires, the Sandon Tornado, the Brisbane floods of 1974 and the Sygna Storm.

This handy little book will help you stay alive. It tells you how bushfires behave, how to prepare for a bushfire, what to do when a fire threatens and how you can safeguard your home and yourself.

Whether you're in the bush, in your car or at home, there are lots of ways to limit the risks. *Firewise, Fire-safe* provides emergency contact details, vital checklists and first aid approved by St John Ambulance.